"*Choose Your Self* is an empowering guide for any woman who gets that the relationships we desire with others start with the relationship we have with ourselves. Megan has pulled together many inspiring, practical, and enlightening ways to stop feeling bad about your relationship status and instead focus your energy on exploring and enjoying the deeper vs. superficial path of self-love."

Christine Arylo
leadership advisor, author, and
founder of The Path of Self Love

Praise for *Choose Your Self*

"*Choose Your Self* is a relatable and clear guide for embracing the relationship you have with the most important person in your life—you. I highly recommend it!"

Elizabeth Earnshaw, LMFT
author of *'Til Stress Do Us Part*

"*Choose Your Self* by Megan Sherer gives such beautiful, accessible tools to come home to your truest self and to fall in love with your life along the way."

Ruthie Lindsey
speaker, transformational coach,
and author of *There I Am*

"*Choose Your Self* is a breath of fresh air for all the women who have been choking on incomplete dating advice that leaves self-compassion out of the equation. This is a book for a generation of women who, more than anything, long to be seen. Megan's words will leave you feeling lighter, yet somehow more whole at the same time."

Parm K.C.
author of *You Will Feel Whole Again* and *Eggshells*

"Relationships come and go . . . but the relationship to yourself always remains. Megan Sherer is both correct and insightful in her assertion that the relationship we have to ourselves is perhaps the most important one we ever have, and navigating that with compassion, doses of self-care, and a healthy amount of self-worth is critical for developing strong relationships—first with ourself, before anyone else. I applaud Megan's forthrightness in acknowledging the plight of the modern woman who is saddled with so much pressure and expectation, and giving her the freedom to choose what is most right *for her*."

Alanna Kaivalya, PhD
author of *The Way of the Satisfied Woman*

"*Choose Your Self* is a liberating guide for every woman ready to embrace her own worth, heal deeply, and find fulfillment from within. Megan Sherer's compassionate wisdom provides the tools to break free from societal expectations, nurturing the most crucial relationship we have: the one with ourselves. If you're ready to put yourself first and build a life you genuinely love, this book is a powerful place to start."

Wendy Valentine
host of *The Midlife Makeover Show* and
author of *Women Waking Up*

"*Choose Your Self* feels like a warm hug and a wake-up call rolled into one. Megan beautifully reminds us that the love we are fervently searching for is already ours and begins with the person in the mirror. This book is not here to tell you that you should just be OK with being single—it's about realizing that nothing from the outside can make you whole. You are already whole! Her words shake you up from the inside and rearrange the belief that romantic love is superior in such a way that both single-dom and partnership become extraneous when you are able to drink from the well of self-love each and every day. If you're ready to stop waiting for life to start and ready to choose love, this book is for you."

Samantha Chung
cohost of the *Spiraling Higher* podcast

CHOOSE YOUR SELF

CHOOSE YOUR SELF

HOW TO EMBRACE BEING SINGLE, HEAL CORE WOUNDS, AND BUILD A LIFE YOU LOVE

MEGAN SHERER

BOULDER, COLORADO

Sounds True
Boulder, CO

© 2025 Megan Sherer

Sounds True is a trademark of Sounds True Inc.

All rights reserved. No part of this book may be used or reproduced in any manner without written permission from the author(s) and publisher.

No AI Training: Without in any way limiting the author's and publisher's exclusive rights under copyright, any use of this publication to "train" generative artificial intelligence (AI) technologies to generate text is expressly prohibited. The author reserves all rights to license uses of this work for generative AI training and development of machine learning language models.

This book is not intended as a substitute for the medical recommendations of physicians, mental health professionals, or other health-care providers. Rather, it is intended to offer information to help the reader cooperate with physicians, mental health professionals, and health-care providers in a mutual quest for optimal well-being. We advise readers to carefully review and understand the ideas presented and to seek the advice of a qualified professional before attempting to use them.

All names used throughout the book have been changed to protect patients' privacy.

Published 2025

Cover and jacket design by Charli Barnes
Book design by Meredith Jarrett

Printed in the United States of America

BK07221

Library of Congress Cataloging-in-Publication Data

Names: Sherer, Megan, author.
Title: Choose your self : how to embrace being single, heal core wounds, and build a life you love / Megan Sherer.
Description: Boulder, CO : Sounds True, 2025. | Includes bibliographical references.
Identifiers: LCCN 2024041358 (print) | LCCN 2024041359 (ebook) | ISBN 9781649633927 (trade paperback) | ISBN 9781649633934 (ebook)
Subjects: LCSH: Single women. | Interpersonal relations. | Self-acceptance. | Self-esteem.
Classification: LCC HQ800.2 .S5185 2025 (print) | LCC HQ800.2 (ebook) | DDC 306.73082--dc23/eng/20241129
LC record available at https://lccn.loc.gov/2024041358
LC ebook record available at https://lccn.loc.gov/2024041359

*To all of my teachers, healers, and mentors along the way:
thank you for reminding me of my light when I couldn't see it.*

*To my younger self: breathe, love. It all works out
better than you can imagine, so trust your timing.*

To all of the men who didn't choose me: thank you.

Disclaimer

This book contains advice and guidance pertaining to mental health and interpersonal well-being. It is not intended to replace medical or psychotherapeutic advice and should not be used to replace guidance from your doctor or mental health professional. This book should be used as a supplement to any physical or mental health plan you are currently following under the guidance of a professional.

All names of individuals mentioned in this book have been changed.

Contents

INTRODUCTION 1

Part 1: Finding You 15

CHAPTER 1: **The Real You:** Discerning Truth from Lies as You Rediscover Your Authentic Self 17

CHAPTER 2: **Self-Care in Action:** Improving Your Relationship with the Most Important Person in Your Life 39

CHAPTER 3: **Understanding What You Want:** Reclaiming the Power of Your Desire 67

Part 2: Hello, Love 89

CHAPTER 4: **Called Out:** Getting Clear on Your Patterns and Cleaning Up Old Habits 91

CHAPTER 5: **The Big Loves:** My Relationship Journey Through All of Its Highs and Many Lows 95

CHAPTER 6: **What Have You Learned about Love?** How Your Attachment Style Impacts Your Relationships 107

CHAPTER 7: Getting Off the Situationship: The Secret to Why You Keep Choosing Emotionally Unavailable People 119

Part 3: Unraveling Your Past 129

CHAPTER 8: Getting to Know Your Nervous System: Aka Managing Your Reactions and Becoming Grounded 131

CHAPTER 9: We Need to Talk: Leveling Up Your Communication Skills 145

CHAPTER 10: Losing Yourself Isn't a Good Look: Self-Betrayal and Finding Your Inner Compass 155

CHAPTER 11: Drop the Judgment: Changing Your Relationship to Being Single 163

CHAPTER 12: What Else? All the Ways We Get in Our Own Way 171

CHAPTER 13: Dear John (or Kyle, Claire, Quinn, or Whoever): Letter Writing Practices to Let Go of Your Past 181

Part 4: Making Magic on Your Own 187

CHAPTER 14: Your Inner Child: The Part of You Who Needs Some TLC 189

CHAPTER 15: The Body Talks: Learn to Befriend Your Greatest Ally 205

CHAPTER 16: It's Okay to Feel Good: Reclaim Your Relationship with Pleasure 221

CHAPTER 17: Your Wild Moment: Do the Things You Think You Need a Partner For 233

Part 5: Something New 245

CHAPTER 18: **Building Community:** Romantic Love Is Not the Only Kind 247

CHAPTER 19: **The L Word:** Redefining Your Relationship with Loneliness 257

CHAPTER 20: **Mining for Gold:** Getting Clear on What You Really Want in "the One" 265

CHAPTER 21: **Love Me Well:** What It Looks Like to Choose Love from Your New Standard 279

CONCLUSION: **Happily Ever After:** You Are Perfectly on Time 285

WITH LOVE 291

RECOMMENDED RESOURCES 293

NOTES 297

ABOUT THE AUTHOR 299

List of Practices

As you move throughout this book, you may want to revisit some of the practices and journal prompts that stood out to you most strongly. Reference this list for a complete overview of the practices we explore together.

CHAPTER 1
Affirm Your Singlehood 24
Witness Your Self-Talk 31
Reflect on the Origin of Your Self-Talk 33
The Self-Talk Reframe 38

CHAPTER 2
Practice Imperfection 44
Living Vision Board 47
Intentional Self-Appreciation 49
Feelings Inventory 52
Self-Respect Check-In 54
Let Yourself Off the Hook 56
The Art of Letting Go 59

CHAPTER 3
The Real Me Journal Prompts 71
Figure Out What You Want 75

List of Practices

Communicate Your Desires 78

Past, Present, Future Method 83

Guided Writing 84

Freewriting 85

Guided Future-Self Meditation 86

CHAPTER 5

Your Relationship with Love 106

CHAPTER 6

Identify Your Core Wounds 113

CHAPTER 7

Check in on Your Emotional Availability 127

CHAPTER 8

Get Regulated: Solo Regulation 140

Get Regulated: Social Regulation 142

CHAPTER 9

Acknowledge Your Communication Patterns 151

CHAPTER 10

Identify Your Core Values 161

CHAPTER 11

Find Your Self-Judgments 168

CHAPTER 12

How You Get in Your Own Way 178

CHAPTER 13

Letter Writing for Healing 182

CHAPTER 14
Meet Your Inner Child 191
Additional Practices for Inner Child Connection 193
Your Beliefs about Discipline 196
What Does Inner Child Self-Care Mean to You? 198
Take Your Inner Child on Playdates 203

CHAPTER 15
Shake, Scan, and Breathe 219

CHAPTER 16
Contemplate Your Sexual Journey 225
Body Connection Through Pleasure Practice 230

CHAPTER 17
What's Your *Wild* Moment? 243

CHAPTER 18
Friendships Inventory 251
Strengthen Your Friendships 252

CHAPTER 19
Somatic Healing for Loneliness 263

CHAPTER 20
Lead from Your Values 266
Identify Your Nonnegotiables 269
Identify Your Deal-Breakers 271
The Main Character List 274

CHAPTER 21
Are You Ready for a Relationship? 281

Introduction

> "When you say 'yes' to others, make sure you are not saying 'no' to yourself."
>
> —Paulo Coelho

Our never-ending quest for true love in the form of a singular soulmate leaves so many of us lost and disconnected from ourselves. Our efforts to win the affection from some hypothetical special person inevitably distract us from the real work of becoming our own first and ever-present true love. When you can decentralize dating from your life for long enough to put the spotlight on your relationship with yourself, you will be planting seeds of love that will bloom for the rest of your life, regardless of who else comes and goes.

I know, it's easier said than done. But I'm living proof that this journey is well worth it.

The truth is, *I'm so grateful that the universe wouldn't let me be impatient in love.*

That every time I eagerly said, "I'm ready," the response was, "Not yet."

And every time I said, "This is it, he's the one," I was met with, "Not him."

That despite all of my protests and breakdowns and bargaining, I wasn't allowed to settle.

Because every "not yet" and "not him" was leading me to something better all along, in a story I could never have imagined writing in my wildest dreams. And after all that time I was looking for someone else to fill the void, I found something even better, something I didn't even know I was missing: me.

I came to realize that even though I may someday spend decades with someone I deeply love, the truth is that I am only ever forever mine.

And the same is true for you. You are your own person before you are anyone else's. You will always be yours first.

The Plan

I always had what I thought of as "the Plan." I was a fairly timid kid who tried to keep my head down and not be noticed too much, but I had big dreams for my life. I was going to go to the best college, start a successful business, do lots of philanthropy work, get married by twenty-four, and start having kids by twenty-five. I wanted to be a cool young mom with an amazing husband, and I also wanted to be a self-made entrepreneur. I demanded perfection of myself in everything I did, so I was going to have it all, and you couldn't convince me otherwise.

At this point you are probably either nodding along because you can relate and you're hoping I will tell you how all that is possible, or you are laughing and rolling your eyes because you know how this story plays out.

Here's how it actually went down: I waded through rocky teen years with plenty of high-functioning anxiety under my belt, went to college and struggled to recover from an eating disorder, started a business that was quickly sidelined by a traumatic car accident, began to experience severe depression and panic attacks, and ended up in a string of terrible relationships that tanked my self-worth even more. Suddenly I found myself at twenty-five single, childless, building a new career, financially struggling, emotionally overwhelmed, and realizing that I had a whole bunch of trauma to heal. So much for the Plan.

On the one hand, I was finally beginning to understand how misguided my original plan was. I'd wanted children from a young age, partly because that's the prescription we're sold and partly because I was forced to grow up really fast to get my needs met and was basically cosplaying as a little adult from the age of ten on. It made me feel in control to be the "adult," and control was my lifeline. It didn't hit me until well into my twenties that I could pretend to be an adult all I wanted, but there were very real parts of me that were stuck at wounded younger ages. I needed to work on healing my own childhood wounds before being fully responsible for another human life. I was also willing to admit to myself that there was a lot I wanted to explore and accomplish before adding kids into the equation.

On the other hand, I still felt the pressure of those prescribed time lines and was incredibly impatient in my quest to check all the right boxes at precisely the right moment. I was masking feelings of desperate inadequacy under the guise of my desire to find "the One." I became obsessed with the idea of meeting my soulmate and threw myself headfirst into an overhaul of my love life. On the eve of my twenty-fifth birthday, I decided to end an unhealthy situationship that I had been in far too long and resolved to break that cycle for good.

Spoiler alert: I didn't. While I did leave that particular relationship (and proceeded to agonize over it for an embarrassing amount of time), the cycle was certainly not broken. I went on to repeat that pattern a couple more times, because I clearly had not learned my lesson. One of my mentors calls it "doing the research." Our own life experience is the best research for discovering who we are, what we want, what we don't want, and what our values are. But the key that many people miss is that once you collect the data, you have to actually do something with it—and be willing to pivot if the results aren't what you were looking for.

So many of us end up in a perpetual cycle of trial and error, making the same errors over and over again because we refuse to course correct along the way. And I get it. Sometimes you need to repeat the same mistake a few (dozen) times before you're finally ready to take the lesson and move on.

For ages I focused on getting the wrong guys to choose me rather than doing the inner work of choosing myself first. It took a lot of trial, error, confusion, and forced surrender to finally learn that *I* was the one I'd been looking for all along.

This book is your step-by-step guide to breaking the cycle of giving your power away and to rediscovering the gift of your own presence along the way.

Now, I don't want to kick off our time together by bumming you out. If you have a plan that hasn't been working and you were hoping for advice on how to get the things you want, all hope is not lost. I want you to have what you want. You get to have the most wonderful relationship and all of your other desires as well. But there's a really important pit stop you must make first. I'm going to invite you to be willing to believe that there is an even *better* outcome for you than you had originally planned. A life that's even more aligned and beautiful and love-filled than the best thing you've conjured up in your mind so far. And I'm going to help you get there.

The reason why most women are uncomfortable being single is because we feel like there's somewhere we need to get to. It often feels like being in a relationship is a finish line in a race that we're abruptly going to be eliminated from if we go too slow. (Have you ever seen a first-time marathoner escorted via golf cart from the race course after ten hours of giving it their absolute best? Even though participating is a massive accomplishment in itself, most people unfortunately see not finishing as some kind of personal failure.) And because of this, so many women rush themselves and choose the next person they see, whether they're a good match or not—and they're often not.

The important truth for you to grasp is that a relationship isn't a finish line. It's not even a milestone. It's a living, breathing organism in the landscape of our lives. Healthy romantic relationships require tending, and nourishment, and fertile soil in which to grow together. It's not just a box you check. At least not if you are the type of person I think you are.

You're someone who can't settle for a basic connection that leaves you wondering if there is something more. Deep down you want someone who engages all of your senses and challenges you while simultaneously making you feel so safe and loved. And like I said, I want that for you too. But in order to get there, we've got to address some important things first. You need to learn why your relationship with yourself is the most important one you will ever have. So that's the new plan. Are you ready?

Becoming Your Own Best Friend

In this book we're going to explore what it takes to become your own best friend and why you would ever want to. When you're young, the idea of being your own best friend probably sounds incredibly lame—as if no one else likes you and so you have to spend all of your time alone. The older you get, the more you (hopefully) realize that becoming your own best friend doesn't equate to social isolation and loneliness, nor does it mean that you're uncool and no one likes you. Instead, you begin to see how cultivating this special relationship with yourself actually provides a much more solid foundation for the rest of your relationships to flourish and for your life to improve overall.

And personally, I am an advocate for learning this lesson sooner rather than later. As I began to learn many of the principles and practices that I will share with you throughout this book, I noticed an interesting trend. When I'd open up about what I was going through with the older women in my life (moms, aunts, pseudo-big sisters, and mentors), they would all express one common sentiment: "I wish I had learned that lesson earlier on." Some would say things like, "I didn't learn to put myself first until my fifties." Or, "I didn't even know self-love was an option until I turned forty." Or the most common one: "I wish I hadn't wasted so much time caring what other people thought."

Hearing those remarks made it feel abundantly clear that no matter how difficult this path might be, it would pay off. I was determined to continue to learn what self-love was really about. I took their experiences as a cautionary tale: we can either wait until shit really hits the fan in our lives and go decades without being our most authentically expressed selves, or we can do the hard work of figuring out who we are and fully embodying that now. Given the choice, I'd rather use the time I have now to get ahead.

Besides the obvious fact that I was an overachiever and wanted to somehow be ahead of the rest of the class in learning life lessons, I've discovered many other valuable reasons for wanting to become your own best friend sooner rather than later. A few of which include:

- **You are the only one there from start to finish.** Yes, we're surrounded by people when we come into the world (or at the very least the one person who birthed you). And maybe you'll be blessed to be surrounded by people who love you when you leave it. But the reality is, we are the one and only constant throughout our entire lives. We are the only one who is present from start to finish and every single moment in between. And that's what really matters here: all of those little in-between moments. Not just the big celebrations and heavy traumas, but the small, seemingly inconsequential moments when we're just brushing our teeth, reading a book, or sitting by ourselves. If you are the only one who is guaranteed to be there for all of it, then it stands to reason that you may want to enjoy the person you'll be spending so much time around. Which brings me to my next point . . .

- **You will never be bored.** Do you remember those moments growing up when all of your friends were busy and it felt like there was absolutely nothing to do (especially if you grew up pre-social media)? You could be sitting at home by yourself doing absolutely nothing and feeling bored out of your mind, but if you were sitting with your best friend doing absolutely nothing, you might feel completely content. So it stands to reason that if you become your own best friend, then it's literally impossible for you to be bored—you are always in the company of someone you love! Anything you do will feel meaningful, whether it's going on an exciting solo adventure or lying on your floor and contemplating life while listening to your favorite artist on vinyl. This was one of the biggest shifts that surprised me on this journey. I'd hear friends exclaim how they could never travel alone or go to a restaurant alone. They'd complain that they hated not having plans because they didn't like feeling lonely and bored. I grew amazed at how much I actually loved doing things by myself, and any fears of loneliness quickly began to fade. I came to realize that being alone was a powerful opportunity to get to know myself on a deeper level, and I saw just as much value in that as I did in the opportunity to get to know someone else. So just know that a happy side effect of this process is the eradication of boredom from your life forever.

- **Your relationships become so much healthier.** Loving yourself often improves your ability to love others. When you have a better understanding of who you are, what you value, and what makes you tick, you can show up for your relationships (family, friends, and partners) in a healthier way. This is partly because you will have a newfound ability to communicate your feelings, needs, and desires to the people around you more effectively. (Don't underestimate how incredibly life-changing this skill is. We'll dive deeper in a later chapter.) But it's also because befriending all the parts of yourself, the good ones and the parts you may feel are bad, gives you a greater capacity for compassion. Understanding yourself helps you understand that everyone around you has a story and parts of themselves they may not feel proud of. We're just each at different points in our journey. Compassion and communication are two of the best relationship deepeners that I know of.

- **You'll stop settling for less than you deserve.** Becoming your own best friend is the shortcut to finally being able to cut unhealthy relationship patterns from your life. Because when you know that you are comfortable being alone, you're not reliant on anyone else to make you feel worthy or lovable.

And when you're not seeking that external validation, you are much less likely to settle for people who offer less than you deserve or desire. You become so much more comfortable being single and waiting for the right partner, which allows you to raise your bar as high as you want it to be. (We'll explore how to set standards, boundaries, and deal-breakers in chapters 20 and 21.) Plus the more you learn to love yourself, the more you realize what you bring to the table and how valuable your presence can be in someone's life.

- **You'll heal things you never knew you were holding onto.** You know how the longer you know someone, the more you uncover about them? Most people don't show all their cards up front. It takes time to peel back the layers of who someone is, where they hide their pain, and what makes them feel seen and loved. The same is true for you. When you really commit to showing up and getting to know yourself, it takes time to peel back your layers. You'll most likely discover things about yourself that you had no idea were impacting you. This process can certainly be emotional, but mostly it's liberating. Becoming your own best friend is like finally discovering the correct owner's manual after decades of trying to navigate life without one. Suddenly things will start to make a lot more sense. Everything will begin to feel a little easier and a lot lighter as you let go of things you no longer need.

Not to mention the fact that choosing yourself is quite possibly the most empowering feeling you will ever experience. And I really want that for you. Like, *really*. So think of this book as a companion guide to getting to know and love yourself. Because just as in any relationship, it's going to take work. You don't just create a best friendship or amazing love story overnight. It takes time to build trust, intimacy, connection, and love. And most of us weren't given a handbook on how to do those things growing up, so they might not feel natural, innate, or intuitive at first. Give yourself the gift of showing up for yourself anyway. And know I'll be here to guide you along the way.

If I had to distill the process of becoming your own best friend down into a few bullet points, it would be these:

- When you are going through something difficult, soothe and nurture yourself as you would a really close friend who needs your help.

- When you've accomplished something, celebrate yourself as you would a really close friend whom you're so freaking proud of.

- When you're feeling big feelings, ask good questions and hold space as you would for a really close friend who needs to feel less alone.

- And when you're feeling lost and unsure of where to go next, encourage yourself as you would that really close friend.

Essentially, learn to treat yourself like someone you really love and care about. That's the basic idea. The reality is a little more complex, because we often have lots of baggage that we've been carrying in our relationship with ourselves, and we have to sort that out before that healthy and loving connection is possible. You've gotta dredge up some things from the past to clear up misunderstandings and make way for a new way of relating to yourself. My invitation for you as you are doing this work is to be as patient and compassionate toward yourself as possible. There may very well be moments of frustration, annoyance, and big feelings. That's okay—let them be there. Trust the process of coming home to yourself.

Getting to the Good Stuff

For so many single people, life can feel like it's on hold. Celebrations and recognition often seem to be reserved for when you're engaged, getting married, or having a baby. Making big life decisions, like moving to a new location or buying a house, can feel much more difficult on a single income. It's no wonder so many single people feel less than. But I'm here to make sure you know you are more than enough right here and now and that your life isn't on hold until you meet a partner.

As a holistic therapist and coach who specializes in attachment trauma, I've heard just about every limiting belief and core wound in the book. Honestly, I pursued this line of work because I needed it so badly for myself. As you'll learn in this book, I kept finding myself in frustrating patterns that talk therapy wasn't helping me get out of. So I began to learn about alternative modalities and finally started to see some progress. Over the years I've been trained and certified in many modalities, including dialectical behavioral therapy, clinical hypnotherapy, Integrative Somatic Trauma Therapy, emotional life coaching, breath work, meditation, Reiki, energy healing, and yoga. I see the most progress when we take a whole-person approach and work with the mind, body, heart, and spirit all together.

I've been doing this work for ten years now and have witnessed so many beautiful transformations in that time. In full transparency, many of my clients are women who come to me in the aftermath of a breakup or wanting to get out of an unhealthy relationship dynamic. More often than not, they want to heal whatever there is to heal in order to find their person. And time and time again, once we start working together, their goal eventually evolves. They do start to heal, and they realize that the person they actually want to find is themselves. They want to feel at home being who they are and be able to create joy and beauty and love in their life, even before a partner shows up. They want to get to the good stuff. And in our work together, they do.

I want that for you too. Whatever your story has looked like up until now, this is your era of choosing yourself. So let's take a moment to explore what you can expect in this book and in our time together. First, I'd like to note that the content of this book can be applied to anyone who wants to heal their relationship patterns and improve their relationship with themselves. Because many, but not all, of my clients tend to be cisgender women in heterosexual relationships, I will sometimes default to that language. But please know that regardless of your gender identity and sexual orientation, there's a lot to be gained from this book. We will explore some societal narratives and conditioned norms that apply primarily to women, but even those sections are full of powerful reflections for all of us.

We'll delve into topics like actionable self-care, understanding your nervous system and attachment patterns, healing core relationship wounds, setting clear standards, learning to be in your body, and how to meet your authentic self. We'll start by reintroducing you to the most important person in your life, then examining your past and using it as a mirror for growth, before finally learning to choose something new and claim what you really want out of life. While most of this book is devoted to helping you get to know yourself better, we're often doing that through the vehicle of relationship patterns. There will be guidance on how to approach future romantic relationships, but if you decide that single life is where you're most satisfied, then feel free to reframe those lessons as relevant to *all* relationships in your life, not just romantic ones.

As you move through the material in this book, you'll find a blend of new ideas to get you thinking, storytelling, questions for reflection, and personal practices for you to try. In each topic I introduce, I weave in some examples from my own life experience as well as some client stories to give you a frame of reference for how these themes might show up in your own life. In almost every chapter you'll also come across exercises and tools to help you put these ideas into action, including journal prompts, reflection exercises, somatic practices, visualizations, nervous system regulation, and inner child work. I recommend that you try each practice once before moving on to the next chapter or material in the book. You can also bookmark the exercises that stand out to you the most and come back to them anytime you wish. Once you've gone through the entire book at least once, then you can go back to the chapters you'd like to spend more time with. There's no prescribed time line or right or wrong way to go about the healing work of choosing yourself. It's just an ongoing journey of consistently showing up for yourself, one step at a time. Some days you will make massive leaps, and some days you will take wobbly baby steps. No matter your pace, you will never be behind, as it's all about *your* timing for *your* life.

Before we dive in, I'd just like to say what an honor it is to guide you in this process. I know that this work can be tender, vulnerable, and sometimes even a little scary. But I want you to know I've been where you're standing, and I've also seen firsthand how powerful this journey you're embarking on is and how sweet it gets on the other side. I'm happy to be your guide as you find your way back home to choosing yourself.

PART 1

Finding You

> "In an ideal world we would all learn in childhood to love ourselves. We would grow, being secure in our worth and value . . . letting our light shine. If we did not learn self-love in our youth, there is still hope. The light of love is always in us, no matter how cold the flame."
>
> —bell hooks

Welcome to the first day of your new relationship with yourself. This part of the work is about getting to know yourself, maybe for the very first time, because that's what you have to do in order to choose yourself. It's about sifting through your limiting beliefs and conditioned ways of being, so that you can let go of anything that isn't you. Mark this date in a journal somewhere—you'll want to remember it.

Throughout the next three chapters, we're going to explore what it takes to strengthen your relationship with yourself. I want to make it clear that the guidance that follows is not about becoming the "best" version of you. That language can often make us feel like we're already failing before we've started. Nothing we'll explore together will make you more worthy. That's because your worth doesn't wait for you at the end of a new book, tool, or self-care practice. This work isn't about fixing what's broken, because you're already whole. This work is about reconnecting to your *favorite* version of yourself. The version that makes you feel most confident, radiant, self-accepting, and alive. The version that gives you permission to bring your full self to your life, messiness and all. The version of you that feels most like home. Bookmark and highlight the practices that feel most empowering to you so that you can come back to them anytime you need a little reminder of who you are.

Chapter 1

The Real You

Discerning Truth from Lies as You Rediscover Your Authentic Self

As humans, we're hardwired for connection. From the time we're born, we look to the facial expressions, movements, and voices of our caregivers to inform our sense of self and safety in our environment. Later, we look to our peers to help us figure out how to fit in and feel accepted. Ultimately, most of us look for the love of another person to affirm that we're good enough and that we have a place in the world. And in all that looking to others and favoring their opinions, we often disconnect from our own internal compass. Many people learn early on to trade their authenticity for belonging.

Learning to be comfortable in solitude is one of the most powerful gifts you can give yourself. Because in that solitude, you get to meet all of the unguarded parts of who you really are when no one is around telling you who to be. As much as I love being around (the right) people, I know well enough by now that I need regular time alone to quiet the external noise and reconnect to myself.

The roles we play for other people in our life do matter: daughter, sibling, parent, friend, teacher, therapist, caregiver, partner, and so on. But at a certain point, it's valuable to take inventory of those roles and reflect on whether our choices have been rooted in authentic expression or are simply the result of conditioned behavior and people-pleasing tendencies. There comes a time in everyone's life when it serves us immensely to start asking ourself the hard questions and journey back to the core of who we are and who we want to be, even if that means letting some people down along the way. Because in becoming willing to let them down, we'll lift up the version of us who's been silently aching to be seen and known.

Societal Expectations

Let's get one of the big conversation topics out of the way early on: what other people think—the thing that I dedicated a couple decades of my life trying in vain to control. The fact is, most of us have been conditioned to believe there is something wrong with us if we aren't in a relationship. Especially for women, there's often a strong social or familial pressure to hit certain milestones by a particular age. Find your person, get married, start making babies, and make sure you do it all before you turn thirty, or it's too late. That's the plan many of us were taught we must follow.

So intentionally choosing to be single and focus on yourself is an act of rebellion that can feel *super* uncomfortable. In all honesty, it's not fun to have to constantly field questions about why you're single. It's also not fun when those questions and societal expectations become your own inner dialogue. Someone asks,

"So why are you still single?" and your conditioned mind automatically shames you into thinking, *This is so embarrassing. There must be something wrong with me. Why am I still single?*

That shame and pressure are the very things that cause so many people to dive into relationships they never should have been in or to stay stuck in patterns much longer than they need to. We'd rather drown ourselves in the distraction of being with the wrong person than to bear the weight of failing to achieve societally imposed milestones.

Which—let's be honest—is a heavier weight for women to carry thanks to a certain biological clock, as well as narratives about where our worth comes from. Whether or not you even want to have children is a massive conversation in and of itself and one that should never be rushed or pressured. But add in your mother's desire for grandchildren, plus the endless stream of pregnancy announcements from girls you went to high school with, and you've got a recipe for shame. Suddenly everyone is an expert on *your* fertility and feels entitled to know what you plan to do with your womb.

The realities of that biological deadline are valid for some, but this isn't a book about fertility. It's about possibility and growth and building a loving and honest relationship with yourself, which happens to be an invaluable resource if you choose to be a parent. It's the foundation that all relationships, especially ones with children, are built on. Believe me, I've spoken to plenty of women who've done it the other way around. And they all told me they wished they had started working on themselves before having kids, because it feels infinitely more challenging after. But we're taught that becoming a mother is our life's purpose, the thing that will complete us. And since so many of us are desperately seeking that sense of wholeness, we believe people when they tell us it exists only in marriage and babies.

The looming pressure of those arbitrary time lines and milestones tends to be heightened when we also have uncertainty in other areas of our life. Personally, I've never felt more behind in life than when I was turning twenty-five. It was a quarter-life crisis in the truest sense. I remember, the week before my birthday, filling pages of my journal with all the things I thought I would've achieved already but hadn't. Remember the Plan I shared about in the introduction? It was basically a checklist of everything that I was failing to measure up to. I hadn't gotten a master's degree, I wasn't a millionaire, I didn't have a husband or even anything remotely close to resembling a healthy relationship, I didn't have kids. I had no clue what I was doing but was still trying to maintain a perfect exterior image so I would seem like I had it all together when I inevitably bumped into Mr. Right. It was exhausting.

And the truth is, I *was* a mess at twenty-five. I was about to jump from one situationship into another, unaware of how much underlying trauma I still had to heal. I was constantly dissociating from my body in ways that resulted in lots of unhealthy choices for me. What I didn't know at the time was that your twenties are *supposed* to be messy.

Societal expectations (and maybe a bit of biology as well) will have you thinking that your twenties are the prime time for choosing a mate and settling down. The word *spinster* might come to mind—a term that was originally coined to refer to a yarn spinner's profession but evolved to connote an unmarried woman older than prime marrying age. Which probably seems ridiculous now, but somewhere in our DNA is the memory of the many centuries when the role of women was just to procreate and tend to their men.

In fact, a growing body of research in intergenerational trauma suggests that trauma can leave an imprint on a person's genes, which can then be passed down to future generations.

Much of this research focuses on extreme circumstances like famine, war, and the Holocaust. But we can also imagine the ongoing trauma and repression that women in our ancestral lineages likely underwent and see how the genetic memory of those experiences may still enforce a drive within many of us to adhere to these prescribed time lines for partnership and the expectations of dutifully fulfilling our role in the evolution of the species.

So if you're still single in your thirties, the pressure is definitely on. These days there's more leeway, especially if you are pursuing lofty career goals (as though that's the only viable excuse for waiting to "settle down"). But the underlying message is still that you'd better hurry up and meet someone by thirty-five, or your time is up.

And if you're still single in your forties? Forget about it—all hope is lost. These are beliefs that are so pervasive, we regard them as facts.

So it made sense that turning twenty-five made me feel like I was failing at the basic requirements of being human. I didn't realize until years later that I was not at all alone in that sentiment. Just about every young woman I talk to had a moment like that in her twenties: one where she was convinced she was broken and unlovable and doomed to be single forever.

Carrie's Comparison Issue

I met Carrie when she was twenty-six and navigating an ugly divorce from a narcissistic and abusive man. She was one of those people who seemed like she had it all together. She was a badass in her career, had achieved incredible success at a young age, and exuded confidence and effortless beauty. On the surface, you'd wonder how she ever ended up with a man like that. The reality is, there were plenty of reasons why. But she didn't ever have the chance to explore and heal them, because she dove into that commitment at such a young age. So when she came out the other side and started to ask herself the hard questions, she couldn't help but feel like she was behind in life.

I remember her telling me one day that she was scared of turning twenty-seven and being alone. She felt like twenty-seven was such a big age and that there was something wrong with her for being single again. Her fear came from a mixture of wondering what other people would think, not wanting to have to date again, worrying about having kids, comparing herself to younger married friends, and feeling like her past experience made her too broken to be loved. That's a lot of pressure to put on one birthday.

She couldn't believe it when I told her that I was in my thirties and happily single. Her disbelief is a product of the fact that many of us weren't given a model of what self-empowerment looks like. We're taught that the words *happy* and *single* cannot be in the same sentence.

Carrie eventually embraced this new era of her life and practiced the principles that I'm going to teach you in this book. She learned to choose herself, and I had the pleasure of watching her come back to life (which happens to be my favorite part of my job).

It can feel a little (or a lot) rebellious when a woman chooses to prioritize herself over seeking a partner. And for so many of us, Carrie included, who were taught to be "good" girls growing up, rebellion doesn't feel like an option. We convince ourselves that in order to be of value, we have to live our life for other people, measuring up to their yardstick to get them to accept us.

The reason that this pressure often feels more significant in our twenties is because we've just left childhood and are still wearing that good girl mask—without even knowing it's a mask.

Tessa's Good Girl Pattern

Take Tessa, for example. She was the epitome of a good girl. She had a great job, was an incredibly thoughtful friend, and always played by her family's rules. She was kind and soft and sweet, as well as witty and incredibly intelligent. And yet beneath the surface, you could sense a sadness and heaviness in her. She came to me, as many women do, when she was going through a breakup. Just as she was about to move in with her boyfriend, he broke up with her and moved to another state. Though the focus of our work was on her breakup, we always get into childhood wounds as well (something we'll explore in chapter 14). With Tessa, we discovered that her good girl exterior was actually a response to growing up in an abusive household. She learned that if she was "bad," she'd get hurt. So being good was quite literally a lifeline. That kind of programming can run deep.

It was clear to me that, as an adult, Tessa had been unconsciously seeking relationships that reminded her of the instability of her childhood. So it also wasn't a shock when I discovered that she was really resistant to being single. After a couple of months of processing the grief and pain of her breakup, she wanted to believe that she was ready to date again. I knew that dating was just a distraction from doing the painful work of healing from her childhood abuse, the root of all her relationship issues. But she wanted to hurry up and get into another relationship so she could be one step closer to getting married and giving her parents grandchildren. She was desperate to fulfill her good girl role.

Taking off her good girl mask and straying from her family's expectations felt too unsafe for her nervous system. So she repeated this pattern a few more times before she was finally ready to admit that it wasn't working. And when she finally did commit to doing that deeper inner healing work, she became an entirely different person. Everything about her felt lighter and brighter and, most importantly, more authentic. It was so beautiful to see her finally embrace being single and build a healthy relationship with herself before choosing a partner.

Try This

AFFIRM YOUR SINGLEHOOD

Whether it's your family's expectations, societal narratives, or the discomfort of being the last one in your friend group to settle down, the pressure is real. Or, rather, it feels real. It feels heavy—until you finally decide that your time line is the only one that matters. When you begin to challenge your internalized beliefs about singlehood and affirm your choices to those around you, something really wonderful happens. You begin to believe, and to truly feel in your bones, that you are always on time for your life. That the relationship that is meant for you is coming in the timing in which it's meant to come. And that in the meantime, you want to soak up every precious second of time you have alone with yourself. That is the magic of this process.

Let's address the practicalities of this unique work. I'll be the first to admit that choosing this path is absolutely going to cast you as different from the norm. It's likely going to make other people around you uncomfortable, because it's unfamiliar for them too. So it can be helpful to have some canned responses ready to fire off to the people who will inevitably question your life decisions. My first inclination is to have you tell them, "It's my life, it doesn't impact you, so kindly fuck off," but since that might not go over too well, I'm going to share some other statements you can rehearse for those inquiring minds.

When someone asks, "So why are you still single?" you can say:

- "I am taking some time to focus on myself and reach some personal goals first."
- "I'm working through healing some stuff from my past that I want to address before getting into a relationship again."
- "I'm taking this time to get really clear on what I want and don't want in a relationship."
- "I'm just not ready yet."
- "I'm really happy right now and want to enjoy this chapter on my own a little longer."
- "I just haven't met someone who aligns with my values yet, but I trust the timing of my life."
- "You know, I'm actually not comfortable talking about my love life at the moment. Can we talk about something else?"

Pick whichever one resonates with you and make it your new mantra. It's a lot more difficult for people to challenge someone who is confident in their beliefs. You get to own your decisions and this chapter of your life, even if it makes people around you uncomfortable.

Self-ish

I grew up believing that "selfish" was a harsh insult and a terrible thing to be. I thought that you were either selfish or loving and that those two things were mutually exclusive. Combine that belief with a history of complex trauma, and it's no surprise that I spent most of my life in people-pleasing mode, much more attuned to others' needs than to my own. Having a dissenting opinion was out of the question, so I adopted the views and preferences of the people around me, like a codependent chameleon. While I thought it was helpful, I couldn't see that my defense mechanism was slowly killing the real me.

Somewhere along the way, I realized that this way of living—being so disconnected from myself—wasn't sustainable. I learned that the world of "self" is actually incredibly important. *Self-help, self-love, self-care,* and *self-talk* slowly became staples in my new vocabulary. I discovered that giving from an empty cup isn't selfless, it's self-destructive. And it turns out that prioritizing your own needs and filling your own cup first actually gives you the capacity to be the most loving and whole version of yourself. That is better for everyone involved, even if they don't like the boundaries you have to set to get there.

The key is to focus on convincing *yourself* of this truth rather than trying to convince those around you. Remember when we talked about societal expectations? This is another one: society would rather have us be good girls who follow the rules and put everyone else before us. It appears to benefit those around us when we give and give until there's nothing left. God forbid we learn to take care of ourselves and get called that ugly word: *selfish*. We girls grow into women who are masters at adapting and bending to the wills of people around us. We practice becoming who we need to be in order to be safe, to be loved, to be accepted, and to be chosen. It's time to flip that script. Because the truth is, there's a reason we're told to put on our own oxygen mask first. We have to have our own needs met before we can be of use to others. We have to learn to meet our own needs. Even more importantly, we have to advocate for them, because it's likely that people around us will not.

Though I've had many opportunities to practice what I'm about to teach you, the chapter of my life that I spent healing from chronic illness taught me more about being selfish than any other chapter. Getting diagnosed with chronic Lyme disease at age thirty was like being plunged into an advanced course in identifying my needs and putting myself first. It threw me into the deep end of using everything I had learned over the prior years. I had to practice saying no more than I was used to in order to prioritize what I needed for my healing, like doctor's appointments, treatments, nourishing food, a low-stress environment, and plenty of rest. For the sake of healing my body, I had to learn to be okay with disappointing friends and family and to know that my worth did not lie in my ability to show up for others at all times.

Sometimes it felt frustrating; sometimes it felt empowering. Setting boundaries and saying no are not exactly a walk in the park. But learning to be a little selfish was honestly one of the greatest gifts I could have ever given myself, because it's what allowed me to heal so much faster than I could have otherwise.

What if we didn't have to wait until we got sick or something else traumatic happened in order to prioritize ourselves? What if that could just be a regular practice? Not to shut people out, but to fill up our own cup in order to have more to give, both to ourselves and to others?

Because that's the thing: there's a healthy way to be selfish. Think of the phrase "full of yourself," which usually negatively implies someone is being egotistical. The reality is, you should be *full* of yourself. You should be full of your passions and curiosities, full of the unique sense of self that helps you feel confident in who you are—not full of the stories and demands and pressure of who others want you to be. Knowing and embracing your authentic self helps you show up more fully in your life and relationships.

And then, you don't just stop at embodying this empowered form of selfishness. I believe (as you might have gathered by now) that love is the reason we're here. It's what makes us human. Learning to love and be loved, being in relationships, and building community are all vital tasks of a healthy life. So we don't learn to be selfish just to live in isolation for the rest of our lives. We learn to prioritize ourselves so that we know what it's like to go into the world fully resourced and to give from an overflowing cup. When you do it this way, you have more love to give, more sustainably. If the idea of centering yourself makes you uncomfortable at first, know that you're ultimately doing it for the greater good.

What Is Your Relationship to Your Self Like Right Now?

That's what the first part of this book is all about. Because in order for someone to be your best friend, it's kinda important that you get to know them. There may very well be moments in this journey when you look in the metaphorical mirror and don't like what you see. You may feel confronted, critical, and judgmental as you shine a light on the parts of yourself that have been long hidden.

As you catch yourself in those feelings, I want you to try taking a new approach. Respond to yourself the way you would to your very best friend if they were working through the same issues. For example, if your bestie was doing some inner healing work and discovered that a childhood wound had left her with the tendency to become a little snarky and passive-aggressive when she felt rejected, what would you do? You probably wouldn't actively try to make her feel even worse about herself by calling her a piece of shit, telling her that she's stupid for acting that way, or demanding that she should just get over it. Because you love and care about her, you would probably validate her emotions and let her know that what happened to her was not okay and her reaction to it as a child was understandable. You would hold space for her to evolve as she processed this pain and worked to change the pattern. And you would celebrate her progress along the way, however small or slow.

I am asking that you do the same for yourself. If you are to become your own best friend, you need to act like a best friend would. Yes, you will be calling yourself out on your shit (in a loving way, as any great friend would). You'll also be learning to love the hell out of yourself in the process. When you discover something that feels scary or uncomfortable, love yourself harder. Do as a best friend would do.

Self-Talk

You will spend more time talking to yourself than to any other human on this planet. Whether you realize it or not, the thoughts you repeat to yourself on a daily basis become your reality. It has been said, "We are what we repeatedly do. Excellence, then, is not an act, but a habit."[1] This quote, though commonly attributed to Aristotle, was actually written by philosopher Will Durant in a summary of Aristotle's work. It's often misattributed because the assumption is that Durant was directly quoting Aristotle. Kind of like a game of philosophical telephone, which is a lot like how our inner dialogue gets formed. Isn't it interesting that when we're told the same lie enough times, we cease to question its validity?

Now, this is not me taking aim at either philosopher, but I think there is something very important left out in this statement. I do agree that our habits, in large part, define who we are as people. But it's also important to acknowledge that a habit of action is always preceded by a habit of thought. Say, for example, you get out of bed and make coffee every morning (the habit of action) because you have the thought that caffeine will help you start your day. After doing that for long enough, you come to identify as a coffee drinker (the habit of thought). The beliefs we hold and the things we think about on a regular basis are the impetus for which actions we select in the first place, whether consciously or unconsciously.

And that is why we need to talk about our self-talk. The words that we speak to ourselves each day, whether consciously or not, ultimately shape the relationship we have to ourselves and the world around us. The crazy thing is, most of our self-talk actually is unconscious, often just an echo of beliefs we've picked up from other people throughout our life. More often than not, these thoughts and beliefs that aren't actually our own are unequivocally *not* serving us.

So What Is Self-Talk?

Self-talk is your internal dialogue—basically just the conversations you have with yourself on a daily basis. Your self-talk is influenced by your subconscious mind, and it reveals your thoughts, beliefs, questions, and ideas about yourself and the world around you. Self-talk can be both negative and positive (and also neutral). On the positive side, it can feel uplifting, empowering, and confidence building. On the negative side, it can often stem from or lead to feelings of anxiety, overwhelm, insecurity, and/or unworthiness. Most people aren't actually aware of their self-talk or that they have the power to change it. If you haven't been aware of it, that's okay! I'm going to walk through the whole process of becoming conscious of your self-talk with you.

Without you realizing it, your self-talk can impact every area of your life, including your health, relationships, career, finances, family, abundance, and more. That may sound overwhelming, but it can actually be an incredibly powerful realization. Because your self-talk originates from you, you have the power to control it. It may seem out of your control, since many of these thoughts are automatic. But we actually have the ability to work with our subconscious minds, and our brains are much more malleable than you might realize. That's good news. The less good news is that it's not an overnight process. Creating new patterns of thought and building new neural pathways takes time, repetition, and consistency.

Try This

STEP 1: WITNESS YOUR SELF-TALK

To change your self-talk for the better, the first step is just to observe it. Initially the goal is simply to start to become aware of what your self-talk sounds like. Not to change it, only to notice it. We aren't aware of most of our automatic thoughts until we're in a situation that triggers them. It can be helpful to keep a journal in which you jot your thoughts down every time they pop up. Even keeping notes in your phone to refer back to can be a great way to begin to build this awareness.

You can also reflect on whether a recurring thought is positive or negative by tuning in to how it makes you feel. Do you feel uncomfortable, anxious, or not good enough when you think the thought? Or do you feel optimistic, joyful, and vibrant? In your journal, you can put a little star or heart next to all the self-talk patterns you observe that feel good and circle the ones that don't feel so great.

This is an important step because it allows you to take agency over your experience. Many people aren't aware of the connection between our thoughts and feelings, much less the power we have over them. Humans are so conditioned to remain the same that we don't challenge our own thoughts or question how they make us feel. We assume that our thoughts are facts and our feelings are something that just happen to us. The reality is, you are not your thoughts. The more often you can practice observing your thoughts, the more you will experience yourself as separate from them. You are the witness of your thoughts and the director of your experience.

Why do we focus on feelings first when we're working with our self-talk? Because feelings are the most powerful driver of the human experience. It's our feelings that often determine the actions we take (or don't take), the relationships we have (or don't have), and the version of ourselves that we show up as in the world. Feelings are powerful energetic impulses that animate our body and guide what we do. So it makes sense that we'd want to have some degree of conscious relationship with them.

Here's an example. Let's say you're trying to do something new and you make a mistake in the process. If you think the thought *Ugh, I am such a loser. Why do I always fail at everything?* it's likely that you'll then experience shame or dejection. Your brain and body learn in that moment that trying new things is scary and will result in negative feelings. To avoid those unwanted feelings in the future, your brain will create a pattern of avoiding trying new things that you might fail at.

Now let's look at that scenario through a different lens. Say you try to do the new thing and still make the mistake, but this time you consciously choose to think, *Making mistakes is just part of the process of trying new things, and I can try again!* This time, your thought leads to feelings of determination and self-compassion.

Those feelings inspire you to continue to try new things, which ultimately leads to feelings of success and pride. The situation is the same, but the feelings and aftereffects are very different, simply because you decide to think a thought that feels more empowering.

Feelings are our biggest clues in this process of growing our awareness of our self-talk. And I'm not saying that you'll never again have a thought that makes you feel bad. But when you do, you'll remember that you have the power to direct your thoughts in a direction that ultimately results in you feeling better. It's always up to you. Sometimes there is great benefit to sitting with the unpleasant feeling for a while to learn what it has to say and allow it to be fully expressed before choosing a more empowering thought. There is no right or wrong way to go about witnessing your self-talk, as long as you put self-love and acceptance at the heart of it.

Try This

STEP 2: REFLECT ON THE ORIGIN OF YOUR SELF-TALK

The next step in the observation process is to reflect on where these thoughts come from in the first place. Most of our self-talk is born of conditioning that we picked up from our parents or caregivers, siblings, friends, communities, and the media we consumed while growing up. For example, you might often find yourself saying, "My thighs are so big," because you heard your mom say that and you have a similar body type to hers. Or whenever you make a mistake, you might tell yourself, "I'm such an idiot," because your brother used to say that to you when you were little. Or maybe the movies you watched as a teenager taught you that you need to look and act a certain way to fit in, so you find yourself in a spiral of self-judgment every time you're in social settings.

After you've spent some time with step 1, look back to the list you've created and see if any obvious origins to those thoughts come to mind. Spend some time reflecting on whether these thoughts are yours or if you've picked them up from someone else. You will likely discover that many of your thoughts are not actually your own. The things you've been telling yourself all these years are just code written from someone else's belief system. Do you see why creating this clarity is so vital to changing your self-talk? When we realize we've been carrying something that's not ours, it can be easier to let it go. It was never our burden to carry.

It might be a little disconcerting to realize that you've adopted all of these disempowering thoughts from other people. But don't worry, it happens to everyone. You are 100 percent normal. And, like I said, you have the power to change the thoughts that aren't working for you. We'll get to that in a moment.

"What If?"

The first question to ask yourself in the process of improving your self-talk is perhaps one of the most simple yet magical questions that exists: "What if it weren't true?"

This query is an invitation for you to consider the possibility that the thoughts you've been recycling over and over in your head might not actually be the truth. They might not be the cold, hard facts you've believed them to be. When you invite in the possibility that one particular thought might not be true, it opens your mind to feel into any number of other possibilities. I've found this experience to be incredibly permission-giving and liberating, especially if you are someone who is used to being really hard on yourself.

Let's take this whole dating and love life thing as an example. If you're like most people, you look at your past experiences and translate them into future probabilities. If you've had a string of failed relationships or have never been in one in the first place, you might have the thought *I'm doomed to be alone forever.* When you assess how that thought makes you feel, the answer is probably *Not so good.* Your brain then starts to look for patterns and external reinforcement of that thought, and so you continue to stay single and feel bad about it.

But what if that thought weren't true? When you invite in that question, it can change your love life dramatically. It might play out something like this:

Original self-talk: "I'm just doomed to be alone forever."

Question: *"What if it weren't true?"*

New self-talk: "Okay, so what if I wasn't doomed to be alone forever? Well, that would be nice. I would feel more confident about being single if I knew that I was going to meet the right person for me eventually. I would feel more optimistic and hopeful on a regular basis. That would probably make me feel even better in my career and friendships as well. If I felt better about myself, I might put myself out there more. And then if I met my person, rather than coming from a place of scarcity and insecurity, I would feel so good. Okay, I guess I am willing to believe that I'm going to meet the right person for me at some point, because it feels better to think that and I can see that being a possibility."

What's amazing about that is you got yourself into a better feeling state within just a couple minutes all on your own, simply by asking yourself one powerful question. And this is where it gets really good. Because when you realize that you have the power to change how you feel by changing what you think, you learn that your feelings were never dependent on the outcome. You never had to find a partner in order to feel loved or get a promotion at work in order to feel valuable. You can create those feeling states in yourself, which then creates more favorable conditions for what you want to show up. Like attracts like.

"What Would Feel Better?"

The last stage in the self-talk improvement process is where you get to tune in to the possibilities you created in the previous stage and choose what you actually want to feel. As you observe your self-talk, ask yourself, "What would feel better?" My recommendation is to always reach for the thought that gives you the next best feeling. In other words, you wouldn't jump from a really crappy-feeling thought all the way to the most joyful and empowered thought possible. You want your choice of thought to be believable. If it's not believable to you, then it'll feel inauthentic, and the change won't stick.

Here's the example I always give: If you frequently think thoughts of self-hate or self-criticism, you wouldn't jump straight to thinking, *I love myself, and I'm amazing!* If you did, you wouldn't believe it, and your corresponding feeling state wouldn't change much. You might even feel *more* frustrated as a result. But if instead you changed your thought to, *I'm not where I want to be yet, but I am willing to be open to the possibility that I could like myself more,* then you've created space for something new. That statement might feel more believable, which then brings in some feelings of hope and self-compassion. Little by little, you might even get to the point where you really do believe that you're amazing and lovable. But it starts with the next-best-feeling thought.

One of the amazing things about improving your self-talk is that it takes you from a world of finite possibilities to one of open-ended possibilities. This matters, because many of us grew up in a culture in which being happily single was not modeled to us as a possibility, nor were we shown what healthy romantic relationships look like. When we operate from finite thinking, the only things we'll ever experience are ones that we have reference points for. In order to create new experiences, we have to train our brain to perceive endless possibilities—and, even better, endless possibilities in which we can get what we want out of life.

As you make progress in improving your self-talk, experiment with asking yourself (and whatever higher version of yourself or higher power you believe in) these two questions:

- "What's the best possible thing that could happen?"
- "How can I allow the best possible thing to happen?"

These questions are a potent way of signaling to the universe that you are open to things unfolding for you in surprising and exciting ways. It's about remaining open to all possibilities. Because the truth is, there are possibilities that you don't yet even know exist. There are people out there experiencing things that haven't yet even crossed your mind. You can't yet see all the wonderful and magical ways that life could be for you, but you can invite those experiences in by having a brain that's attuned to possibility.

You picked up this book because some part of you believed in a possibility that you could start to love yourself and experience life in the most beautiful way before finding a partner. And the first step to realizing that vision is to consciously choose to speak to yourself in enlivening and empowering ways. This conscious self-talk process is something that you will use regularly in the beginning, until you're doing it automatically. As humans, we'll never get to the point where we don't have any negative thoughts. Our brains are designed to look out for perceived danger. So our job isn't to make all the thoughts go away, but to learn to respond to them in a new way and lovingly replace them with thoughts that feel better.

Try This

THE SELF-TALK REFRAME

Unfortunately, changing your self-talk usually isn't as simple as repeating positive affirmations until you're blue in the face. That's kind of like putting a Band-Aid on a gaping wound that really needs stiches. In order to become someone who treats themselves with respect, you have to get in the practice of witnessing, understanding, challenging, and reframing your self-talk. Use this simple five-step inquiry anytime you notice yourself having disempowering thoughts:

1. What is a thought I find myself having frequently?
2. How does that thought make me feel?
3. Where did that thought come from? Is it mine, or does it sound like someone else I know?
4. What if it weren't true?
5. Is this a thought that I want to keep thinking? If not, what is the next-best-feeling thought I could replace it with?

Chapter 2

Self-Care in Action

Improving Your Relationship with the
Most Important Person in Your Life

It was barely six in the morning, and I'd just woken up. I was thirsty and needed to go to the bathroom, but I lay motionless in bed, trying with all my might not to breathe too loudly. I resisted the urge to toss and turn and squirm, like I would if I were in my own bed. I didn't want to wake him up and scare him off, the man in the bed next to me, whom I'd been dating for months but who showed no signs of interest in commitment. I thought if I could just spend enough time with him, eventually he'd see how great we could be together. If I could just be perfect enough, inevitably he'd ask me to be his girlfriend.

So every chance I got, I shrank my needs. I made myself small and amenable, almost as if I believed that if I was nearly imperceptible, then he wouldn't mind me being around all the time.

I wanted him to see me as someone easy to be with, someone easy to choose.

What I didn't realize then was that all that time I spent vying for his love, I was ignoring the only person in the room who actually had the capacity to love me in the way that I craved: me. What I'd eventually come to learn was that love really is a verb. It's an actionable state of being that is most effectively expressed through gestures of care. The beauty of self-care is that you're both the giver and the receiver, so you benefit twice. And guess what? Sometimes self-care is as simple as getting up to drink some water when you're thirsty or go to the bathroom when your body tells you it's time.

Self-Love

Be totally honest with me: Do you cringe a little bit when you hear the term *self-love*? It's okay if you do—a lot of people do. I used to. First off, it's such a vague term. Like, *Okay, I know I'm supposed to love myself, but what does that even mean? And how do you do it? And is it really that important?*

Second, since we're taught not to be too full of ourselves, the idea of self-love can feel dangerously close to having a big ego. So we secretly think to ourselves, *Who am I to love myself and take up that much space?*

And third, many people didn't have a healthy example of what love looks like modeled to them. So if we don't really know how to love and be loved by others, why would we know how to love ourselves?

When the term *self-love* first came into my orbit, it was a totally foreign concept to me. I didn't even try to understand it. I just brushed it off as something that was for other people to figure out, not me. I didn't think I needed self-love, because I had discipline. I had goals, and drive, and rigid rules, and structure to get me where I wanted to go. Self-love sounded like something frivolous that would just make me soft and slow me down.

Sometime later I heard those words again, and I heard them in a new way. I was in recovery from an eating disorder at the time and was finally ready to admit a difficult truth: I didn't like myself all that much. Forget love—I was still learning to treat myself with the basic respect and decency that you would a casual acquaintance. I realized that I was pushing myself too hard and punishing my body and choosing unhealthy partners because some part of me believed that I wasn't good enough. It made sense that they weren't choosing me, because I wasn't choosing myself. I saw that my harsh inner critic, my people-pleasing tendencies, and my inability to set boundaries were all symptoms of my lack of self-love.

And thus began the journey of learning to treat myself in a way that signaled that I mattered. After spending some time on that journey, I realized that *self-love* isn't some fluffy term that's used to help people feel better about themselves. Self-love is an internal choice that you make, not because you earned it, but simply because you exist and that's enough.

Over the years I was able to pinpoint why that term gets confusing. Societally and culturally, it can often appear that self-love is just about superficial things. It's portrayed as the process of indulging in luxurious spa treatments and feeling like you're beautiful. But that portrayal doesn't get to the heart of the matter—and we can sense that. It makes us feel like self-love is all about vanity and narcissism, but that's not the real definition at all.

Here's my definition: Real self-love is not just face masks and bubble baths; it's messy. Real self-love is engaging in radical honesty and having the courage to revisit past pain and trauma in order to heal and grow from them, rather than staying numb. It's admitting when you are out of alignment, and seeing where your patterns come from, and realizing that your parents were just imperfect people doing their best even though their best may have hurt you, and understanding that it's your job to heal those hurts. It's ending relationships that don't serve you and learning to set boundaries. It's finding joy in the quiet moments alone with yourself, being willing to feel all of your emotions with no distractions. Real self-love isn't glamorous, but it is so worth it.

Wherever you are on your self-love journey, I can tell you that you're light-years ahead of most people. How do I know that? Because you bought this book. You've invested time and money and attention in having a better relationship with yourself. These are powerful acts of self-love. Developing a strong relationship with yourself helps you to appreciate who you are, prioritize your happiness, and forgive yourself when you mess up.

In my opinion, that's the beauty of real self-love. It's not about thinking only positive thoughts or pretending that you're perfect or feeling warm and fuzzy about yourself 24/7. It's about giving yourself permission to accept who you are even when you feel like a total mess. It's knowing that you can feel upset and disappointed with yourself and still love yourself.

The reason this is so powerful is because not everyone got to experience that level of unconditional love growing up. For many people, when a parent was mad or disappointed at them, it resulted in punishment or a withdrawal of love, an experience they may have internalized and interpreted to mean that they didn't deserve love when they did something wrong. Or, even worse, that they were not worthy of love at all. They learned that their lovability was tied to their achievement, obedience, and ability to serve. So how do we unravel those things? We diligently and compassionately unlearn those childhood lessons about our worth through practices of self-love and care.

Some of my favorite real-life ways to practice self-love on the daily include ditching perfectionism and comparison, tuning into internal and external gratitude, feeling your feelings, treating yourself like you matter, forgiving yourself, and letting go.

Ditch Perfection

I could have spent the rest of my life getting lost in the pursuit of perfection. And I likely would've died trying—that is not an exaggeration. Anyone who has dealt with extreme levels of perfectionism knows the toll that it can take on one's physical and mental health. Because nothing about life is or ever will be perfect, perfectionism is a losing game. You set yourself up for failure again and again and then beat yourself up for never being good enough. But it's not your fault. Perfectionism is most often a response to our surroundings feeling out of control and scary. It's neither a strength nor a weakness nor a character defect. It's just something your subconscious mind decided would serve you in navigating a crazy and unpredictable world.

For me, like many young girls, perfectionism showed up as an ally to help me navigate an imperfect household. We think that if we can just do everything "right" and have everything figured out, then we'll feel in control. No one will need to worry about us, and we'll get the love and attention we need, and the world won't feel so scary anymore. I used to desperately try to convince myself it was that simple. But we don't live in an $a + b = c$ world. Taking a specific action or being perfect at something doesn't guarantee a specific and perfect result. Believe me, I've tried to bend reality to fit that equation.

The more I tried to force a specific outcome, the further I'd end up from it. Then the more I felt like I'd done something wrong, the more I would search for what I could do better the next time around. It was a maddening cycle. The most loving thing I ever did for myself was to become willing to admit that perfectionism wasn't working for me anymore. It was an adaptation response from childhood that was making adulthood harder and more painful for me. However, I quickly realized that just deciding to be done with the pattern wasn't enough to actually change it. So I decided to work on healing the wound that had created the pattern in the first place. (This is one of many instances where I recommend working with a trained practitioner. Whether it's a therapist, a counselor, or a trauma-informed coach, it is so beneficial to have a trained expert holding space for your healing and guiding you in the right direction.)

For me, healing that original wound meant a combination of things: learning to accept that there are many things in this life I can't control, being willing to believe that I am worthy of love even if I'm flawed and messy, and understanding that perfection doesn't equate to safety. Little by little I learned to be flexible, and soft, and compassionate with myself. And I learned that imperfection is beautifully human. We're not here to have it all figured out all the time. We're here to experiment, play, and adventure our way through life. More often than not, those experiments and adventures will include setbacks and mistakes and messy moments. And that's exactly the point of it all.

Try This

PRACTICE IMPERFECTION

As much as we think it's helping us, perfectionism often comes at a cost. The more rigidly you need to control yourself and your life, the less room you have to actually live it. So give this simple somatic practice a try in order to begin to create some room for life to be messy and imperfect and for that to be okay.

Set the timer on your phone for one minute and press start. Then, stand up and start jumping up and down and shaking your head at the same time. If you are unable to jump, try shaking your arms or your head from a seated position. During this time, don't fix your hair or clothes or anything around you. After the minute is up, stand or sit in silence without correcting anything about yourself. Just notice what it feels like to have messy hair and disheveled clothes for a moment.

If you're ready to take that practice to the next level, try the same challenge in other settings, like a yoga class or on a hike. Let your sweaty hair get in your face, let your pants ride up a bit, let your mascara run. See how long you can go without needing to fix anything. There's no right or wrong way to do this—it's just a practice of flexing your muscle of pliability.

Ditch Comparison

While we're on the topic of ditching patterns that don't serve us, let's talk about comparison. Our brains are wired to look for perceived differences: better or worse, safe or dangerous, friend or foe. It's what helped us survive and evolve as a species. But there's a big difference between comparing external conditions to keep you alive and comparing yourself to strangers on social media. There is nothing inherently wrong with contrast and differences. They're what make life interesting. The issue is when we hold harsh judgments about the comparisons we're making, which we almost always do. It's probably rare that you would think to yourself, *Wow, that woman is so much prettier and more successful than me. That's awesome, good for her!* Instead, we see someone whom we perceive to have things we don't, and then we feel bad about ourselves for not being good enough.

We hold judgments about levels of attractiveness, success, wealth, relationship status, popularity, and so much more. And then we use those judgments as weapons against ourselves. So it seems the first thing to do when ditching the comparison game is to reevaluate our judgments. Why have you decided that someone else having something good says something negative about you? Why do you need to label one as "better" and one as "worse" than the other? Judgment will always leave one person superior and one person feeling inferior. One of my favorite ways to work on the habit of comparison is by practicing changing it to celebration. Instead of seeing what the other person has as a threat or insult or source of shame to you, practice seeing it as a clue pointing toward your desires. If someone has something that you want to experience, take that as an opportunity to celebrate the fact that this thing is in your orbit. They are showing you, by example, what it looks and feels like to have that experience, which you can use as a signpost to help you get even closer to having it for yourself.

I believe that our authentic desires are ours because we're meant to fulfill them. They guide us to take the steps to be ready to create them, and sometimes that means showing us what it looks like on someone else. So we celebrate those moments by learning to find appreciation for the clues along our path showing us what we want. And when it comes to someone's physical attributes that we can't "have" for ourselves, it's still an opportunity for celebration. We get to celebrate the fact that there are so many different types of beauty in the world and that someone else's doesn't take away from our own. Remember, differences are not a bad thing. It's our judgments about them that get us into trouble. So your invitation is to practice celebrating rather than comparing. Simply because it feels better, and that's a self-loving, affirming thing to do.

Try This

LIVING VISION BOARD

Think about something you recently felt a sense of negative comparison about. Maybe it was someone's dreamy vacation photos on social media or a friend's seemingly perfect relationship. Take a moment to reflect on why that thing matters to you and write down two or three feelings you think it would give you (for example, "I'd feel relaxed and peaceful on that vacation" or "I'd feel happy and connected in that relationship").

Next, your job is to shift your perspective to one of expansion and possibility. See that representation of the thing you want as evidence that it exists and it's possible to have. And if it's possible for them, it's possible for you too. It's almost like you're creating a living, breathing vision board. Every time you see something on it, you get to practice cultivating those desired feelings. So find at least one thing you can do in this moment to give you access to one of the feelings you wanted to feel. Maybe you can't hop on a plane to go on vacation right this second, but you can probably go for a nice walk or visit your local bakery and get a treat that brings you joy. Maybe you can't find your dream relationship right here and now, but you can reach out to a friend to feel more connected.

When you stop seeing others as competition and the world as scarce, you can start getting in the practice of simply adding good things to your living vision board each day.

Internal and External Gratitude

If you've been in the self-help world long enough, you're probably tired of hearing the advice to keep a gratitude list. Having a gratitude practice is often hailed as the best tool for lowering depression and anxiety. In the field of positive psychology, gratitude is simply acknowledging the things we find to be good in life. And for a lot of people, it really does make a difference in their mental health and overall outlook on life. But I've got a few secret tricks to share with you that I've observed can really increase the potency of a gratitude practice.

The first is that when we are practicing gratitude, it's not as simple as saying, "I vam grateful for X." I've found it to be much more powerful when you come at the practice from a sensation state first. In the moment when the good thing happens, take a few seconds to intentionally open your heart and be present to what your body is feeling. If it's a beautiful sunset, maybe you feel warmth in your chest. If you're enjoying a delicious meal, maybe you feel your tastebuds dancing and your stomach satisfied. If someone does something kind for you, maybe you feel a sense of internal joy lighting you up. By paying attention to these little nuanced feelings, you're actually amplifying them and changing your energetic vibration to match your emotions. You're not just thinking happier thoughts by making a gratitude list at the end of the day—you're teaching your body what it *feels* like to be in joy and appreciation on a regular basis. The former helps you change your outlook, but the latter helps you actually change your lived experience. Life becomes a whole lot sweeter, richer, and more satisfying when you focus on amplifying the feelings first.

My second secret trick is to notice the subject of your gratitude. Nine times out of ten, we're focused on our external circumstances, environment, and relationships. But how often do we intentionally find things to appreciate about ourselves? Not often enough. I love inviting people to search for things to feel grateful for about themselves, because it can really cause them to view themselves in a new light. It's not so much about saying, "I'm amazing and perfect and wonderful" (and feeling like a liar because you don't believe that to be true). It's more about giving yourself permission to appreciate the wonderful things that have shaped you into the unique human that you are.

If that sounds challenging, you're not alone. We've had it drummed into our heads that focusing on what's good about us is egotistical, vain, or even narcissistic. But being grateful for what makes us strong and unique is actually powerfully healing. It orients you toward bringing more of your authentic magic into the world. Here's a simple exercise that, when done regularly, will help you build self-appreciation as a healthy habit.

Try This

INTENTIONAL SELF-APPRECIATION

Here are a few examples of things you might appreciate about yourself on any given day: your strength, your creativity, your resilience, your kind heart, your curiosity and wonder, the way you love, the freckles on your nose, how good a friend you are, the way your eyes sparkle when you're happy, your commitment to self-care, the fact that you make the world's best brownies. There are an endless number of things that you can appreciate about yourself, physical and nonphysical.

I challenge you to practice having a self-appreciation moment daily for one month straight. Bonus points if you challenge yourself to find something different every day! If that feels too hard, just finding one thing and focusing on that same thing every day will help you build momentum in learning to appreciate yourself in a bigger way.

Start right now by closing your eyes. Breathe deeply until you come up with at least one thing you genuinely appreciate about yourself in this moment. Keep your eyes closed for at least ten deep breaths while you allow the sensation of appreciation to build in your body.

Feel Your Feelings

Feeling your feelings is hard—at first. Most of us weren't taught how to feel and express our emotions in a healthy way growing up, or we learned that we'd be judged or shamed for them. So we got into a pattern of repressing and disconnecting from our feelings, and now our tendency is to numb out at the first sign of discomfort arising. We reach for our phones, use substances, binge Netflix, overeat, or bury ourselves in work. We never learned to sit with the discomfort and see what it had to teach us, nor did we learn that it inevitably passes. I promise you that you are strong enough to feel that uncomfortable thing and that it won't be as bad or last as long as you fear it will. And once you do feel it—once it has permission to take up space and get your attention—then it softens and is eventually free to leave.

So how do you practice feeling your feelings if you're used to repressing or ignoring them? First, set aside time to sit with discomfort. When you feel those uncomfortable sensations starting to stir, give yourself permission (if you're able) to go to a safe and quiet place and explore what's coming up. Then, start by simply identifying the physical sensations you're experiencing in your body. You might feel a tight chest, a racing heart, a pit in your stomach, shaky hands, or pain in a specific area. Once you've identified the physical sensations, see if you can put a name to the underlying emotion(s). Maybe you feel embarrassed, sad, angry, betrayed, guilty, scared, resentful, or confused. Maybe it's a familiar feeling, or maybe it's one you've never given yourself permission to admit out loud before. Either way, your job is to not judge the emotion. Your job is to feel into your body and allow the emotion to be expressed in whatever way feels right. Maybe that means punching pillows, or crying, or shaking your body, or jumping up and down, or just lying there and feeling it all. Notice there is pent-up energy in your body that wants to be released.

That's all emotion is. It's energy that wants space and permission to be seen and felt and then released. Once you feel like your body has done what it needs to do, I encourage you to spend a few moments taking deep breaths with your eyes closed. Sit or lie down with your hand on your heart as you breathe and notice what it feels like to hold space for such big emotions. Give yourself acknowledgment for feeling something that perhaps used to scare you.

If you're not feeling ready for that step and you'd rather start with intellectual reflection, I've included some journal prompts for you to write about. These are great tools to help you move toward understanding your emotional patterns and your relationship with feelings in general. But remember, we can't think our way out of feeling. Believe me, I've tried.

I spent many years logically processing and intellectualizing my feelings but not letting myself feel them. The profound healing and big changes in my life didn't start to occur until I practiced actually *feeling* things. That's when I came to understand that feeling our feelings is an act of self-love. Why? Because witnessing and validating our emotions is one of the most compassionate things we can do for ourselves, and compassion is an extension of love. Giving yourself full permission to let go of something heavy that you've been struggling to carry is profoundly kind.

Reflect

FEELINGS INVENTORY

Choosing yourself means choosing all of you, including the range of emotions you may have gotten very skilled at hiding or ignoring. This work will bring up big feelings—there's no way around that. So the best thing you can do is to become fluent in your emotional language, though that may require patience. Set aside some time to observe your past patterns around feeling and processing your emotions using these journal prompts.

- One at a time, call to mind several emotional experiences from your life and look at how you reacted. Do you have a tendency to feel things really deeply? Or do you feel mostly unaffected by things that happen? Maybe some emotions are okay, but others aren't?

- When you were growing up, what was the narrative in your household about feelings and emotions? What would happen if you cried? Got angry? Got excited or loud?

- What do different emotions feel like in your body? For example, when you are angry, where in your body does it show up, and what does it feel like? What about sadness? Jealousy? Fear? Joy? Love?

- Do you feel safe letting yourself express a range of emotions? Which ones feel unsafe to you?

Treat Yourself Like You Matter

Stop going around and looking for proof that you're not good enough. You might not realize that's what you're doing, but you are. At some point in your childhood, you might have learned through someone's words or actions that you weren't enough or that you didn't matter. That your feelings and needs didn't matter, that you weren't lovable enough, that you didn't measure up. So now your clever little brain goes around and seeks out conditions that confirm that feeling of not-enough-ness. And thus begins—again—the cycle of you treating yourself like you don't matter and unconsciously seeking out people and situations that will confirm that for you.

But here's the kicker: it's not even true. It's just a story you learned and have been telling yourself all these years. So when someone doesn't want to commit to you, that aligns with your inner narrative. When you keep ending up in toxic relationships or work environments, that checks out. And when you struggle to set boundaries with people or stick to healthy habits, that adds up too. Because some part of you believes you deserve these kinds of experiences.

I am here to tell you, unequivocally, that you matter. You deserve to be treated like you matter. And you deserve to treat yourself like you matter. That means honoring your boundaries, respecting the needs of your body, ending unhealthy relationships, being kind to yourself, and choosing to put yourself first. You don't have to earn the right to do this. That right is yours, simply because you exist. And the more you treat yourself like you matter, the more you'll attract people and situations that reflect the same.

Here's what it looked like when I was treating myself like I didn't matter: I was overworking and undernourishing my body; I was continually pursuing men who didn't want what I wanted; I put up with hurtful behavior from friends and partners; I struggled to communicate my sexual boundaries; I let my peers pressure me into drinking when I didn't want to; and I constantly felt anxious and disconnected from myself. And by the way, when I was treating myself the worst, I had convinced myself that I was doing everything "right." That perfectionism that we talked about earlier was the disguise I wore to cover up my poor self-worth. I thought that working so hard to be better at everything meant that I cared about my well-being, when really it was a signal of how little I thought of myself. As hard as it was to heal and give up this pattern, it would have been harder to live the rest of my life believing that I didn't matter.

If you can relate to any of that, I invite you to start being really honest with yourself about this topic.

Reflect

SELF-RESPECT CHECK-IN

Take a few minutes to reflect on the way you treat yourself on a regular basis in comparison to the way you treat the people you love the most. Here are some questions to get you started:

- When a loved one makes a mistake, how do I respond to them? When I make a mistake, how do I respond to myself?

- Do I hold myself to unrealistic standards and then punish myself if I don't reach them?

- Am I able to honor my needs and desires, even if it means disappointing others?

- Do I treat myself like I'm someone whom I respect, love, and care about?

Forgive Yourself

Once you start to see all the ways that you have treated yourself like a jerk and stayed in dynamics that were unhealthy for you, it can be tempting to be pretty mad at yourself. We love finding someone to blame, even if that someone is us. It's like you're wielding this double-edged sword: you're beginning to realize that you deserved better, but also that many times you were the perpetrator of your own torture. So your quest to treat yourself better leads you down a path where instead you just feel really angry at yourself.

I'll give you an example. I had a client who was introduced to me while going through a divorce. She was young, in her mid-twenties, and had met her soon-to-be ex-husband when she was just eighteen. He was her very first relationship, and she had no other context for what a healthy marriage should look and feel like. He turned out to be manipulative, deceitful, and emotionally and verbally abusive, and she stayed for longer than she now feels she should have. When she finally got some distance from him and began to do the work of healing, she didn't like what she saw. She looked back at that younger version of herself who stayed in an unhealthy marriage, and she felt anger and shame. She was having thoughts like, *How could I have been so stupid? What was wrong with me that I stayed so long? Why did I waste so much time with him and let him treat me like that?* While it was important to give these feelings space to come up, those thoughts were ultimately unproductive in her healing.

Because the truth is, we always do the best we can with what we know. It's easy to look back and say what you could've or should've done differently. But you're looking back with the advantage of time, wisdom, lived experience, and new tools in your arsenal. You didn't have any of that back then. So forgive yourself for not knowing better. Forgive yourself for being human. Hindsight really is 20/20. And our relationship wounds tend to give us the blurriest vision. I stayed in so many situationships and unhealthy relationship dynamics far longer than I "should" have. But my vision was blurred by my low self-worth, my insecure attachment style, my abandonment wounds, and my subconscious fear of being alone. Those versions of me needed love and healing, not more punishment and abuse for my perceived shortcomings.

Learning to forgive myself was one of the most gracious acts of self-love I've experienced. It felt like a boulder being lifted from my chest so that I could finally take a deep breath again.

Self-forgiveness will be a valuable tool for you when we get to part 3 of this book. As we explore some patterns and experiences from your past, notice whether any tendency arises to want to blame yourself and make yourself wrong. If those feelings creep up, see if you can practice a bit of compassion and forgiveness instead. Give yourself permission to not know what you didn't know back then. (In other words, accept your past.) And know that forgiveness might not happen in one fell swoop. Instead, it's something that you practice and return to over and over again, until you feel that boulder lifted.

Try This

LET YOURSELF OFF THE HOOK

Read through these instructions fully first and then take yourself through this mini–guided practice for embodying self-forgiveness.

Close your eyes and picture a young and innocent version of yourself. If you have a hard time imagining your younger self or feeling compassion toward this version of you, try picturing a niece or nephew or another child you love. Imagine this child knocked over a glass and is upset and embarrassed about the mess they made. Imagine how you'd comfort this child and let them know that it's okay; accidents happen, and now they'll learn for next time. See if you can locate a place in your body where you feel a sense of care and compassion for that child (for example, maybe a warm sensation in your chest).

Now, hold onto that feeling as you imagine an adult version of you who made a choice that hurt you or ended poorly. Go to that version of you in your mind, whether it was one week ago or many years ago, and imagine yourself sharing this compassionate feeling with that part of you you've been blaming. See that, just like the young child you comforted earlier, this version of you was doing the best they could with the information they had at the time. Let that version of you know that it's okay to make mistakes and learn and grow from them. Let that younger you off the hook for not being able to access another choice.

Now spend some time reflecting in your journal: How did that practice feel?

Let Go

Letting go is a similar concept to forgiveness, because in the process of letting go, our acceptance of what is and our release of resistance ultimately create space for something new to come in. So often we cling to our stories and our attachments because we fear that if we let go, nothing will come to take their place. We stay in bad relationships because we're afraid that this is as good as it will get. We hold onto limiting beliefs because we're unsure of who we'd be without them. We might even stay in abusive relationships for fear of what could happen if we left. For many women in that position, staying, rather than risking retaliation from the abusive partner, feels like the safer option. And we stay in unfulfilling situations and places in life because it feels more secure than venturing into the unknown. We love safety and certainty. And if you're anything like me, you crave control and having all the answers.

There was a period of time in my twenties when I became really invested in healing and doing inner work. Feeling overwhelmed by trauma, I was desperate for any clarity and guidance that I could get. I was a regular in the self-help and spirituality sections at my local Barnes & Noble, I'd seek out conversations with anyone who would give me advice, I hired therapists and healers whenever I could afford it (and even when I couldn't), and I'd end every day lost in the rabbit hole of Google searches and YouTube videos. I was constantly seeking and sometimes begging for answers. But the funny part is, I didn't always listen when I got them. I met a stretch of time when I kept getting one message over and over again: *let go*. Multiple mentors and guides were telling me that I needed to loosen my grip, release my attachments. Everyone I talked to and everywhere I turned seemed to be conspiring to teach me the same lesson, and I didn't want to hear it. The thought of loosening my grip felt akin to throwing out my life vest when I was drowning in a storm. So instead I just nodded along and said, "Okay, I let go," even though I had no concept of what that really meant. I just hoped that saying their magic words might make everything better.

It took me quite some time to learn that letting go is really about permission and allowing. Giving yourself permission to change and grow and evolve. Giving yourself permission to give up on the things not meant for you. Allowing the universe to guide you in a direction that feels better, even when you can't see what's coming. Allowing for the possibility that your plan might not be the best one for you and that even better things are in store if you only let go of your attachment to the way you think things need to be. Sometimes letting go means releasing people, places, and things that no longer serve us. And sometimes letting go actually means opening up to a greater vision of what's possible for your life.

Letting go is expansive. It creates space and new possibilities. That's why it's such a beautiful act of self-love: it gives you room to grow into who you really are, regardless of who you believe yourself to be in this moment.

Try This

THE ART OF LETTING GO

Curl your left hand into a fist, squeezing it as tightly as you can for about ten to twenty seconds. Keep squeezing as you feel your hand start to tire. Now, wrap your right hand around your left fist with some gentle and steady pressure. Notice that as you cradle your fist, it naturally starts to soften and loosen its grip. It doesn't have to work so hard to hold its shape, because it has the support of your right hand to maintain the shape.

That's what we're going for when we practice the art of letting go: finding small comforts that support you in being able to loosen something you've been holding on to too tightly. That support might come in the form of literal rest, time in nature, prayer, asking a therapist for help, or anything else that makes you feel more capable of surrendering some control.

Here are some questions to reflect on after you try this practice:

- What am I holding onto for fear that nothing better will take its place?

- What do I need to loosen my grip on right now?

- What am I afraid will happen if I let go? How can I support the part of me that holds that fear?

So, as you can see, these suggestions go far beyond massages, facials, and bubble baths. Self-love is a commitment to the belief that you are worth doing hard things for and that you're deserving of the payoff that comes afterward. The seven practices in the "Self-Love" section in this chapter—ditch perfection, ditch comparison, internal and external gratitude, feel your feelings, treat yourself like you matter, forgive yourself, and let go—are a crash course to help you prepare for what's to come. When you practice these concepts in your daily life, little by little you'll come to regard yourself as someone who is deeply worthy of love. And that's ultimately what this work is all about. It's time to learn how to love yourself better, so that your solitude is sweeter and you'll never accept anything less in any of your relationships.

Self-Soothing

Continuing down the lineup of practices in our self-oriented learning program, we have to talk about self-soothing. Self-soothing is any behavior you might use to regulate your emotional state all by yourself. It's the process of comforting and nurturing yourself with healthy tools and activities—the key word being *healthy*. I'm sure you can think of a time you used coping mechanisms that were unhealthy or destructive. But before we get into some self-soothing methods that you can practice (or might already be using), it's helpful to understand a few reasons why you might struggle with self-soothing.

It's believed that our ability to soothe ourselves is developed in childhood when we internalize the experiences of being soothed by our parents or caregivers. Basically, we learn to imitate the way that they treated us when we were upset or overwhelmed. So if you had parents who were neglectful, inattentive, or just not attuned to your emotions for any reason, you might have internalized the experience of your needs not getting met in a loving way. As an adult this may have left you with a belief that you are not deserving of receiving this type of care from yourself or others or that taking care of yourself is shameful in some way. Maybe you had parents who yelled at you when you were crying, and now you find yourself being enormously self-critical anytime you have a big feeling.

Alternatively, maybe you had helicopter parents who always stepped in to fix things for you and never helped you learn that you're capable of doing things on your own. In that case, you might hold the belief that others are solely responsible for soothing you, which can lead to unhealthy patterns in relationships. Some people also fall prey to overusing soothing strategies to the point of emotional avoidance ("If I just focus on doing this thing that makes me feel better, then I don't ever have to face the actual problem").

If it's not clear by now, most of us don't get out of childhood unscathed. Even really loving, well-meaning parents aren't perfect, and we don't always learn the tools we need in order to be emotionally healthy adults. It can be helpful to do a little skills audit and see where your blind spots are. Self-soothing is a valuable skill to explore now. We'll be touching on some sensitive, potentially painful subjects throughout this book, and it's important to be confident in your ability to know when and how to soothe yourself, as well as when and how to lean on your support system for help.

You want to learn to effectively self-soothe so you can decrease anxiety, panic, and stress while increasing your ability to tolerate pain and stay present in a moment of distress. Essentially, you're expanding your capacity for feeling safe in the midst of discomfort. This can help you make less impulsive decisions and overcome difficult situations with more grace and groundedness.

What Are Some Healthy Ways to Self-Soothe?

This is my tried-and-true list of tools and practices that are accessible, free, and work wonders on soothing a dysregulated nervous system. I recommend trying several of these practices, if not all of them, more than once. They might feel immediately grounding, or you might need some repetition with them before you notice their effects. It's helpful to remember that there's no one-size-fits-all—different tools work for different people.

- **Slow, deep belly breathing.** This helps to activate the parasympathetic nervous system and get you out of fight-or-flight mode (we'll explore this more in chapter 8).

- **A hot bath.** A steaming bath with Epsom salts and calming essential oils, like lavender or eucalyptus, takes the soothing to the next level. Ending with a cold shower can further support regulating your nervous system.

- **Soothing touch.** As a very tactile person, I'm a huge fan of surrounding myself with comforting textures. Use objects (a soft blanket, a smooth stone, a cozy pillow) or sensations (petting an animal) that induce a calming feeling.

- **Self-touch.** Try rubbing a hand on your heart, giving yourself a hug, stroking your own arm or cheek, or giving yourself a hand or foot massage.

- **Body scan and muscle relaxation.** Mentally scan your body from head to toe, taking your time and observing what you're feeling in each part of the body. Then, try tensing and relaxing one muscle at a time, noticing how that induces a sense of grounding.

- **Scents.** Use comforting scents, in the form of candles or essential oils, to boost your mood and signal to your brain that you are safe.

- **Sounds.** Listen to calming music, white noise, or nature sounds.

- **A weighted blanket.** Rest under a weighted blanket in a dimly lit or darkened room.

- **Tea meditation.** Mindfully sip some warm herbal tea and notice the sensations as it moves down your throat and into your body.

- **Moving meditation.** Quiet your mind by intentionally moving your body: take a walk, practice yoga, or do any other form of movement that brings you joy.

What Are Some Unhealthy Strategies People Might Use to Cope?

The habits on the following list may or may not be familiar to you. Our society normalizes and even encourages many of these behaviors, so some of them may feel like the only things that help you cope with overwhelming feelings or daily life stressors:

- Substance use
- Overeating or restricting food
- Overexercising
- Self-harm
- Overspending and/or gambling
- Excessive scrolling and/or binge-watching

These behaviors help us check out, and sometimes that's what's needed. In small amounts, dissociation can be a helpful tool when we've reached the point of overwhelm. But when occasional checking out turns into an ongoing harmful habit, it's time to reevaluate our coping mechanisms and possibly enlist the support of a therapist to help us get on a healthier track.

We rely on unhealthy coping mechanisms when either we don't know there's another way to cope or some part of us believes that we don't deserve good things and loving experiences. It takes time, practice, and intentionality to develop a self-soothing tool kit that works for you—and you need to be willing for your tools to change. You might go through a phase when breath work is super effective in helping you manage stress, and then suddenly it doesn't work as well anymore. So you shift to using mindful movement, or meditation, or body scans. It's normal that you may require different approaches during different seasons of your life.

People often want one magical approach that will fix all their problems. They want to know what pill to take or what special mantra to use that will make everything better forever. I know, because I was one of those people. And unfortunately it doesn't work that way. My desire to find the one magical solution is part of what drove my obsession with certain behaviors along my healing journey. I spent many years obsessively controlling my food intake and overexercising on a daily basis just to run away from the many uncomfortable feelings that I didn't know how to face. When I finally realized that these tactics weren't working, I became just as obsessed with finding a healthier method that would be the key to solving all my problems. Every time I learned a new practice, I'd fixate on it to the point of excess. If someone told me twenty minutes of daily meditation was great for you, I'd assume more was better and meditate for two to three hours. If a self-help book suggested working with three affirmations a day, every morning I'd write out ten pages of affirmations I desperately wanted to believe. Spoiler alert: more isn't better. My obsessive behavior only made things worse.

I've learned that there is no single magical solution to making ourselves feel better. It's about having a robust toolbox of self-soothing practices that we can rely on, depending on the feeling and situation at hand. This toolbox must also include the ability to increase our tolerance for feeling and sitting with our emotions in the first place. That's how we discern what it is that we need in any given moment.

Let's take going through a breakup as an example. The classic image of self-soothing after a breakup almost always includes binging on ice cream and sappy movies. While there's nothing inherently wrong with either of those things (I am a huge fan of both sweet treats and rom-coms), they're certainly not a cure-all for heartbreak. As much as I wish I could tell you that time and ice cream heal all, they do not. Being intentional and going within and clearing out old misunderstandings and trying out new tools and practicing new ways of being—these are things that provide healing. You have to actually feel your heartbreak, reflect on your relationship and why it ended, and get clear on what you want moving forward. And in those moments when it just feels like too much to bear, you pull out your self-soothing techniques. That's when you need to be kind and gentle with yourself, just like you would with a small child who is hurt.

So your assignment now is to make a list of all the practices you have tried and enjoyed, as well as ones that you would like to try next time you're in need of some love and care. You can use the list of healthy ways to self-soothe on page 62 as a starting point, then add anything else that feels healthy and nurturing to you. Put this self-soothing toolbox list somewhere special and refer to it in times of need.

Chapter 3

Understanding What You Want

Reclaiming the Power of Your Desire

Not long ago, I was leading a retreat for a dozen women to help them reconnect to their authentic self-expression. About halfway through the event, the alchemical energy of transformation started to fill the room in a way that everyone could feel. When that happens, it's a special moment that I like to call the homecoming. See, in the beginning of these events, there's often a lot of excitement mixed in with a bit of guardedness. As women share their intentions one by one, I have a subtle sense that something is being held back, which is entirely understandable when you're being asked to share something vulnerable in front of a group of strangers.

But as I guide them through practices and we start to move our bodies, they begin to shed their armor. They let go of the to-do lists they came in with and dissolve the worry of what other people in the room might think of them. And inevitably, they reach that moment when they come back home to themselves. You can actually see it when it happens. When a woman starts to fully inhabit her body and remember herself and own her desires, a life force radiates from her.

I lived a lot of my life disconnected from that life force, and I'm willing to bet you have too. But the good news is, it's never too late for a homecoming.

Self-Discovery

Much of this book is about discovering who you are, what you value, what you want, and how you like to show up in the world.

One of the most common patterns I see in women in the dating world is that they hide pieces of themselves for the sake of conforming to what their partners want. Most of the time this isn't done consciously. When I was dating in my twenties, I had no idea how much of myself I'd lost and hidden and given away just to try to get guys to choose me. I wouldn't think twice about adopting a crush's favorite foods, favorite music, date preferences, and even communication style. A lot of this behavior stemmed from my unhealed attachment wounds, codependency, rejection sensitivity, and low self-worth. But we'll get to that later.

Relationships can actually be a great vehicle for self-discovery. Several chapters in this book give you the opportunity to explore important lessons and takeaways from your past relationships. While we can certainly learn much about ourselves in solitude, we can also learn a lot about ourselves in the context of interacting with other people. Relationships truly are our greatest teachers and our biggest mirror for what's going on inside.

The key words to remember when using relationships as clues for self-discovery are *discernment* and *authenticity*. You have to become adept at discerning what your truth is, so that you are coming from a place of authenticity, rather than taking on your partner's truth as your own. Here's a simple example.

I once dated a guy whom I was completely enamored with. He was older than me, was very successful, and exuded a sense of self-confidence and carefree joy; naturally, I put him on a pedestal. I had this problem back then: I couldn't allow myself to have strong opinions around anyone I was attracted to and/or intimidated by. So when he asked me before our first date if I liked seafood, I impulsively said yes. Seafood is the one type of food that I strongly and categorically dislike. But in an effort to be the cool girl, I decided to just go with the flow. Maybe he was onto something and I'd magically learn to love eating seafood at the swanky restaurants that he'd take me to. I spent many nights swallowing sashimi and oysters and seared fish without chewing because I didn't want to gag at the taste, and I couldn't admit that I had been pretending to love what he loved.

On that same first date we also got to talking about music, which has always been a big part of my life. He asked me if I liked house music or EDM. My perception of those music genres at the time was that they were intense rave music and not something that I had any interest in. So what was my answer to his question? "Totally, I love it!" You're probably sensing a theme right now. When he started mentioning artists, I said I was really bad with remembering names, so he offered to play some of their songs for me later. He did, and, surprisingly, I truly loved everything he played. We spent an entire evening listening to music together and bonding over it.

So did I learn to love seafood because of him? Definitely not. But I did learn to love a genre of music that I probably wouldn't have given a chance to otherwise. In the context of that relationship, I had too much of my own healing to do to be honest with him about what I liked and didn't like. But years later, I can still look back and appreciate what I discovered about myself because of him.

How much of what you do is because you actually like it, and how much of it is just a conditioned habit from past relationships? Which of your preferences are truly yours, and which are the remnants from years of people pleasing? I'd invite you to consider what it would be like to release those habits. Start to observe how much space is freed up when you're honest with yourself about what you like and what you don't.

That's what self-discovery is all about: becoming radically honest with yourself (and eventually others) about what's true for you. And the only way you can discern what's true for you is by living life and paying attention. Seek out experiences and interactions with the world that shape who you are. As you begin to do this, you might find that the version of yourself you've been showing up as is really a melting pot of other people's desires and preferences. Just as with self-talk, we can sometimes take on the personalities and interests of those around us. The more permission you give yourself to be radically honest, the more some of those traits and preferences might naturally fall away. This is a good thing! It means you are getting closer to knowing your authentic self.

Your work now is to notice if you, like me, have had a tendency to betray or ignore parts of yourself for the sake of fitting into someone else's world. If you have, then this is a powerful moment for you to start cultivating your own sense of identity again.

Throughout this book there will be moments when I ask you to try new things, take new actions, and experiment with new ways of being. The point of these assignments isn't only to get you out of your comfort zone. It's to help you rediscover who you are. It's to help you build a sense of identity that is separate from any romantic partner or external validation.

The two things that are required for self-discovery are introspection and new experiences. Self-discovery is less about asking the question "Who am I?" and more about observing what lights you up and how your brain is wired and how your past has shaped you. It's about discovering how you feel about the world around you, what you value, what you need and want, and what attachments you can let go of in the process. And then it's about deciding who you want to be and taking steps to show up as that version of you. I believe that self-discovery is as much an active, ongoing decision as it is a gentle allowing of what already exists.

The reason that we're going through this process is to help you ensure that the things you are doing and the people you are choosing to have in your life are reflective of what you really want and who you really are. Not who the world wants you to be, but who you *are*. And that's a choice that only you can make.

Reflect

THE REAL ME JOURNAL PROMPTS

Getting to know yourself is the same as getting to know a new friend or romantic interest: it's all about asking good questions. Have you ever been on a date where you were the only one asking questions? It probably felt pretty lackluster and one-sided. That's because it feels good when someone is genuinely curious about us and our interests! So why would it be any different in your relationship with yourself? It's time to start asking yourself the juicy questions. Here are a few to get you started, but feel free to get creative and add more to this list.

- What events in my life have shaped me the most?
- If no one else were around, what would I love to spend my time doing?

- What is a subject I could talk about for hours? Why do I love it so much?

- Have there been moments in my past when I ignored my truth to please someone else?

- What is the ideal version of me like? What's the difference between her and who I'm showing up as now? How can I fill in that gap?

I recommend writing out your answers in a journal so you can come back and reread them later. If journaling isn't your thing, you can record your answers out loud in a voice memo on your phone.

Defining Your Desires

"What do you want?"

These seemingly innocent words, when strung together in this way, used to feel like a direct threat to my safety. For many years this was an impossible question for me to answer.

A friend would ask me where I'd like to eat, and I'd respond, "Wherever you want to go!" Someone would ask my opinion on a topic, and I'd just agree with whatever they said. Relationships always progressed on the other person's timing because I never dared to express what I wanted. And if a partner asked me what I desired in the bedroom? My brain would immediately shut down, malfunction, lose all ability to process.

What did I want? That question didn't make any sense to me (at least not in the context of relationships). First, it required me to identify my desires, which I'd become completely detached from in my quest to shape-shift to fit with the people around me. Then it meant that I'd have to actually use my voice to share an opinion that might be different from that of the person I was speaking to—and risk a disagreement? Out loud? Impossible.

The sad thing is, I didn't even know I was doing this. Everyone around me playfully called it indecision or chalked it up to me being a Libra. As if my astrological sign had eliminated all of my desires and preferences at birth. But it's not just me: society does this to little girls every day. Strips them of their unique voices and then makes fun of them when they become just silly, indecisive women who don't know what they want.

At some point you probably learned that your own desire, or the aftermath of it, was not safe to have. You wanted something and were reprimanded for throwing a tantrum when you didn't get it, and you began to equate desire with punishment and lack of belonging. We disconnect from our wanting when we learn it's not safe to feel the feelings that arise from not getting something we want. We also lose confidence in our desires and decisions when they've led to loss of love in the past and it becomes seemingly safer to default to what others prefer.

The truth is, desire is power. Desire is strength. Desire is the force that causes you to show up fully for your life and make changes when something doesn't feel aligned. Desire gives you permission to be a "Hell, yes" and pursue anything that lights you up from the inside out. But first, you must learn to give yourself permission to define and connect with your desires and to own them 100 percent.

Some people are really great at owning their desires. They never lost the part of themselves that knows what they want is important and that they deserve to experience it just because they exist. When we're babies, our whole life is about getting our needs met. We need to be fed, we need our diapers to be changed, we need to be held and nurtured and rocked to sleep. That's about it.

Then, as our basic needs are met and we begin to grow and interact with the world more, we start to experience desire. We see things that we want to play with, places we want to go, people we want to talk to. As a baby or toddler, we have no judgments or preconceived notions about our desires. We just want them fulfilled, and so we ask for them (or we go after something without pausing to ask, because we don't even consider that we may need permission). Some of those babies grow up into people who continue to pursue their desires without self-judgment or shame or trying to make themselves small.

But somewhere along the way, many of us learn that we can't always have what we want. Or that we shouldn't want particular things. Or that going after something we want will get us in trouble or lead to pain. And so we slowly disconnect from our desires, because it hurts to want something that you feel like you can't have.

Well, it's time for you to learn to *want* again. Because you can't show up as your most authentic self (in life or in relationships) if you're not fully owning both your needs and your desires. Desire is just a natural extension of who you are. A desire is your internal self seeking to have an external experience through your senses that satisfies a curiosity in you. I like to think of desires as clues that lead me further along the path of my truest self. Every time I honor one, life seems to flow better. Every time I shame myself for having a particular desire or try to repress it, life feels sticky and clunky and frustrating.

When it comes to desire, you might be in one of two places:

- **Camp No. 1:** I need to figure out what the heck I actually want in the first place. Desire is a totally foreign, maybe even scary, word to me, and I don't know where to start.

- **Camp No. 2:** I know what I want, but I have no idea how to say it out loud. I've gotten so used to being quiet and submissive and flexible that I don't know how to own my desires around other people.

Let's address each of them and give you a road map of where to begin.

Try This

IF YOU'RE IN CAMP NO. 1: FIGURE OUT WHAT YOU WANT

Your homework involves a little investigative digging. Start by identifying some moments in your past when you know that you made a decision to please someone else, even though you really didn't want to do it. Here are a few examples to get you thinking:

- Your friend asks you for a ride to the airport. Normally, you'd be happy to drive them, but this time you'll have to miss something important to make it work. You feel bad letting them down, so you say yes anyway.

- You've been overextended at work. Your boss asks if you can stay late to take on a new project. You know you really need sleep, but you say yes anyway.

- Someone asks you out on a first date to a venue you're not comfortable going to. You don't want them to think you're too picky, so you say yes even though you know it won't feel good for you.

As you reflect on those moments, feel into your body and see if you can identify any physical sensations that came along with your choices. Maybe some heaviness in your chest, or a pit in your stomach, or a lump in your throat? What did it feel like to say yes when you really meant no?

Then, spend some time in self-inquiry about why you prefer to please others over pleasing yourself. Why are their wants and needs more important than yours? Maybe people-pleasing was the only way to create peace in the chaotic household of your childhood. Maybe you've experienced big pain on the other side of letting someone down. Or perhaps you were taught in your culture, family, or religion that selflessness is an important quality to possess. Get curious about the part of you that decided to disconnect from your desire.

Once you have an understanding of why this part of you exists, you are free to change its role a bit. It's likely that this part of you was just trying to keep you safe, loved, and accepted in some way. But as an empowered adult, you get to decide what's true for you. And you can decide that it's possible to be safe and loved *and* to own your desires. Those things are not mutually exclusive.

Now, the fun part. (Okay, maybe it'll be a little uncomfortable too, depending on how resistant you are to owning your desires. But I promise you this is a good kind of discomfort to push through.) I want you to set aside five minutes in your day when you can be completely alone in a quiet room to try out the following practice. Start by closing your eyes and putting one hand on your heart and one hand on your belly. Take a deep breath, and with your eyes closed, I want you to think of something you want and internally say the word *yes*. Notice any feelings or subtle sensations in your body when you say it. Next, say *yes* out loud. Again, notice any shifts or sensations in your body. Go through this same process for all of the following words and phrases, keeping your eyes closed and hands on your heart and belly. Remain present to any physical sensations you're feeling.

"Yes!"

"YES!!"

"Hell, yes!"

"More of that!"

"I want that!"

Open your eyes, get out your journal, and write responses to these prompts:

- How did it feel to practice having desire and giving a full-bodied yes to something?

- Did any resistance come up to what you were saying and feeling?

- If you held back because it felt uncomfortable, what would it take for you to feel that yes with your full body?

You might need to come back to this practice for a few rounds before you begin to get comfortable with the sensations of owning a desire. But once you do, I want you to identify what it specifically feels like in your body for you to be a "Hell, yes!" Do you get butterflies or feel a lightness in your chest? Do you feel grounded and certain? Do you feel warm and expansive inside? It's important to identify the physical sensations, because these are what you will use as clues later on to identify your desires. And anytime you feel those sensations telling you that something is a yes, you get to practice owning it. You get to ask yourself, *What would it be like to give myself full permission to have this thing I want?* After you've played around with that for a bit, you're ready to move on to the next step.

Try This

IF YOU'RE IN CAMP NO. 2: COMMUNICATE YOUR DESIRES

Your work is all about the practice of having what you want. Sometimes it can help to start small. Begin by making a list of anything and everything that you've been desiring lately. It could include big things, like having a loving relationship, getting a raise at work, moving into a new home, or going on a month-long vacation. This list can also include more easily achievable desires, like getting your favorite pastry from the local bakery, taking a full day to binge-watch a new show, or dancing around the kitchen while you cook dinner. Write down anything and everything that has felt like a yes for you lately, whether you've actually done it or not.

Then, go through your list and practice owning each thing out loud. For each item, say out loud, "I give myself permission to desire X and to let myself have X." An example might be: "I give myself permission to desire a healthy relationship and to let myself have a healthy relationship." Or: "I give myself permission to desire a cinnamon roll from my favorite bakery and to let myself have that cinnamon roll." Then, notice if you are giving more importance to some of your desires than others. Is it easier for you to own some things on the list than others?

After you've rehearsed the feeling of owning what you want, now it's time to practice actually having it. You'll start by fulfilling a desire that isn't dependent on anyone else. So go get that cinnamon roll, or have your movie day in bed, or buy yourself the thing you've been really wanting. Then spend some time luxuriating in what it feels like to have something you've desired. Again, notice any discomfort that arises, as this is valuable information too. Maybe when you get something you want you feel guilty, or shameful, or afraid that you might lose it. These feelings are neither good nor bad—they are just feedback about where you are in your healing.

Once you've gotten a little more comfortable with giving yourself the things you want, it's time to practice with other people. Again, allow yourself to start small if that feels better. Next time your friend asks you where you want to eat, practice sharing what you really want rather than defaulting to their favorite restaurant. Or if they've already suggested a place you're not into, you get to say, "I'm not really feeling pizza tonight, but I'd love to go to that new Thai restaurant!" Let that land in the space without following up with a placating "If you want," "Only if that sounds good to you," or "But I'm fine with whatever!" You may need to give the people in your life time to get used to you voicing your desires, but I promise you won't lose any relationships over your food preferences (at least not any healthy relationships).

Communicating things that we're not used to communicating is an uncomfortable process. It can feel awkward and unsettling at first. But the more you practice it, the more empowered you will feel to speak your truth and honor your desires.

For a long time, I was so disconnected from my sense of desire that I truly thought I didn't have any. I believed that my only desire was to give other people what they wanted and that's what would make me happy. And while it's not a bad thing to derive pleasure from making other people happy, it cannot be your sole source of satisfaction. It took me a long time to undo this conditioning and to realize that there is nothing inherently wrong with having my own individual desires and preferences.

In fact, I was so disconnected, I had to start by using other people's desires as a road map. I'd tune into something that someone else wanted, then ask myself how that thing felt in my body. If it was a yes for me, then I'd practice having it or pursuing it. If it was a no, I'd give myself permission to let "No" be a full sentence. By doing this, eventually, my desires became my own personal road map on the path to living a life that lit me up from the inside out.

You don't do yourself a favor by hiding your desires. Imagine yourself as someone new you're wanting to get close to. It's hard to have a good relationship with that person if you don't know who they are, what they want, and what makes them unique. That would be like bonding with someone over a shared love of country music, only to realize years later that they hate country and were just trying to make you happy. In order to truly get to know them, you need to learn what kind of music they actually love. So start being honest with yourself about what you want and watch how new possibilities start showing up in your life left and right.

Your Future Self

There is a version of you that exists in the future who already has everything you want and many things that you haven't even dreamed of wanting yet. And if you're into the science of quantum mechanics, where all possibilities are present in any given moment and time is irrelevant, then you know that this future version of you also exists in this moment, here and now. Or if spirituality is more your thing, you can think of your future self like a guide whom you have access to for support, clarity, and advice. Either way, it can be helpful to get in the habit of connecting with this future you. I'm going to teach you how.

Developing a practice of regularly connecting to your future self serves two important purposes. First, it instills you with the confidence that what you want to have is not only possible but probable. In those (inevitable) moments of doubt or confusion, you can have faith that everything works out in the end. If you're feeling brokenhearted today, you can connect with the version of you who is happy, fulfilled, and in love. You can get a sneak peek from this future you of what it feels like to be in the most wonderful, healthy, fulfilling relationship, and you can start to bring those feelings into your present-day life to relieve your heartbreak. If you're feeling lost today, you can connect with the future version of you who is totally aligned with your life purpose and surrounded by loving community. Essentially, connecting with your future self opens up the door to realities that may not feel possible for you yet, and it helps bring them closer to you.

Second, having a future-self practice helps you to make your future goals more tangible and effectively reverse engineer them into your life. Because if you believe that what you want is inevitable, then you can focus on the aligned action steps it will take to get there. We often don't take action because we're afraid that the thing we want isn't possible for us. We fear failure, rejection, loss, embarrassment. And so we stay confined to the circumstances of our present reality, even if deep down we want to experience more. When instead we allow our future self to guide us, we can connect with the best actions to get us where we want to go.

Let's use a simple, tangible example. Say you have a huge presentation at work tomorrow, and it needs to go well. You can imagine a future version of you, twenty-four hours from now, who has totally nailed the presentation and is brimming with confidence because your boss told you that your impressive work put you in line for a big promotion. That future version of you might guide you to run through a practice round of your presentation without note cards tonight so that you feel really comfortable with the material. They might also guide you to drink some herbal tea and go to bed early, so that you wake up well rested and with plenty of energy. Those simple actions are what will lead you to give a stellar presentation, and they came from the version of you who already has the outcome you want. If, instead, you were to take action from the part of you that is afraid things will go poorly, you might make unnecessary changes to your slides that throw you off and spend all night tossing and turning in anxiety, leaving you completely exhausted by morning.

If you can believe that there is a version of you who already has the life experience you desire, it makes it so much easier to take aligned action. Even if you're experiencing some feelings of anxiety, you might take comfort in the fact that some future version of you has already created a successful outcome. The reality is, sometimes both things might be true. All that means is that you are a totally normal human—welcome to the club.

So now for the fun part. Let's connect with your future self! For the sake of committing to the rest of the suggestions in this book, let's make a few assumptions. Let's assume that a future version of you exists who has the most beautiful and fulfilling relationship with yourself imaginable. This version of you has done some powerful inner healing work and has set the stage for healthy, expansive relationships to come into your life. Your friendships are strong, your work is fulfilling, your life feels full of joy and magic. And maybe you go to a point in the future where you have that romantic relationship you've always dreamed of. Future you has met your person, and they're everything you wanted and more. Let's assume that all of that is 100 percent true and already exists in a future time line. Because in making these assumptions, you will have a deeper subconscious motivation to take the actions that will get you there.

Now, here are four ways to practice connecting with your future self.

Try This

PAST, PRESENT, FUTURE METHOD

This method can be done either as a meditation, with your eyes closed, or in written form in your journal. I love it because it gives you a tangible experience of what it's like to connect with different versions of yourself and where the conversation might start.

Begin by imagining that you as your present-day self are talking to a version of you from five to ten years ago. Pick an age that you still feel somewhat connected to, but one far enough back that your life has changed in significant ways. Now, offer younger you instructions and advice on how to live the life you are now living. You can start with practical, logistical things, like handing them your keys (in your mind) and telling them how to get into your current home, water your plants, drive your car, and so on. Then, move on to any guidance you think they need to hear at that age. Things like, "You're going to want to spend a lot of time at the bookstore, because self-help books are the beginning of a really important healing journey for you." Or like, "Start making lists of all the places you're excited to travel to and what you want to do there, because in a few years you'll have the money, time, and freedom to be able to travel often." The advice you're giving them is relative to the season of life they're in, but is meant to inspire them to move toward where you are now. It's like you're leaving a trail of breadcrumbs for your younger self.

Once you feel that present you has connected with past you, we'll move on to the next phase. Now you will allow future you to connect with present-day you. Again, pick an age in the future that gives you enough time to believe your life could be different in meaningful ways. So if you are twenty-five years old now, maybe you choose to connect with your thirty-five- or forty-year-old self. Imagine that older, wiser version of you is speaking to you and telling you all about what your life is like at that age. You want to set the intention to connect with the most ideal version of yourself so that you can glean what you need to shift in order to get there.

First, notice what they look like and feel like. How do they carry themselves? What's their energy like? What are they wearing, and what do they do each day? Similar to how you did in the first stage of this process, you can imagine them handing over any keys or instructions to get into their world, and then let them give you guidance on how to get there. Don't judge or question anything that comes up—just allow the process to flow. Again, you can do this with eyes closed in a meditation, or you can freewrite these conversations in your journal.

You might find yourself thinking, *I feel like I'm just making this up.* So what if you are? If it ultimately makes you feel better, inspires you to believe in greater possibilities, and helps you take action on the things that matter to you, that's a win. Plus it's normal to feel like you're making it up, since this information *is* coming from you. It's coming from a future version of you, but that version exists within you already. Don't let doubts discourage you from experiencing the magic that this process can bring.

Try This

GUIDED WRITING

If you need a little help to get the conversation started with future you, you can try the process of guided writing. In this method, you will write a question at the top of a page as your present self and then respond to the question as your future self. You can ask any question that you want. But know that if you aren't getting an answer, there's a reason for that too. It might not be the right time for you to have that information, or it might be completely irrelevant to your future. Trust whatever comes forward. Here are a few questions to get you started:

- Where are you working, and how do you feel about it?
- What are your relationships like?
- What is something you've learned that is important for me to know?
- How do you spend your time?
- What is something you really love to do?
- What is a goal you have or something you're looking forward to?

Try This

FREEWRITING

This method is pretty simple but can yield some surprising results. You'll start by freewriting a letter to your future self. Freewriting simply means putting pen to paper without a prompt or specific structure. You can write whatever you feel inspired to, however it wants to come out. It doesn't have to make any logical sense. Tell them everything that is going on in your life right now and how you feel about it all. Then ask the question "What do you want me to know right now?" and answer as your future self. Write for as long as it feels good. Maybe set a timer for five or ten minutes, or make an intention to fill up a page.

When you finish writing, read what you wrote and make note of any changes or action steps that your future self wants you to take. Identify ways that you can begin to take those actions today. The more that you can show your future self you're really listening, the stronger the connection will become. You can do this practice daily or whenever the mood strikes.

Try This

GUIDED FUTURE-SELF MEDITATION

Okay, I get that if this concept is new to you, it might feel silly or strange to be talking to some seemingly made up future version of you. Sometimes, it can help to have a little guidance to make the process easier. I've actually found that guided meditations can be one of the most powerful ways to facilitate a relationship with your future self, because in a relaxed state you tend to accept the suggestions that are being given to you. It can be easier to conjure an image of your future self and listen for messages from them when you're in a meditative state. Or, even better, in a hypnotic state. As a licensed hypnotherapist, I love teaching about the practice of getting in touch with your subconscious mind. You can use guided hypnosis essentially like a deep guided relaxation to help you open up to suggestions and new possibilities. The difference is that while meditation is intended to create active mindfulness, hypnosis is intended to induce passive suggestibility. They're often formatted and experienced similarly, with the main difference being the induction, a brief technique offered at the beginning of a hypnosis practice to help tap into the subconscious mind. (Note that guided hypnosis is different from a hypnotherapy session, which would be led by a trained practitioner and include therapeutic techniques focused on one particular area of your life.) If guided hypnosis is something you're curious to try, I have a guided hypnosis for meeting your future self on my website. Head to megansherer.com to explore.

If you'd prefer to take yourself through a guided practice, you can record yourself slowly reading the following script and then listen back to it.

"Close your eyes and take several deep, slow breaths. As you breathe, allow your body to drift into a state of deep relaxation. Each breath brings more calm to your body . . . five . . . four . . . three . . . two . . . one. You now find yourself in a beautiful place in nature, feeling peaceful. As you imagine yourself in this place, you see an older and wiser version of you coming over to greet you. You immediately feel safe and connected to this version of you, and you ask them to share any guidance they have for you. Allow your future self to speak to you now, receiving their words of wisdom for as long as you like. And when you feel ready to come back to full awareness, you'll bring this new insight with you."

The whole point of these processes is to get you in alignment with the things you say you want. Oftentimes we prioritize temporary pleasure (going back to the cute but emotionally unavailable person) over long-term satisfaction and joy (doing the inner healing work to choose yourself first and create space for healthy love). But when you begin to integrate a future-self practice into your life, you build a compass to help you make decisions. In any given choice that could affect both present you and future you, you can start asking yourself what future you would do.

You can also ask yourself if your choices reflect the desires of future you and if future you would be grateful for the choice you are now making. Remember the example I gave in the beginning of this chapter? Would future you rather have you go to bed early before your presentation or stay up all night stressing about it? When you approach decisions from this lens, the choice almost always becomes more clear. Building a relationship with your future self is really just enhancing the relationship you have with yourself overall. It's taking a more holistic view of your life and learning to take action from that place, rather than getting lost in irrelevant details. Plus it's fun to feel like you have a secret mentor at your disposal anytime you need advice.

PART 2

Hello, Love

> "Your task is not to seek for love, but merely to seek and find all the barriers within yourself that you have built against it. . . . The special love relationship is an attempt to bring love into separation."
>
> —Helen Schucman, *A Course in Miracles*

This is the moment when you come face-to-face with love. It's when you say goodbye to the version of you who felt like love was something you had to strive for and earn, and you say hello to the version of you who is learning that love is who you are. And in order to do that, it's important for you to be willing to unknow yourself.

What the heck does that mean?

Essentially, it means having a willingness to release your attachment to the untruths you've been telling about yourself. So often, we go through life telling our stories and asserting that those stories are who we are. But while our past experiences are certainly woven into the fabric of the person we've become, they don't dictate who we can be in the future.

You have to be willing to let go of who you've convinced yourself you are if you find that it's not working for you. For me, I had to let go of being the perfectionist. I had to unknow myself as the person who pushed past every edge just to try to prove my worth, and I had to become willing to know myself as someone who was soft, kind, and compassionate toward myself. I had to let go of being Miss Independent-and-Can't-Ask-for-Help. I had to unknow myself as someone who had to have it together and have all the answers figured out so that I could begin to know myself as someone who was willing to be vulnerable and let people in. I had to let go of being the quiet, go-with-the-flow girl. This meant being willing to unknow the version of me who didn't have a voice or speak my mind for fear of rejection, abandonment, or judgment. And in doing so, I learned to know myself as someone who takes pride in my perspectives, confidently uses my voice, and advocates for my needs.

In the chapters that follow, you'll be invited to reflect on some of your origin stories when it comes to love as I share some stories of my own to get you thinking. But remember that these origins are not your endings and that from here on out you are the only author of your story. Be willing to rewrite the parts that don't feel right to you. Be willing to see yourself in a different light. Be willing to believe that greater possibilities exist for you than the ones you've come to believe in.

Chapter 4

Called Out

Getting Clear on Your Patterns and Cleaning Up Old Habits

One of the great advantages of spending time intentionally single is having time to self-reflect, to learn from your past, and to experiment with new ways of being. Key word: *intentionally*.

During all the chapters of my life when I felt like I was single against my will, I was so focused on what I could do to meet the right person that I lost sight of the fact that I needed to first become the right person for myself. Actually, I didn't lose sight of that fact—it never occurred to me to begin with. I knew I could change my body and my clothes and my outer achievements to appear more attractive (all of which I obsessed over at different times). But I thought my patterns and habits and triggers and beliefs in the realm of love were predetermined, so why bother addressing them?

I finally realized that I was focusing too heavily on doing manifestation rituals and getting lost in the details of where and how to meet a guy because it felt easier and safer than doing the real work—the inner work. Let's be honest: it's scary as shit to come face-to-face with the parts of yourself that you've spent years skillfully hiding or avoiding. It's confrontational and uncomfortable to call yourself out for the sake of cleaning up your patterns and showing up in a new way. It was especially fear inducing for someone like me, who had a visceral aversion to getting in trouble. I translated all feedback I received to *I'm wrong and bad and guilty and shameful, so no one's gonna love me, and I will die alone.* Yep, real dark, real fast. So admitting to myself that *I* was the problem was scary. It felt easier to blame it on emotionally unavailable guys, bad timing, and the flaky Los Angeles dating scene. It felt easier because those things were out of my control, and therefore there was nothing I could do but sit around and wait for the perfect guy to show up and save me from all that drama.

The distinction I was missing is that calling yourself out is very different than self-blame. Calling yourself out is about taking radical responsibility for yourself, everything that happens in your life, and your reactions to those happenings. It's not about making yourself wrong for those things. It's about taking your power back from all the people and places you've given it away to and realizing that you've always had the ability to author your own story in the way you see fit. And that starts with admitting to yourself where you've been out of alignment with how you want to show up in your life and relationships, where those patterns come from, and in what ways you're willing for it to be different.

To make this process a little less scary for you, I'm going to be taking you through lots of personal examples of my own. Yep, the girl who was petrified of getting in trouble for doing things wrong has grown into a woman willing to openly call herself out in front of you and share all the ways I needed to clean up the mess in my love life. That should give you some indication of how impactful this work really can be. I have no fears about sharing my challenges and shortcomings anymore because I recognize them now as valuable sources of information that helped me become more of who I wanted to be. I also recognize them as simply part of being an imperfect human, which we all are. And now, hopefully, they can be helpful clues for you to do the same.

Remember, as we explore our past, we are not doing so through the lens of blame, shame, and attachment to stories. As much as you have to be willing to call yourself out and face your patterns, you have to be just as willing to unknow the version of you who created them. My hope is that you walk away from this process feeling empowered. And instead of thinking, *Oh, no, I'm anxiously attached, and I keep choosing emotionally unavailable partners, so I must be totally broken*, you think, *I'm so glad I'm now aware of my romantic tendencies and where they came from so that I can choose differently next time.*

Before I bare my soul and call out all the ways that I was engaging in unhealthy patterns and dynamics in my love life, we're going to go on a little journey back in time. I want you to have some context for the various types of relationships I've found myself in. It's a journey of love and loss and plenty of questioning of my sanity. But ultimately each relationship (or even pseudo-relationship) I was in taught me so much about myself—at least, when I was ready to see the lessons. And what I want you to keep in mind as you reflect on your own history with love is that no connection is too small to teach you something about your relationship with love and feelings and connection. That person you had a crush on in the seventh grade but never actually spoke to?

That counts. That unrequited romance with your coworker? Definitely counts. Even if you have never been in any romantic relationship, I promise you have a history that will give us clues as we call out our patterns.

Chapter 5

The Big Loves

My Relationship Journey Through All of Its Highs and Many Lows

Love shapes us. When it's present, it can soften our edges and help us grow. But the truth is, we're shaped as much by the love we didn't get as the love we did. The way you weren't soothed when you needed it, the way you felt you had to earn love with your grades or your compliance or your looks, the relationships where you felt like you never quite measured up . . . these experiences shaped you and often made you learn to play small in love. But the beauty is, your heart is a muscle that can be reshaped like any other. It can be strengthened by experiences of being seen, known, cherished. It can be opened wide and poured into, taught that it's safe to feel again.

I, like you, was shaped by the impactful and formative relationships that have marked my romantic history. We'll call them the Four Big Loves—although I use the term *love* loosely here. Much of what I experienced wasn't a healthy dynamic of love. It was often more of a mixture of wanting to be chosen, engaging in codependent behavior, putting men on a pedestal, and thinking that securing a committed relationship would be the answer to all of my problems. What's funny about that is that love was actually the source of most of my problems in my twenties. My own dysfunctional relationship with what I thought love was, at least.

But that's exactly how we learn. We look to our past experiences to show us what we've come to believe that love is and then compare that with healthier examples so that we can better understand what love isn't. This process of honestly examining your past to find out where you gave your power away to false depictions of love will teach you about the way that your brain and heart have been wired. Then, you will get to choose how you want to rewire them.

One thing that's important to me is not to get lost in the specifics of these particular men, because the story isn't about them. It's about the lessons that their presence offered. I'm not even going to bother using names for them (fake or real), not because they didn't matter, but because in the context of this work I want you to see what it's like to use your past as a mirror without getting lost in the details.

So let's start at the beginning.

Love No. 1

I was fortunate in that I had a fairly healthy first love and long-term relationship that set the bar pretty high. It was certainly not without its drama and angsty behavior, but that's to be expected when you meet as teenagers in high school.

Overall, my first love was safe and fun and playful. There were plenty of big emotions and some massive misunderstandings that led to hurt feelings on both sides. But with Love No. 1, it was mostly innocent and respectful, with a healthy dose of adventure thrown in. We spent a lot of time laughing at our own little inside jokes, sneaking out past curfew to get pizza with our friends, and talking about our enormous dreams for the future. He burned CDs for me with our pictures printed on the front, brought me my favorite ice cream when I was sad, and regularly left flowers in my car for me to find when I got off work. We had a few big fights, but most of the tears we shed were because we loved each other so much and didn't always know how to deal with it, especially when the relationship became long distance in college. He was a great first boyfriend, and I learned a lot from our relationship. But to be honest, I learned even more from our breakup.

The heartbreak of that first love ending was searing and took me years to get over. It didn't help matters that the lines were always a little blurry with us. We were together three years, but it always felt like longer because we spent a lot time in the gray zone afterward. But eventually, with time, the sting wore off. We even reconnected and became great friends later down the road.

Ultimately, our breakup taught me that heartbreak is not a cut-and-dried formula, with a linear set of instructions to follow. I learned that healing the heart is a process that's often more messy, unpredictable, triggering, and slow than you'd like it to be. But I also learned that heartbreak has the unique capacity to teach you, make you stronger, and expand how much love you're capable of holding. And, most importantly, I learned that when you're young, everything feels like the end of the world. All of your firsts are big and emotionally charged, and you don't yet have the perspective to see them clearly. So if you're young and in pain over losing love, give it time. This too shall pass. It's one of those funny things where you think back years later and almost forget how intense it felt. When you're proactive about healing from a breakup and not just steeping in bitterness as time passes, you get to the point where you can look back fondly and appreciate it for what it was: a stepping stone to the next version of you.

Love No. 2

My second love and heartbreak made me swiftly forget that lesson about perspective. It was earth-shattering and devastating and somehow expansive all at once. This love came in hot and strong and full of toxic drama. It pressed up against every wound I didn't realize I had spent my entire adolescence trying to bury. We were in a never-ending dance between my insecurities and fears of abandonment and his charming manipulations and punishing silences.

I was constantly in fear of upsetting Love No. 2, and he was quick to anger and disapprove. It was a codependent's dream (or nightmare, depending which way you look at it). In fact, this relationship was the one that helped me realize I had strong codependent tendencies in the first place. Our dynamic played perfectly into my desire to please other people, to feel responsible for everyone and everything, to absorb their feelings, to ignore my own needs and be extremely self-critical in the process. I was rarely able to identify my emotions, let alone communicate them in a healthy way. Guilt, shame, fear, and perfectionism had reasons to rear their heads every day, and there wasn't a single moment of our time together when my nervous system was calm and regulated. I set zero boundaries with him, in true codependent fashion, so he never had an incentive to change his behavior toward me. Nor do I think he would've even if I'd tried.

I chose to fall deeply in messy, tangled love with someone who would confirm all of the dark and self-defeating thoughts I had about myself. In one moment he'd go on about how he was my number one fan and how much potential he thought I had. In other moments he'd ask me why I was so unbelievably stupid and naive and say there was something seriously wrong with me. He was convincing enough that I started to believe him, and eventually his voice took over my self-talk. This often happens in toxic relationships like ours, where the person on the receiving end of the abusive behavior ends up convincing themselves that the other person must be right—we must deserve this for some reason.

That reason is that somewhere along the line, usually in childhood, we learned that we weren't good enough or lovable enough or fill-in-the-blank enough, so a part of us has always shown up in the world with either the fear or the belief that we don't deserve good, healthy love. And when a partner shows up and proves that to us, we take it as cold, hard evidence that seals our whole "unlovability" case. When the truth is, we're just choosing a relationship that mirrors something going on inside of us that needs our attention. It doesn't mean that it's true. But when you've convinced yourself that it is for long enough, it's going to take time and serious work to undo. That was the gift of this relationship for me.

Even with all of its faults, this connection cracked the lid wide open on all of the work I needed to do on my relationship with myself and my understanding of love. For me, it was necessary. Do I think that everyone should go get themselves into a harmful relationship just for the sake of learning? Absolutely not. But if you've found yourself in one at some point, you can use it as incredibly fertile soil for your growth and self-knowledge.

What Love No. 2 taught me, more than anything, is that our relationships are reflections of our inner world. So if you're someone who has a harsh inner critic, it will be nearly impossible to spot red flags in people who treat you poorly, because it's what you've taught yourself to expect. I learned a lot about what was lurking in my inner realm that I hadn't yet paid attention to, because he brought it all to the surface. But seeing it and actually healing it are two different things. I give myself plenty of credit for being willing to dive deep into inner healing work after this relationship dramatically imploded. I threw myself headfirst into therapy, energy healing, self-help books—anything I thought might alleviate the intense despair I was feeling.

Unfortunately, it wasn't long before another big lesson came my way.

Love No. 3

My third love can be summed up in one word: *escapism*. The wild and fantastical life of Love No. 3 allowed me to get lost in playful visions of a future that would, in fact, never come to pass. Anything to help me avoid feeling the depth of the pain I was in.

This love taught me how deeply (and covertly) I wanted a savior to come in and make it all better for me. Me, Miss Independent, secretly dreamed of a heroic man showing up and burying all my pain under his love. I couldn't admit this or even see it at the time, but I eventually learned that it was a recipe for losing my sense of self for the sake of getting someone else to choose me. I began to observe how easily I threw my own values out the window just to impress others or try to fit myself into their world, rather than doing the work of learning to feel safe and at home in my own.

Almost every single one of my stories with him involves me doing something that contradicted my core values—again, all because I had such a deep need to be chosen. It felt easier for me to get lost in his fantasy land than to admit to myself that I still had a long way to go in my relationship with myself.

And speaking of fantasies . . . I learned from my time with Love No. 3 just how easy it is to get lost in our own delusions when we are determined to avoid painful truths. This was a guy who was actually very clear with me from the beginning that he wasn't looking for a relationship. It was obvious that he was still stumbling from a breakup of his own and thoroughly enjoying living his Peter Pan lifestyle. But that didn't stop me from convincing myself that I had fallen in love with him and therefore it was all going to work out.

Fleeting glimpses of his vulnerability made me believe that some part of him also wanted the future I was secretly envisioning for us, and thus the delusion grew. I used everything I could find as "a sign from the universe" that he was the One—all the while keeping up my chill-girl facade and pretending like I was totally fine with the late-night-text nature of our relationship. It probably sounds ridiculous, but at the time it comforted me to think that the universe wanted us to be together. This hopeful delusion kept me from having to face just how uncomfortable I was with being single and how much pain I was burying.

But ultimately, I knew I couldn't go along with this charade any longer. I realized I was betraying myself every time I was with him, and I wanted to be done with that pattern. The pain of begging to be chosen was finally greater than the pain of facing my inner shadows in order to learn to choose myself. The end of this relationship marked an important milestone for me, because it was the first time I consciously decided to make different choices in my love life. My deliberate resolve to end this situationship was truly the beginning of my journey to become my own best friend. I still had a couple more big lessons in love to learn, but I was determined to not fall back into old patterns. Instead, I found myself discovering a new one.

Love No. 4

My fourth love was an *almost* love who taught me the value of consistency and stability. What's an almost love? It's one of those relationships where the dots never fully connect. One or the other is always just a little bit out of alignment, and you can't get it right, no matter how many tries you give it. (And I gave it a lot.) An almost love is when someone has almost everything that matters to you in a partner . . . except that one key thing. And you're almost willing to justify it and make an exception, because they check all the other boxes. But deep down you know that would be a lie.

What's fascinating about Love No. 4 is that there is no doubt in my mind that I manifested him. I mean, I believe that we're always creating our realities, whether we're doing it consciously or unconsciously. So I manifested Big Loves Nos. 1 through 3 out of my unconscious state of mind at the time and what I believed love looked like and thought I deserved. But with Love No. 4, it was different. This was the first time that I intentionally sat down and wrote a list. You know, a compilation of all the things I wanted in a partner. The only problem was, I made this list from a wounded place and was still very unaware of some major underlying patterns in my love life. I was fed up with the experiences I'd been having in relationships, and I wanted to create something different.

I'm not kidding you when I say that within a matter of days, I met Love No. 4. And he had everything on my list—*almost*. He had everything I had gotten clear I wanted at that point in my life (down to our love of the same music), except the single most important thing: he didn't have certainty, especially when it came to being with me. We fell into a will-they-won't-they pattern, and I can't even tell you exactly how long it lasted. Over the years it blurred together with other crushes and distractions that I used to try to get over him.

I was finally consciously working on the part of myself that believed I wasn't worthy of being fully chosen, but I hadn't quite healed it yet, so I kept choosing to stay in this dynamic. There would be moments when I'd get a burst of courage and self-worth and feel genuinely uninterested in a man who wasn't able to commit to me. But then there would be other moments when he'd show interest in pursuing me again, and I'd invariably fall back into my feelings for him. We could never quite get it right.

What this dynamic ultimately taught me was that I could write affirmations about being worthy and feeling lovable all day long, but until I did the work to actually heal those wounded parts of myself, nothing would ever change. I realized that some part of me was always keeping the door open to him, even when I pretended to move on. My closure finally came when I decided to lay all of my feelings on the table with him, knowing I had nothing to lose. He was seeing someone else at the time, so I was able to say my piece and put it to rest. The sting of feeling like I wasn't good enough for him to be with but someone else was, blended with the liberation of knowing I could finally be free of him and this pattern, was the strangest sensation. I had to come face-to-face once again with my unworthiness wounds and the part of me that believed I'd never be good enough. But this time, I knew I was facing these beliefs in order to heal them. This was the moment that, in retrospect, finally turned everything right side up in my love life.

Love No. 5

. . . was me.

There you have it: the four pivotal loves from my twenties, who led me to do the hard work of learning to love myself. I've come to understand that our experience of what we think love is is a direct reflection of our state of consciousness at the time, combined with all the stories and misunderstandings from our past. That doesn't mean that young love isn't truly love or that toxic love isn't love either. It just means that, in my opinion, those are lesser versions of love than what you could experience if you were honest with yourself about what parts of you need healing. It's a lower standard of what's available to you than if you learn to choose yourself first.

I think we have different soulmates for the different versions of ourselves that we show up as, and you could choose to be with any one of them along the way. But the more you choose to commit to your inner healing and growth, the more you expand what's possible for you in the realm of love and relationships. Like attracts like. It's just something you may want to consider when you reflect on your own love life. If you have a big vision for the type of partnership that you want but you're not sure it's possible, keep expanding.

Don't camp out somewhere that does not fully offer what you want just because you're afraid something better might not come along. Almost isn't good enough when it comes to love. Someone who is almost everything that matters to you isn't your person. Someone who almost chooses you isn't your person. Someone you almost love isn't worth settling for. You deserve more than an almost true love, and so do they. When you let go of all your almosts, you make room for the real thing to show up.

After Love No. 4, I no longer wanted to have a tolerance for dating guys who didn't align with my values, and I didn't want to pretend any longer. I stopped doing anything that felt inauthentic. I was finally letting go of the need to be the cool girl or to contort myself into a version that they might like more. Once in a while, out of comfort and familiarity, I would try to fall back into the old pattern, but it would feel glaringly out of alignment.

I don't use this word often, but *icky* is the best way to describe it. When you're out of integrity with yourself, it feels like there's this slimy coat of grime on your skin that you can't wait to shower off. That's exactly how I felt when I was dating with the wrong intentions. I had achieved a certain level of empowerment, but I still hadn't created the space to fully choose myself.

Don't get me wrong, it was fun to date when I finally had higher levels of self-worth and confidence to bring to the table. I was newly twenty-nine living in New York City at the time and dating was an exciting way to get to know my new home. I let myself enjoy that period of empowered, in-my-worth dating for a while, and even met a few good people. Until I knew I couldn't ignore that little voice inside me any longer. The one that was telling me I still had some work to do, and this work had to be done while I was completely, intentionally single. Not while saying yes to dates or texting guys on dating apps to distract myself. But truly solo, just me and my inner world. And I knew I was ready for that, because it mostly excited me (mixed with a little fear and apprehension).

To not be dating completely contradicts our societal expectations. To decide just to be happy and self-sufficient and focused on yourself is something that most people have not done and do not understand. I was going into this without a playbook and with a lot of potential resistance coming my way from those around me. But I was certain that it was something I needed to do. At the time, I was still making decisions for the purpose of doing whatever it would take to get closer to meeting my soulmate. It was partly to fulfill my desire to be my own biggest love, but mostly it was to chase an ideal vision of relationship that I had been dreaming up. With that dubious end in mind, I committed to being intentionally single for one year. And in a little bit we'll explore what that year entailed. But first, we've got some patterns to clean up.

Reflect

YOUR RELATIONSHIP WITH LOVE

As you begin to reflect on your own relationship to the idea of love, different people may come to mind. We learn about what love looks like first from our parents or caregivers, then our siblings and peers, the media, and, finally, actual romantic interests. The relationship dynamics you witnessed can be just as influential as the relationships you were a part of. Here are some helpful journaling questions to get you started on reflecting about your own journey with love:

- What is my earliest memory of having feelings for someone? What did I learn from that experience?

- What did I learn that love looked like growing up? How did my parents or caregivers relate to each other? How did they express their love to me?

- Which relationships, situationships, crushes, and attractions have felt significant in my life and why?

- Are there any patterns in the types of people I have been attracted to?

- Are there any patterns in the types of people who are attracted to me?

- Have I seen any examples of the type of relationship I want to experience?

Chapter 6

What Have You Learned about Love?

How Your Attachment Style
Impacts Your Relationships

I mentioned earlier that humans are social creatures who are wired for connection. But sometimes those wires can get crossed. Childhood trauma, distracted caregivers, and heartbreak can all impact the degree to which we feel safe in connection with other people. Those sorts of relational ruptures impact our attachment patterns and can have powerful implications for our adult relationships.

In the field of psychology, attachment theory describes how our earliest attachments (most often to our parents and caregivers) leave an imprint on us that affects the way we form emotional bonds as adults. Attachment is our natural impulse and desire to feel connected to and safe with the people around us so that we have a sense of belonging and well-being. We learn from a young age what is safe and not safe in our relationships with others, as well as how we need to behave in order to get our needs met. Those behaviors become embedded, so to speak, in our nervous system and show up in our adult relationships, usually in one of four attachment styles: secure, anxious, avoidant, or disorganized.

Now, your attachment style isn't a crystal ball that tells you everything about your relationship patterns. But it can offer a pretty great explanation of why you're attracted to certain people, why you repeat the same patterns in relationships, and why your relationships started and ended the way that they did. These tendencies play out because we unconsciously expect our romantic partners to act in similar ways to our parents, and then we respond accordingly. You might also notice that different attachment tendencies show up in different relationships. This is the normal result of some of your wounded parts getting activated by the wounded parts of a partner, which can vary from person to person.

About Attachment Theory

Attachment theory as an area of psychology has been around since the 1950s; there is plenty of fascinating research you can explore if you're interested in doing a deep dive. If you want to have a full understanding of the origins of the four main attachment styles so you can map them onto your own childhood experiences, a great place to start is the book *Attached: The New Science of Adult Attachment and How It Can Help You Find—and Keep—Love* by Amir Levine and Rachel Heller. For the sake of our work here, we're just going to touch on the four different styles and how you might be experiencing them in your relationships today.

Secure Attachment

Secure attachment is considered the ideal baseline or healthy expression of attachment styles; it is what allows us to have strong and long-lasting relationships. Someone who is securely attached will have high self-esteem and a solid ability to regulate their own emotions in relationships. They genuinely feel worthy of love, so they are able to easily form connections with others and to give and receive love. Some other signs of secure attachment include trusting others, communicating easily, managing conflict well, and feeling comfortable being alone as well as being in a relationship. Securely attached people tend not to struggle with extreme jealousy, fear of intimacy, or fear of abandonment.

If you're reading this description and thinking, *How is any of that possible???* keep reading until you see a style that you can identify with among the other three.

Anxious Attachment

This attachment style is rooted in a deep fear of rejection and abandonment. It's characterized by dependence on your partner for emotional validation, and it is often associated with needy or clingy behavior in relationships. Someone who is anxiously attached might also experience overlap with some codependent tendencies as well—for example, feeling like they're responsible for taking care of the feelings of others. With this attachment style, you might get anxious when your partner doesn't text back right away, or you might constantly worry that they don't care about you. There's a feeling of unworthiness for love and a general sense of low self-worth. Other signs of anxious attachment include high sensitivity to criticism, jealousy, trust issues, a constant search for approval, and difficulty being alone.

As you can imagine, it's challenging to form a healthy and lasting relationship if you're being driven by these behaviors. It's important to note that while it's normal to feel anxious when someone is inconsistent or unavailable (even for a securely attached person), in someone with anxious attachment tendencies, these behaviors are present even when there's no overt trigger to justify them.

Avoidant Attachment

Avoidant attachment style is often expressed as the classic "I don't care about anyone and I can do everything on my own because I'm independent and I don't need you" attitude—in other words, a fear of intimacy. Ironically, this fear is also rooted in fear of abandonment or emotional pain. People with avoidant attachment are unable to build long-term relationships because they don't believe their needs will get met. That strong, independent exterior isn't bravado: it's a defense mechanism they developed early on from learning that no one was going to be there for them. Someone with avoidant attachment shapes their life in such a way that they avoid having to rely on others for care, support, or connection—not because they don't want to be connected, but because they perceive closeness as a threat. Other signs of this attachment style include being dismissive and mistrusting of others, shunning intimacy, being unable to express feelings, spending a lot of time alone, and having a fear of commitment. These tend to be the people who ghost others in relationships and seem emotionally cold and distant. Deep down, they believe you can't get hurt if you never let people get too close. But unfortunately, you also can't really experience love.

Disorganized Attachment

Also known as the walking contradiction, the disorganized attachment style is essentially a combination of anxious and avoidant tendencies, alternating between the two. The behaviors of a disorganized person can seem totally confusing because they may oscillate between being aloof one day and clingy and emotional the next. The easiest way to frame this attachment style is, "I really want a relationship, but I'm scared." Someone with disorganized attachment will have an intense fear of rejection accompanied by high levels of anxiety, but they will also have difficulty trusting others and tend to push people away. This constant dance between a desire for closeness and a fear of it can be debilitating.

Making Sense of Patterns

What I find to be most fascinating—and also encouraging—about attachment styles is that they're not static. You might notice that you've exhibited different tendencies at different points in your life or in the course of a single relationship. You and your attachment habits will continue to grow and evolve throughout your life. So the good news is that if you learned an insecure attachment style from your childhood or even from your early romantic relationships, it doesn't have to stay that way.

When I finally took a look at my own patterns, I saw some disorganized tendencies. With my first partner, I often prioritized my own independence as a way to feel in control. It was difficult for me to fully express my emotions at times, and I was sometimes afraid that I'd get hurt if I let him in too close. I even turned him down the first two times he asked me out (we used to joke that the third time was the charm). But overall, those avoidant traits didn't rear their heads too much, certainly not enough for me to notice at the time.

I had been hyperindependent from a young age, so it didn't occur to me that I could experience life and relationships in any other way. Plus I was young and in love for the first time and didn't know the most remote thing about inner healing.

With that first big heartbreak, things started to shift. After we broke up, I felt riddled with anxiety with every subsequent crush, relationship, and romantic interaction I had. And that actually made sense to me. As much as I hated the feeling, it seemed familiar—partly because I had yet-to-be-discovered abandonment wounds and partly because society trains young girls to think that they will always be the clingy ones in relationships. Every early 2000s rom-com that I grew up watching depicted the women as desperate in love and constantly waiting around for aloof guys to call them back. Naturally I assumed that was just how it was for all women. Anytime I was interested in someone in my twenties, I'd obsessively stalk their social media, feel insecure about whether they liked me, and be glued to my phone waiting for them to text me. It was sad, but I didn't know how to shut the anxiety off. And again, it also made sense to me because at the time I was just beginning to explore my own codependent tendencies and intense fear of rejection and abandonment.

What didn't make sense to me was how I could carry this anxious pattern and also have been in a long-term relationship where I didn't feel that way at all. But learning about attachment styles and core wounds, I came to understand why I would flip-flop between being fiercely independent one day and feeling desperate for love the next. I would ride that intense roller coaster anytime I was single, and then I'd latch onto someone in the hope that they'd be the solution to my inner turmoil and I'd finally feel more grounded in love.

Of course, the people I chose only exacerbated that turmoil, because I was choosing them from a wounded place. I was gravitating toward guys who would confirm my deepest fears, not soothe them. If a guy I liked wasn't interested in a relationship with me, I'd go straight into obsession mode and feel consumed by my low self-worth until I could get a crumb of attention from him. And if a guy expressed a clear desire to be with me, I became disinterested and emotionally closed off. The pattern felt like: "The guys I like don't like me, and the guys who like me I don't like." Which, by the way, is a pattern I've now seen in hundreds of women whom I've coached over the years.

Try This

IDENTIFY YOUR CORE WOUNDS

In my work I've discovered eight core attachment wounds that impact our self-worth, identity, and relationships. These wounds often stem from unmet needs in childhood, and they unconsciously drive our relationship dynamics and limiting beliefs as adults. Core wounds lead us to believe that something is wrong with either us or the world around us, and that we are therefore separate from the love we crave. You may identify with more than one of the core wounds. While I personally had three primary wounds I needed to heal, I also experienced resonance with all eight of them in some way. Review the list below and see which wound patterns resonate with you:

1. **The abandonment wound:** patterns of codependence, difficulty being alone, feeling like you don't matter
2. **The separation wound:** feeling alone and misunderstood, like your needs don't matter; feeling invisible or neglected

3. **The rejection wound:** feeling left out, lack of belonging, harsh self-criticism, fear of failure

4. **The unworthy wound:** never feeling good enough, not feeling chosen, overgiving to prove your worth or to earn love

5. **The betrayal wound:** fear of getting hurt, deep mistrust of others, hypervigilance, history of infidelity in relationships

6. **The injustice wound:** feeling like life isn't fair and no one sticks up for you; either overly rigid or lacking in personal boundaries in relationships

7. **The powerlessness wound:** feeling broken and incapable of change, giving your power away, settling for unfulfilling relationships

8. **The shame wound:** suppressing your emotions, low self-esteem, fear of vulnerability and of being seen

Once you have identified the wound(s) that resonate most with you, take a moment to notice how that pattern has shown up in your life and relationships. Then ask yourself these questions: *Am I willing to believe that it can be different? And am I willing to give myself grace and patience as I heal?* When you learn to alchemize your core wounds and turn your past pain into your personal power, life gets sweeter and more abundant in every way. You no longer have to live in the limiting stories of your past, so you're free to write your new story however you'd like.

Healing Attachment Wounds

Now for the good news: you can actually heal your core attachment wounds to become more securely attached in your adult relationships. (I'll share seven crucial steps for doing that in this chapter.) It takes work, but it's quite possible. My clients and I are living proof of it. The point isn't to label yourself as "anxious" or "avoidant" and then run around managing symptoms like you're putting out fires in your dating life every day. The point is to heal so that you can open yourself to fulfilling connections, ones where your needs are getting met. And believe me when I say that those securely attached people have it good. It feels amazing to be confident in your self-worth, comfortable being vulnerable and communicating your feelings, and generally balanced in your relationships *and* on your own (because the more secure your attachment tendencies, the more comfortable you are remaining single as well).

But that doesn't mean that you won't feel fazed if you continue to choose the wrong people. You can spend all kinds of time healing your attachment issues, but if you then go out and date an emotionally unavailable person, don't be surprised if you find yourself feeling anxious again. Here's the difference, though: now the anxiety will be your signal that you're in the wrong relationship, and instead of taking it as an invitation to stay and try harder, you can make a different choice. That's the magic of secure attachment: you can trust that your emotions are signals of misalignment rather than deeply rooted symptoms of a bigger issue. The more you trust and honor those signals, the stronger you build that trust with yourself and, ultimately, others.

I can hear the million dollar question that you're probably pondering by now: But *how* do you go about healing your attachment issues in order to form a secure attachment style? Well, this book is a good start. Truly! You heal your attachment issues by actively working on your relationship with yourself, identifying your patterns, and teaching your body what healthy and safe love feels like. The science around neuroplasticity shows that we can actually create new neural pathways in our brains to learn new ways of being, create new memories, and alter our habits and behaviors. And we do that by taking new actions, consistently. Repetition is key when it comes to creating new results.

This is why I'm so adamant that people spend time single after a breakup, especially if a specific pattern of relationship issues has been playing out in your life. If you're quick to jump into another relationship because you don't like being alone, you're just going to keep repeating old patterns. Now, I'm not saying that healing cannot occur in the right relationship. It can. But the likelihood of you choosing the healthy, emotionally balanced relationship *before* you've done the inner healing work is slim. Plus, in all honesty, I've come to learn that it is a beautiful thing to take dedicated time to become your own safe space before choosing a partner—to teach yourself how it feels to be treated and loved well rather than just waiting and hoping for someone else to do it for you.

I've identified, in both my personal journey and my professional experience, seven main ways to actively heal your wounded attachment style and form a secure one. These techniques are discussed throughout this book:

1. Improve your self-talk (chapter 1).

2. Actively build your self-esteem through internal and external actions (chapters 1 through 3).

3. Practice nervous system work and self-soothing tools (chapters 2 and 8).

4. Learn healthy communication and boundary-setting skills (chapter 9).

5. Heal from your past, including inner child healing to address the origin of your attachment issues (chapter 14).

6. Identify and live by your core values (chapters 15 and 20).

7. Build and lean on a healthy support system (chapter 18).

If that sounds like a tall order, don't worry. We're going to cover (or have already covered) every single item on that list and explain practical ways to go about them in your everyday life. Also, these processes don't necessarily happen in a clean and linear order. Most inner work doesn't unfold like that. You start where you are, and you tackle what feels relevant and reasonable in any given moment. You'll bounce around, and you'll peel back different layers, and sometimes it'll feel like you're taking one step forward and four steps back. But that's okay—know that you're still healing, no matter how random the process feels sometimes.

Calling myself out on my attachment wounds and ultimately being willing to clean up those patterns in my life set the stage for the rest of this work to be so much easier. It made me realize how much of my power I'd been giving away in relationships over the years, when really the power to change what wasn't working for me was always in my own hands. I just had to be willing to admit it and face it—and that is, without a doubt, the hardest part.

Chapter 7

Getting Off the Situationship

The Secret to Why You Keep Choosing Emotionally Unavailable People

Does the following sound familiar? You meet someone, you feel a strong connection, you're ready to take things further . . . and then they hit you with "I'm not looking for anything serious right now." Or maybe they don't even give you the courtesy of saying that—they just string you along and hope you won't notice that you aren't in a real relationship with them. The problem isn't that they are unavailable, though: the problem is that *you continue to entertain the connection knowing that they are.*

There are many possible reasons why someone might be emotionally unavailable. It might be the classic player narrative: they're emotionally immature and play games with people's hearts. Perhaps they haven't done their own inner work and are projecting their unprocessed trauma and attachment wounds onto others. They might be choosing to focus their attention on another area of their life like their career, health, or family issues and don't have the time or energy to show up for a relationship. They may be going through a breakup or still healing from a past one. Or they just might not be interested in a relationship with you and not know how to express that.

I somehow became adept at collecting examples of every single one of these variations of emotional unavailability like they were Pokémon cards. It was honestly quite astonishing. In a room full of guys, I could almost guarantee that I'd fall for the unavailable one. And it definitely wasn't by conscious choice. I spent a lot of time lamenting how badly I wanted to be in a relationship and complaining that I didn't understand why every guy I dated was emotionally unavailable.

Here's how it invariably went down: I'd develop a crush on a guy. Occasionally they'd straight up tell me that they weren't interested, in which case I'd have to go tend to my rejection wounds while secretly still obsessing over them for longer than I should. But more often than not, they'd express enough interest in me to take me on dates, text me sporadically, and feign intimacy. Then, a few dates in, they'd hit me with it: "I'm going through a tough breakup. I'm not really over my ex yet. I'm going to be traveling to Europe for a few months. I'm moving across the country. I'm really focused on my business right now so it's not a good time. I don't believe in monogamy or marriage. I'm kinda messed up about something right now; you don't wanna be with me." And then the kicker: "But we can still keep hanging out! I love spending time with you." And of course, in my arrested emotional development, all my wounded heart could hear was that they liked spending time with me. I'd convince myself that none of the other stuff mattered, that they'd change their minds eventually. And that, my friend, is how I ended up in a countless number of situationships in my twenties.

sit·u·a·tion·ship

noun: **situationship**; plural noun: **situationships**

{a romantic or sexual relationship that is not considered to be formal or established}

A situationship is a relationship dynamic in which you are not really a couple, but often act like you are. The other person is getting all the benefits of being in a couple without doing any of the emotional labor, and you're never really sure where you stand with them. But they give you just enough hope to keep you willing to stick around. That's called "breadcrumbing." They sporadically drop little bits of affection and attention that make you think things like, *Maybe they really do like me too and they're just scared, or they just need more time to be ready to commit.*

Depending on the flavor of emotionally unavailable that they are, it can get really confusing for you. Sometimes they're flaky and inconsistent and barely leave any breadcrumbs at all, which to any reasonably self-respecting person is a clear sign of disinterest. But sometimes they treat you like you are in a full-on relationship and give you everything you want—short of actually committing to being in a real relationship with you. Those are probably the most insidious ones; they can keep you locked in the situationship cycle for years.

I'm not kidding when I say I experienced every variation of situationship. I was with the busy-with-work guy, the always-traveling guy, the not-over-his-ex guy, the emotionally stunted guy, the nonmonogamous guy, and the straight-up player. I was deeply entrenched in that cycle, and though I desperately wanted out of it, unconsciously I believed it was all I deserved.

That little unconscious secret would eventually become my first clue to understanding why I was stuck in this pattern in the first place. Because here's the reality: in almost all of those situations, the guy gave me an out. And even if he didn't, I could have communicated my relationship standard and told them I wasn't interested in this dynamic. Except I didn't have a standard, and I certainly didn't have any experience communicating big boundaries. I was operating out of my deep-seated fears of rejection and abandonment, and I never wanted to risk losing what little attention I was getting from them.

Finally, I started to genuinely ponder that fact. At any point in these situationships, I could have gotten off of the hamster wheel, but I didn't want to lose them. I discovered I was afraid that even if I ended things with a guy, it would just happen again with the next guy I met. Rather than risk being completely alone, it felt easier and more desirable to stay and accept the crumbs I was getting while hoping they'd want more of a relationship someday. So I continued to remain in this cycle, even after I became fully aware of how it was harming me. I hoped that by continuing to heal other parts of myself, this part would magically catch up at some point.

The Root of My Pattern

Now, I can't remember exactly what I was doing when I had the realization that changed everything for me, but I can tell you how it felt. It was like I got punched in the gut by the Hulk while simultaneously skydiving out of an airplane—nauseating and exciting and terrifying and liberating all at once. I can also tell you, without a shadow of a doubt, that I was only able to experience and digest this new understanding because I had gotten to a point in my healing journey where I was willing to set my ego aside.

I had been doing enough shadow work (aka exploring and accepting the not-so-pretty parts of myself) to know that all human traits and behaviors are essentially neutral—they just provide valuable information about what's going on in your psyche. And I'd done enough inner child and interpersonal relationship work to know that the people who trigger us are often mirroring some unhealed wound or trait that exists inside of us. The more we can be willing to own the parts of ourselves that we've hidden and shamed in the past, the more fully we can love and accept who we really are. I'd become ready and fully committed to knowing parts of myself that I had buried or ignored for the sake of keeping my ego's perception of me alive.

So what was this big realization? Suddenly it made sense to me why I kept choosing emotionally unavailable people: it was because I myself was emotionally unavailable. [Insert mind-blown emoji.] Remember that paragraph at the beginning of this chapter where I listed some of the reasons a person might be emotionally unavailable? Let's add a few more reasons to it:

1. They're scared of being hurt, abandoned, or rejected, and so they choose someone they can never fully get close to. On some level they know that it won't hurt as much or feel as scary as real, big, messy love.

2. They never saw what healthy love looks like, and they're just choosing partners who reflect a wound or pattern from their childhood because it feels familiar and therefore safe to their subconscious.

3. They're deeply uncomfortable with their own emotions because they never had a safe space to process them, so they choose people who don't challenge them to open up and have emotionally vulnerable conversations. They haven't committed to themselves on a deeper level, and attract people who don't want to commit to them either.

All three of which applied to me.

Like I said, this realization was nauseating and exciting and terrifying and liberating all at once. Because if *I* was actually the emotionally unavailable one, then *I* had the power to heal and change that within myself. Exciting. But that healing would also come with the responsibility to finally show up fully and openheartedly for love—and face all the risks of pain that come with it. Terrifying. I knew enough to understand that doing this work would pay big dividends, though. And I decided that I really was ready to be done with this pattern. So I started to reflect on why I had been actively keeping healthy love at bay. Why was I unconsciously unavailable?

The obvious reasons were my fear of getting hurt again, like I had in the past, coupled with the fact that emotional unavailability was familiar to me, as it was modeled by both of my parents in different ways. I didn't really know what healthy love looked like or felt like, and that scared me. Even though I had dreamed of it and visualized it and romanticized it, my nervous system had no concept of what it would actually feel like in my body.

Most importantly, I came to realize that I was emotionally unavailable to *myself* as much as to others. There were big emotions that I was rejecting and refusing to allow myself to have. It was no wonder I had a hard time expressing my feelings to others: I could hardly feel them or identify them myself. And even when they did surface, as they inevitably had to, I ran from them in fear. I didn't experience a lot of safety or support around big emotions growing up, so I did not feel safe to have them as an adult. But guess what? Love is a *big* emotion. Perhaps the biggest. So of course I was unconsciously running from any potential experience of real, unguarded, totally exposed love.

Becoming Available to Yourself

The final reason for this pattern—which took me a little longer to uncover—was that I was deeply afraid of losing myself again. In my early twenties, at a time when I was just beginning to discover who I was in the world, I'd been in an emotionally abusive relationship that was full of gaslighting, manipulation, and isolation from my friends and family. I willingly threw myself into the fire and kept giving away pieces of myself to this man. To be clear: I would never insinuate that someone who is a victim of any form of abuse is at fault for the manipulations and consequences of that dynamic. That said, in my own experience, it was ultimately empowering to acknowledge the ways that I actively played a role in losing my sense of self to appease him, because it helped me see the areas in which I needed to heal and take my power back.

And I did. I spent a full two years intentionally healing (with the tools I share in this book, as well as with professional support) from the aftermath of that relationship. I rediscovered my sense of self and felt more grounded and connected to my truth than ever before.

Years later, I discovered with a little more digging that I was harboring a fear of something like that happening again. If I could give so much of myself away to the wrong man in an unhealthy relationship, then what was stopping me from repeating the pattern? My heart was trying to protect me from going through that indescribable pain once more. So it made perfect sense that I would close off the deeper parts of myself by choosing partners who would never really challenge me to open up, since they themselves were unavailable too.

I had to do two things to counteract this fear. First, I had to teach my heart and my subconscious mind that I had healed and grown enough that I would not let that happen again, that I had finally moved forward. And, second, I had to be willing to risk falling in love with someone who could turn out to be the wrong person anyway and trust that I now knew how to be there for myself and put the pieces back together if the relationship went south. Love will always involve risk, because we cannot ultimately control what another person feels and whether they will stay with you or go.

When I say that this revelation changed my life, it's not an understatement. Discovering this pattern in myself gave me the key to unlock what was probably the biggest door that I'd kept closed to experiencing healthy love in my life. But it was also supremely uncomfortable, partly because of my whole perfectionism thing (a little voice inside my head telling me I shouldn't have issues like this anymore and how embarrassing it was not to know how to love, especially as a coach and therapist) and partly because I still had to deal with the fact that changing this pattern meant facing big fears and feeling big emotions.

My message here is that just because you start to get the answers and everything begins to make sense, it doesn't mean everything will be easy and peachy keen from here on out. Knowing what your pattern is is one thing; feeling and healing what arises from this knowledge are a different story entirely. My invitation to you is that once you unearth a big pattern like the one I've just described, take the healing journey as slow as you need to, but always be willing to do it scared. The idea that you have to be fully ready to enter into love is a myth that will keep you playing small, and my hope is for you to make it to the big leagues of love—starting with loving yourself, of course.

Try This

CHECK IN ON YOUR EMOTIONAL AVAILABILITY

Here is a simple somatic practice for checking in on your degree of emotional availability. One by one, read each of the following scenarios and pause after each statement to notice what you feel in your body. Most importantly, do you notice a sensation of contraction, openness, or neutrality? Contraction might show up as tightness in your chest, a lump in your throat, shallow breathing, or clamminess. Openness might feel like a warmth in your chest or belly, a slight smile on your face, or a sense of expansion in your posture. Neutrality is the middle ground, where you can feel your body but don't notice any immediate changes.

- You meet someone you like, and they show a genuine curiosity in getting to know you on a deeper level. They ask you to open up about something vulnerable.

- You had a disagreement with someone you care about and they said or did something that was really hurtful. Now you have to communicate how they hurt you.

- You're in a situation that reminds you of something painful that happened in your childhood and brings up big feelings. You respond by acting out or shutting down, and later you have to go back to the other person to explain what you were experiencing.

- You fall in love with an amazing person and begin envisioning your future together. After some time, the relationship doesn't work out due to unforeseen circumstances.

There's no right or wrong response to any of these statements. See your reactions as valuable clues showing you some of your inner parts that may need attention and healing. Just notice how each of these scenarios makes you feel and what they bring up for you. If you notice a lot of contraction, you'll want to pay special attention to the tools and topics that we're about to explore in part 3.

PART 3

Unraveling Your Past

"We either own our stories (even the messy ones), or we stand outside of them—denying our vulnerabilities and imperfections, orphaning the parts of us that don't fit in with who/what we think we're supposed to be, and hustling for other people's approval of our worthiness."

—Brené Brown

The part of your story we're about to investigate is about the unraveling of everything you knew to be true about love and meeting yourself in the process. All of the stories, all of the patterns, all of the past hurts: this is where you allow all of that to crumble so that you may mine for the gold you'd like to keep.

Together we'll explore your nervous system, your communication patterns, and all the places inside where you self-abandon or self-sabotage when it comes to love. We'll lovingly unwind all of the cycles that are no longer working for you and explore more empowering replacements as you rebuild your sense of self.

When we experience loss or heartbreak or challenge, our first instinct is to wish for things to go back to the way they were and to make the pain go away. But when you can instead learn from the pain and lean into the unraveling, you will end up somewhere more beautiful than you could have ever imagined. You will end up standing inside of a love story between you and yourself that makes the people who couldn't fully love you in the past pale in comparison.

Chapter 8

Getting to Know Your Nervous System

Aka Managing Your Reactions and Becoming Grounded

Years ago, somewhere between Love No. 2 and Love No. 4, I'd spent what felt like ages doing talk therapy and reading books that helped me think about my problems but not take action to change the core wounds causing them. I assumed I was ready to date again and hoped to stumble into a fairy-tale love story in no time. Imagine my surprise when I met a guy, chose to conveniently ignore some glaring red flags, and ended up heaving in anxiety when he ghosted me (as his red flags warned me he inevitably would). I felt that all-too-familiar ache deep in my heart, the one that liked to tell me I'd be alone forever, coupled with racing thoughts and a nauseous stomach. I thought I had healed. I thought I had done all this work. So why did I feel like I was right back at square one?

The answer is because I had tried to work my problems out only in my mind. I'd tried to intellectualize my way through them and logically understand them, but I hadn't yet given my body time to process the new insights and catch up.

Taking healing at your own pace requires you to attune to what's going on in your body—and, more specifically, in your nervous system—at any given time. Let's dive into a quick lesson on what the nervous system actually is and how it responds to different stressors. This is information that I think every single person should be taught when we're young, because having a thorough understanding of how your nervous system works helps you more clearly understand your body, your feelings, and your reactions to the world around you.

Your nervous system is made up of your brain, spinal cord, and all the nerves in your body. It works to keep your body regulated, and when it's healthy you feel calm, resilient, and connected to others while also being able to respond to danger in an effective way. Part of it is under your voluntary control, and part of it operates involuntarily and automatically (which is good, because you wouldn't want to walk around all day needing to tell your heart to beat and your lungs to breathe and your stomach to digest).

A healthy nervous system allows us to respond to stressors with ease and to return to that home base of peace relatively quickly. This is your nervous system when it's in the *parasympathetic state*. The *sympathetic state* is what you probably know as your fight-or-flight response. When your brain recognizes a threat in your environment, your autonomic nervous system responds quickly and automatically by producing hormones to help you address said threat. This is a necessary response in order to help our body deal with big and sudden stressors. Now, dysregulation of the nervous system occurs when we get triggered into a sympathetic state and get stuck there. We end up having an overactive stress response, where small things that would be no big deal to most people cause you to go into panic mode.

Why does this type of dysregulation happen? Well, one of the factors most relevant to what we've been exploring is childhood trauma, which can show up in the form of abuse, neglect, or attachment wounds. That can mean, for a child, one specific traumatic incident or ongoing and repetitive trauma. Particularly if your parents or primary caregivers were neglectful, were hot and cold in their affection toward you, routinely invalidated your emotions, or were chaotic and unpredictable in their actions, you learned as a child that your environment was volatile. Your brain reacted by ensuring your nervous system remained activated and hypervigilant in order to keep you safe—and it stays stuck in this mode even after you're an adult and your environment is different. It's as if you had a scary encounter with a bear when you were little and now, as an adult, you unconsciously look out for bears everywhere you go, even in places they don't exist, like at the mall or in your living room. This makes you extra sensitive to stress, overwhelm, change, and other triggers that vary from person to person.

Understanding Trauma

This is a good time to talk about the t word: *trauma*. First off, since most people tend to associate trauma and post-traumatic stress disorder (PTSD) with events like war and natural disasters, there can be a sense that it doesn't apply to other circumstances. Many of the women I've worked with over the years have come to me to explore their relationship issues, and when we begin to talk about their childhood they're a little bit wary at first. They'll explain how they had a good childhood, or they know their parents really loved them, or that nothing super intense or traumatic happened to them. And so they're resistant to using the word *trauma*, which can then make them resistant to doing any work around supporting their brain/body in healing from past pain. I'm all about using language that empowers, so let's clarify a couple of things here.

Trauma occurs whenever we go through very stressful, frightening, or distressing events that we don't feel capable of dealing with. It exists on a spectrum. That spectrum is not necessarily correlated to the severity of the event but, rather, to how your system interpreted and processed it at the time. One distinction that is helpful to keep in mind is the difference between *big T Trauma* and *little t trauma*. A big T occurrence is something that most people would consider extremely disturbing, such as violent, life-threatening, or catastrophic events. A little t occurrence is something that may not threaten personal safety but is still felt as significantly distressing. Some examples include the death of a pet, being bullied at school, having parents with overly high standards, or going through a breakup. Whether we respond to an occurrence as big T or little t is highly individual and based on personal levels of resilience and inner resources at the time of the event, as well as the availability of interpersonal or social support. Some research has even shown that repeated exposure to little t traumas can actually cause more emotional harm than a single big T event, especially when they occur during our formative years.

All of that is to say that you might be someone who brushes off childhood events as "not that bad"; or you may think that others had it worse, so you have nothing to complain about; or you may not want to vilify your parents. This is your invitation to consider that even if those things are true, you may have still experienced events in your childhood that you weren't yet emotionally equipped to deal with (as is quite normal and understandable). And giving yourself permission to process and reprogram those as an adult is an incredible act of self-love. Just something for you to consider as you encounter certain words and exercises in the pages that follow.

How Your Body Responds to Overwhelm

Now, something you might not know is that *fight* and *flight* are not the only two stress responses. There are actually two more that are less talked about but are just as significant, especially when it comes to our relationships. They are *fawn* and *freeze*. Together they make up the four F's. It's also imperative to acknowledge that each of these responses to stress or trauma are your brain's way of getting you to the outcome it believes is safest or most favorable for you. A dysregulated nervous system is *not* a broken nervous system. Your brain and body are in fact doing exactly what they were designed to do: keep you alive and safe. It's just that they received some misinformation along the way and have learned to perceive threats where there are none. Past trauma may have interrupted your ability to regulate your nervous system responses and ultimately feel safe in relationships. Self-protection becomes more important to your brain than connection.

The Four F's

So how do these patterns show up in our relationships? Let's break them down:

- **Fight**: You see a bear coming, and you instinctively decide to get big and loud and go after it. This response is all about maintaining control in order to get what you want (which, deep down for most people, is the love and acceptance or safety you didn't get in childhood). If this is your go-to response, you might find yourself quick to anger, trying to be louder than those around you, using fear tactics, feeling like you have no control over your rage, and always on the defensive. There's a tendency to charge toward conflict rather than move away from it.

- **Flight**: You see a bear coming, and you immediately run the other way. This response is about avoiding pain at all costs (which can often come from a childhood desire to escape parental abuse, shame, or judgment). As an adult trying to evade pain, you can use just about anything as an escape. Yes, that might include turning toward addictions to numb out. But it can also include insisting on perfectionism, throwing yourself into work, daydreaming, or wearing rose-colored glasses and refusing to look at anything painful. You might also be the person to end a relationship at the first sign of turbulence or to ghost people in order to avoid difficult conversations altogether. As you can imagine, this response tends to coincide with an avoidant attachment style.

- **Fawn**: You see a bear coming, and you speak sweetly and calmly to it, or you give the bear food to make it happy so it won't eat you. Personally, I find this to be the most interesting of all the trauma responses. Fawning essentially offers the experience of safety by pleasing the person who is threatening you in an attempt to disarm them. At some point you learned that making others happy was a tool you could use to minimize harm or guarantee your safety. In childhood this might have kept you safe from an abusive or narcissistic parent, but as an adult it can be a recipe for codependent relationships. You're more likely to lack personal boundaries; engage in people-pleasing, to your own detriment; hide your true emotions; and lack a strong sense of self-identity. The fawn response is an ingenious strategy for staying safe in an unpredictable childhood, but is a massive barrier to healthy vulnerability and strong interpersonal relationships as an adult.

- **Freeze**: You see a bear coming, and you're paralyzed with fear; maybe at best you play dead. In this response, your brain is essentially trying to buy you time to figure out the best next step. The most extreme version of freeze has been referred to as the *flop response*, in which your body may literally go limp or you mentally dissociate from the painful experience. Being stuck in the freeze response in your daily life—what's called a *functional freeze*—can make you feel numb, isolate you from your loved ones, and cause you to look for ways to detach from the world and from uncomfortable feelings and situations. This can often appear to manifest as symptoms of depression, but the good news is there are simple yet powerful strategies to shift out of this state over time (*time* being the operative word, so be patient with yourself).

Again, these stress responses are natural and necessary in cases of extreme danger, trauma, or difficulty. It's when your brain is overactive and hypervigilant and you get stuck in one of these response patterns that it becomes a problem, and you react to nonthreatening situations in a highly activated way. And yes, this overactivation is more likely to occur if you have a history of trauma or an anxiety disorder. When you understand how your nervous system works, you can begin to practice being more mindful with your experiences and separate your old story from your current state of being.

You're Not Broken

Before I understood what was going on in my nervous system, I thought I was crazy, especially when it came to love. It didn't help that the guy I was dating at the time also told me that I was crazy, because he didn't understand what was happening for me either. At age twenty-two I was in a car accident that, in addition to being traumatic in and of itself, simultaneously unearthed years of unprocessed childhood trauma. The whole event also triggered the most unhealthy and emotionally abusive aspects of this relationship. It was definitely not a safe space for me to have big emotions, so I was constantly on the verge of having a panic attack while trying to pretend I was normal.

My tendencies, I learned over time, were to get stuck in fawn or freeze. (It's common for people navigating ongoing or complex trauma to fall into a hybrid of two responses.) I avoided sharing my true thoughts and feelings at all costs and diverted my energy instead to doing whatever I could to make him happy—my fawn response. I thought that if I could pretend everything was okay and make him love me, then all my problems would be fixed, and I wouldn't feel this way anymore. Then, in the moments when I couldn't keep on pretending, I'd freeze. I would isolate myself, numb out by endlessly binging a comfort show I'd already seen five times, and check out from any uncomfortable feelings long enough to feel semi-stable again.

My problem wasn't that I was crazy or that I was broken. It's that I was attempting to find safety in an inherently unsafe relationship during an already very turbulent time in my life. What I needed wasn't to pretend that everything was okay and hope for the best; I needed to address all of the ways my brain and body were very much not okay and needed support. Learning about my nervous system was a game changer after that relationship ended because it gave me a road map to all of my traumas and triggers. The more attuned I became, the more easily I could identify when something felt off and which strategy I needed to use to right the ship. The more I healed my nervous system, the more authentic I could be in relationships.

I began to notice when I would fall into that old pattern of fawning in a relationship. I treated it like a notification light: it meant either that the relationship I was trying to enter into was not a safe one or that for some reason I didn't feel safe in my own body and I needed to address that before I could authentically connect with the person in front of me. When I would find myself in a prolonged period of numbness, I could identify that as nervous system overwhelm (rather than a depressive episode) and take actions to help my body unfreeze. It wasn't easy and it certainly wasn't a linear process, but it was a beautiful thing to feel like I finally had some agency over my brain and body again.

Why is this all so important in the context of relationships, being single, and learning to love yourself? Because healthy interpersonal relationships are vital to a regulated nervous system and because a dysregulated nervous system is more likely to lend itself to unhealthy relationship patterns. Dysregulation can also prevent you from choosing a healthy partner, because your overactive brain may be associating something innocent about this new person (perhaps their haircut or the scent of their cologne) with an unsafe partner or caregiver from your past, and therefore you see only danger. It can even impact to what degree you feel safe or unsafe being on your own.

I've found that people who tend to fall into either the fight or fawn response patterns are generally deeply uncomfortable being single, and they will seek out a relationship at all costs (usually to their own detriment). People who tend toward flight or freeze responses, on the other hand, are more likely to isolate and avoid being in relationships, perceiving them as unsafe. I believe that getting balanced and stable within your own body is one of the best ways to ensure that you'll be able to choose healthy relationships in the future. But the catch is, nervous system healing happens both on our own and in the context of a safe and supportive community. There are practices that fall into two important buckets: solo and social.

Try This

GET REGULATED: SOLO REGULATION

Solo regulation is similar in many ways to the idea of self-soothing that we explored in chapter 2. It's the process of learning first to identify when something is off-kilter internally and then to incorporate habits and practices that will help you return to balance and feel grounded. Many of the techniques we covered in that chapter will apply here as well. But even more specifically, you'll want to use techniques that stimulate the vagus nerve, which runs from your brain down into your digestive system and is the main component that will help you regulate your nervous system. This long, wandering nerve helps control digestion, heart rate, speech, immunity, and mood. Vagal tone, or the strength of your vagus nerve, helps your body more easily recover from stress. Here are a few of my favorite easy practices to promote vagal tone and self-regulation:

- **Breathing.** Slowing your breathing down—in particular, lengthening your exhales—is one of the best ways there is to signal to your body that you are safe. Even better if on the exhale you can vocalize a soothing sigh (like the sound *haaa* or *hmmm*) and feel your shoulders relax away from your ears. You might notice that after making a few deep sighs, your next breaths seem to flow a bit more easily.

- **Use your voice.** Because your vagus nerve is in close proximity to your vocal chords, the vibrations of your own voice can have a wonderful regulating effect on the nervous system. This is why chanting in a yoga class makes us feel calm and singing or humming our favorite song lifts our mood. I personally use singing and humming anytime I'm experiencing physical pain that's causing me to feel overwhelmed, and it makes a big difference every time. So sing, hum, chant—just make sure you focus on emitting low, deep sounds that have a grounding and soothing quality to them.

- **Self-massage or self-touch.** This can be a comforting practice to turn to when you are feeling overstimulated or activated. Try massaging your feet and legs or your hands and arms. You can also use the practice of tapping to stimulate different meridian points along your body to encourage relaxation. My favorite points to tap are in between my eyebrows, on my temples, and in the center of my chest. To practice tapping (at whatever pace and pressure feels good to you), use the pointer and middle finger of one hand to repeatedly tap each of those body parts as if you're gently tapping someone on the shoulder to get their attention. This ancient practice is thought to balance the body's energy system and reduce psychological distress. It's a great way to connect your body's sensations with your emotions.

- **Cold exposure.** Intentionally exposing your body to a stressor like cold water can expand your capacity for discomfort and help you feel more embodied. Though studies on cold therapy for mental health are still in the early stages, preliminary findings show that regular cold showers can reduce anxiety and stress, as well as decrease depression.[1] By intentionally and mindfully using your breath to stay calm in the cold water, you're teaching your brain and body to understand that not all stressors in your life require an extreme reaction, thus building resilience.

This practice is especially beneficial if you find yourself stuck in the freeze response. The previous three practices are soothing, but when you're already flattened by an overwhelmed nervous system, your system actually needs to be activated before you can get back to balance. Think of nervous system regulation like a three-step ladder, as I learned from clinician and polyvagal expert Deb Dana when studying Integrative Somatic Trauma Therapy.[2] At the bottom of the ladder are numbness, freeze, and lack of enjoyment for life. The middle rung of the ladder is sympathetic nervous system activation (fight, flight, fawn). And at the top of the ladder is the safe zone where you feel regulated and able to have healthy social interactions. Repeated cold exposure through cold plunges or daily cold showers can help you get from the bottom to the top of that ladder.

Try This

GET REGULATED: SOCIAL REGULATION

Social regulation is exactly what it sounds like: using a healthy social relationship to coregulate your nervous system with that of another person. We're always sensing into the nervous system states of the people around us. That's why you might go from feeling totally calm one second to absolutely anxious after a stressed-out friend dumps their entire day's worries on you. Or why, when you're in a group, you might suddenly feel the mood shift but not know what caused the change.

We actually learn coregulation long before we learn self-regulation. We coregulate with our mother in the womb and with our parents and caregivers in the early years of our lives. We learn how to deal (or not deal) with big emotions from them, and we rely on the guidance of their nervous systems to inform us how we should respond. Especially if you didn't have examples of safe and healthy nervous systems around you when you were growing up, it's going to be really important for you to practice coregulation as an adult. That can be as simple as finding a therapist you feel safe speaking with. It can also look like learning to communicate your needs to a friend you're comfortable being vulnerable with.

Here are a few examples of ways you might ask for support:

- "I really need a hug right now."
- "Can you just sit here and be with me for a few minutes?"
- "My anxiety is really bad right now. Would you hold my hand?"
- "I'm feeling overwhelmed. Will you breathe with me for a couple minutes while I calm down?"

Take a moment now to think of your own experiences. Is there a moment that comes to mind when you had trouble regulating your nervous system? How might that experience have shifted if you'd asked for support? Think of whom you could have called on and what things you might have said in that instance. Can you think of any other examples of difficult moments and support-seeking requests you could have made? Jot them down in your journal.

These simple requests can have an immediate and profound impact on helping you to feel more calm, and they actually benefit the person you're regulating with as well. One nervous system calms another, and both sides feel relief. The more often you incorporate these types of practices, the more cues for safety your brain will have to draw from in order to keep you calm in future situations.

All of this nervous system work was a game changer for me. I had subconsciously been trying to get romantic partners to help me feel regulated, ultimately putting too much pressure on those relationships to be my sole source of safety. The problem was, I was going about it in the wrong way with the wrong people. I'd feel overwhelmed or anxious or unsafe, then try to get an emotionally unavailable guy to make me feel better. It's no wonder I'd end up feeling worse off!

I didn't start to experience true safety and nervous system regulation until I learned about what was going on in my body and how to properly self-regulate. Then, when I knew what that felt like and was confident in what I needed to ask for, I practiced coregulating with supportive friends and safe therapists and healers in my life. It took time, but eventually I had accessed that feeling of safety enough that I could find my way back to it anytime I was activated. If you don't have a lot of reference points for what safe and calm feel like in your body, please be patient with yourself as you retrain your nervous system. You are worth the time it takes to heal.

Chapter 9

We Need to Talk

Leveling Up Your Communication Skills

I learned a lot of helpful things in my childhood. I learned how to confidently travel and navigate foreign cities from my flight-attendant mother. I learned my love of reading and writing from my thriller-author father. My parents taught me about the importance of kindness, compassion, and generosity in our communities. I learned my way around a kitchen and how to create something from scratch. I learned all kinds of physical pursuits (though nothing involving a ball, because somehow I never mastered hand-eye coordination). And I certainly learned how to follow societal rules and play the game of fitting in and accomplishing things.

But one thing I never learned was how to communicate. We were very much a family of noncommunicators. My dad, writer that he is, has a rich inner world filled with compelling thoughts, most of which go straight from his brain to the page. Whether it's a book he's working on, or a letter he is writing to share his concern about a faulty product, or a thoughtful birthday card he's preparing, he's always been a master of the art of the written word. But spoken word, not so much. He is quiet by nature, a trait I inherited from him, but I also know that he grew up in a family of noncommunicators who believed children were meant to be seen and not heard.

And then there's my mom. Anyone who knows her will tell you that she has, as our Irish relatives call it, the gift of the gab. The woman has no limit to her ability to spout fantastical stories and get a party started. But in my childhood, when it came to talking about hard things, that gift somehow disappeared. I now attribute it to her own upbringing, because we only know what's been modeled to us. Born and raised Catholic in Ireland in the 1950s, she was taught to believe that there are certain things you just don't talk about—and certainly not to anyone outside the family. Everything was about keeping up appearances; even common topics were shrouded in shame and secrecy.

To both my parents' credit, they've each worked on their communication issues over time, and we've been able to talk much more openly in recent years. Again, I don't fault my parents for not knowing what they didn't know. But nevertheless, I was thoroughly unprepared to deal with the many relationship issues that were headed my way in adulthood. What do you get when you grow up in a noncommunicative household and develop a disorganized attachment style, rejection sensitivity, codependency, and a tendency to fawn? You get a girl who is never going to say anything to rock the boat in any interaction, *ever*.

That was me for my entire life until I started to see my communication blind spots. Well, almost my entire life: I'm told that the first few years of my childhood I was strongly opinionated, maybe even bossy; certainly I had the gift of the gab. We are all born knowing how to ask (or scream or cry) for what we need and want; we all have a natural desire to share our unique perspective of the world without any shame. But for many of us, somewhere along the way, that innate ability gets lost in translation.

I didn't even realize that I struggled with communication. Sure, I cried every time I had to have a difficult conversation (particularly with authority figures), and I found it physically impossible to produce an answer when someone asked me what I wanted. But I didn't think that behavior was out of the ordinary. Surprisingly, it was Love No. 2 (the least emotionally healthy of them all) who helped me to see that I was resistant to opening up about myself. I felt like a deer in the headlights anytime he asked me a question that required true vulnerability and authenticity. Partly it was because I was afraid of causing a confrontation with someone who was unpredictable. That relationship wasn't actually a safe space for me to be deeply vulnerable, though I began to try. But I noticed that it wasn't just with him—I was a very passive communicator in every single one of my interpersonal relationships. I'd become so skilled at hiding my truth from other people that I didn't even know I was doing it.

If being a good communicator came easily, we'd all be doing it. The reality is that raw and honest communication will press us right up against our most tender wounds and scariest fears. If we never learned how to do it, telling our truth in an emotionally mature manner feels out of reach at best and a threat to our safety at worst. Either we remain quiet because we think that will make us safe, or we get loud and aggressive to make sure our point is heard, again in an attempt to feel safe. Most of our communication patterns can be traced back to a desire for safety or acceptance, or else they reflect what was modeled to us growing up. When you haven't created that felt sense of safety within yourself, you will always subconsciously fall back on old patterns and defense mechanisms. That's why the nervous system work we explored in the last chapter is so fundamental: it enables us to lay the groundwork for improving our communication in a way that feels safe and empowered.

Avoiding Trouble

Let's explore an example of a communication challenge I've seen in several young female clients. For the sake of this story, I'll consolidate them into a single woman named Kelsey. When Kelsey first came to me, she was fresh from a breakup and wanted some help navigating her heartbreak. As with many of my clients, her initial goal was to get over this breakup so she could move on and find her person. When I see a strong desire to move quickly from one relationship to the next, I know we've got some work to do.

Kelsey and I talked about the breakup and the nature of that relationship. Then we explored patterns and commonalities with her past relationships. Once we had spent a good amount of time in the realm of adult love, we finally visited her childhood. By this time I could see that she had a habit of hiding in relationships—hiding her true self, hiding her authentic desires, and often hiding behind little white lies. Kelsey had learned from her childhood that telling the truth wasn't safe. I discovered that she had experienced verbal and physical abuse growing up and had developed a strong aversion to the experience of "getting in trouble." And so it went in her adult relationships.

Anytime Kelsey sensed the potential for someone to be upset with her or disapprove of her choices, she instinctively reacted by lying. It could be as simple as telling her boyfriend she was at the gym alone, even though she was there with a guy friend, because she was afraid her boyfriend would get jealous. When she finally realized that she had grown accustomed to telling these lies, it rattled her. Naturally, she wanted to see herself as an honest person. She had to become willing to admit that she habitually lied because some part of her felt she needed to in order to remain safe. Then, slowly and methodically, I helped her learn to communicate in new ways and tell the truth in conversations that might have scared her in the past.

I can relate to Kelsey's white lie problem. When I was in the emotionally unsafe relationship with Love No. 2, it often felt like a better option to tell him what I thought he wanted to hear than to tell him the truth. Safety is paramount in the realm of communication. If you're facing any sort of triggering stressor and your nervous system had sounded the alarm, it's going to be very difficult to communicate in a healthy way. Even in other relationships, I found myself passively covering up my truth just to please the person in front of me. (Remember my lies to my date about loving seafood?) That's just the way my brain was wired.

I can tell you from personal experience that this process of cleaning up your communication patterns requires an abundance of patience and self-compassion. It can be really frustrating to start to see your patterns but feel like there's some man behind the curtain in your brain pulling the strings to get you to speak and act in the very ways you're trying so hard to change. It takes time and practice and plenty of repetition for the changes to take hold.

The Four Communication Styles

The challenging job of changing your communication patterns begins with identifying what your communication style is. These communication patterns can most easily be observed in moments of conflict and disagreement. Psychologists generally refer to four basic communication styles:

- **Assertive.** This is considered to be the ideal communication style: a person is able to identify their emotions and effectively express their needs while also holding respectful space for the other person's point of view. Assertive communication often includes "I" statements, such as "I feel..." or "I need..." What's tricky about using the word *assertive* is that it's a term many women are taught to shy away from. Little girls learn they're not supposed to be assertive, and if they are, they're often called names for it later, like "bossy" or "bratty" or "high maintenance" or "bitch." Assertive communication in women is also often mislabeled as "aggressive," another thing we're taught not to be. But we all ideally want to learn to be assertive in our communication in order to advocate for our needs and create a space for honest dialogue in relationships.

- **Aggressive.** People with this communication style typically get defensive and hostile when they feel attacked; in response, they seek to threaten or intimidate the person in front of them. It is very challenging to have a conversation with an aggressive communicator, as they have little regard for the feelings and needs of others. Especially when they sense their needs or safety are being threatened, they can be quick to harm the other person with their words in an attempt to "win." Aggressive communicating leaves no room for another perspective.

- **Passive.** The passive communicator is the classic "Whatever you want to do!" people pleaser. This communication style is marked by a pattern of deferring to what others want in order to keep the peace. Passive communicators rarely voice their own needs and desires and have a very hard time saying no or setting boundaries with others. This can often lead to internal conflict and pent-up resentment—though a passive communicator would never express that, feeling instead that passivity is a safer option.

- **Passive-aggressive.** Similar to those with a passive style, passive-aggressive communicators are not likely to share their feelings and needs. They can appear low maintenance on the surface, but underneath, they are subtly acting out of anger and frustration. Rather than confronting another person directly and honestly, passive-aggressive folks will use passive techniques like facial expressions, body language, sarcasm, and the silent treatment in order to punish others. This communication style is often passed down by parents who give their children the silent treatment when they are upset with them.

Try This

ACKNOWLEDGE YOUR COMMUNICATION PATTERNS

The truth is that most of us do not have perfect communication. Even if we are wonderful communicators, there are always certain types of people or relationships that will challenge our emotional intelligence. And romantic relationships tend to be the most emotionally charged territory of all. So the homework here isn't for you to become a perfect communicator overnight.

It's simply to start acknowledging the patterns you've fallen into and how those may have impacted relationships in the past. It's always your choice to clean up what isn't working for you and to keep what is.

The following journal prompts will get you thinking:

- What patterns do you notice in your conversations and attempts at communication with loved ones?
- Is there any piece of feedback you have repeatedly gotten from different people (typically those close to you)?
- Are there certain conversations you always avoid or feel uncomfortable with?
- Do you tend to be assertive, aggressive, passive, or passive-aggressive?
- What communication expectations do you have of others?
- What assumptions do you make about the ways that other people communicate?

After you've considered those questions, take some time to write letters or scripts of things you wish you would have said in past conversations, using the wisdom and knowledge you have now. (Hindsight truly is 20/20.) Then read those letters or scripts out loud. Hearing yourself communicate in new ways, even if no one is around to hear it, is an incredibly powerful practice.

Here's an example of how you might write a script for this exercise. Let's say you were in a situationship in the past, and when the person you were seeing said they didn't want anything serious, you just went along with it because you didn't want to lose contact with them entirely. Going back and rewriting that communication might sound something like this: "I appreciate you telling me where you're at and what you're looking for. The truth is, I've really enjoyed spending time with you, and I'm looking for more of a commitment. I understand if that's not something you're available for, and I hope you'll understand that I think it's best if we end things. Continuing to hang out without clarity just isn't what I'm interested in."

The intention behind this exercise is not to make yourself feel bad for what you didn't say in the past. It's to create new communication pathways in your brain so that you have more empowering language readily available to you the next time you need to have a vulnerable conversation. Remember, you did the best you could with the tools you had at the time. The more you practice speaking your truth, the more comfortable it will become.

Chapter 10

Losing Yourself Isn't a Good Look

Self-Betrayal and Finding Your Inner Compass

You know the big debate about whether two people could have fit on that floating door at the end of the movie *Titanic*? In case you don't, I'll catch you up. There are two young lovers, Jack and Rose, who are on board the *Titanic* when it hits an iceberg and sinks. It's every man for himself, and they miss out on snagging spots on a lifeboat. In the middle of the freezing Atlantic Ocean, they see a wooden door that's presumably from the sinking ship. Rose gets on the door to escape the frigid water, and Jack . . . he just holds her hand and treads water as they pray someone finds them in time. Major spoiler alert: They're not found in time—at least Jack isn't. He dies in the water. But Rose is eventually rescued and lives a long and healthy life.

So the debate is, could they both have fit on that door? If you've ever seen the movie, you have to admit it was a pretty big door.

Would it have stayed afloat with two adults on it? That's a different question entirely. But let's assume for the sake of this conversation that the door absolutely could have saved them both.

Why is this relevant? Well, in the context of all my early relationships, I was Jack. I constantly sacrificed myself for the sake of the other person and called it love. I abandoned my own needs to make sure theirs were met. And not in a romantic-yet-tragic life-or-death kind of way, like in *Titanic*. Mostly just tragic, because no one was asking me to abandon myself for them. No one's life was at stake. I was just doing it because I wanted so badly to prove that I was worthy of love. And I didn't care that I was betraying myself in the process.

This pattern was quiet and cunning at first. I would pretend to like things I didn't and to be someone I wasn't, but I was convinced that I was just learning to like new things and broadening my perspective. That was an easy enough lie to sell myself from the ages of twenty-one to twenty-five-ish, because I was young and still had much to learn about the world. I couldn't see that I was actually doing it in order to avoid feeling so alone and inadequate. But even as a codependent, anxious, passive communicator, I had core values and preferences of my own that were begging to stop being ignored.

I hadn't yet gone through the process of defining my values, preferences, nonnegotiables, and deal breakers in relationships, so I didn't have the language to identify what I was ignoring. (You'll get the chance to define yours in chapter 20.) But I knew when something felt off—that gut feeling or intuition you get when something about this relationship or that person is not quite right. And I ignored those inner knowings on many occasions just to keep the peace or to maintain my cool girl persona.

Self-Abandonment Isn't Glamorous

One of the core values I found myself neglecting was monogamy. I'm someone who prefers the dynamic of a monogamous romantic relationship. It's the way I'm wired. But as a young twentysomething living in Los Angeles, the land of shiny things, I came across plenty of people who were not interested in monogamy. While there are lots of different ways to have ethically nonmonogamous relationships, I seemed to attract primarily the Peter Pans of Southern California. You know, the guys who never want to grow up and find it impossible to maintain healthy adult relationships? Those guys were my bread and butter.

And rather than tell them up front that I wanted to date exclusively or choose to take my pride and walk away, I usually decided to play the long game. Part of me believed that if I waited them out, this chapter of what I perceived to be immaturity on their part would eventually come to a close, and I'd be there when they were finally ready to settle down. So even knowing they were sleeping around, being crushed by that, and continually having my belief that I wasn't good enough reinforced, I couldn't bring myself to leave. I also couldn't bring myself to ask for what I needed from these men who couldn't have met my needs anyway.

While I was attempting to fit in in Neverland, I was also busy betraying another important aspect of my identity: being a nondrinker. *Sobriety* is the wrong word for my relationship with alcohol, because I've never had a problem with substance abuse myself. But there are many personal reasons why I choose to abstain from drinking. I experimented enough in high school and college to know that, more than anything, I just don't enjoy it. I don't like the taste of alcohol, I don't like accidentally getting more buzzed than I meant to, and I *really* don't like how I feel the day after. I've also never been a huge fan of the venues where people tend to drink. As a highly sensitive person, loud clubs and bars are not my scene. Add to all that the effects of growing up around alcoholism and seeing the damage that excess drinking can do, and you've got a person who understandably abstains.

But that's all hard to explain on a first date, especially for a chronic people pleaser who is trying her best to shape-shift into someone cool and likable. And it seemed like all the cool guys I went on dates with were very much into the drinking scene. So for several years in my twenties, I drank a lot more than I ever wanted to—which for me was zero, so any drinking at all was an abandonment of my authentic self. I didn't feel good while I was doing it, but I was always secretly hoping that positioning myself as the fun girl who likes to party and go with the flow would be my ticket to securing their love.

The Breaking Point

That was the pattern that ultimately led to the night that changed everything for me: my twenty-fifth birthday. By this point, I'd been seeing someone for almost a year, and I was starting to hit my limit with the crazy-making experience of being in a long-term situationship. He was showing no desire to settle down, and I was growing tired of the inconsistency, the late-night texts, his drinking and drug use. He was actually a really great guy—more than a touch hedonistic, yes, but smart and intellectually engaging, bighearted, thoughtful, adventurous, and incredibly charming. That's what kept me around. Can you relate? He had been up-front with me from the beginning, repeatedly telling me that he wasn't looking for a relationship, but I was so focused on all the potential I saw in him to be a great life partner, I just wasn't willing to hear it.

It must have been nearly four in the morning after a signature wild night with him, this time justified by the fact that we were celebrating my birthday, when I was suddenly struck with the clear realization: I was not where I wanted to be. I was betraying my truth and abandoning my values—and for what? A man who didn't even want to be in a relationship with me? So I got up from the party happening in his room without saying a word, walked downstairs, called myself an Uber, and went home. And that was it. I decided right then and there that I would never abandon myself in the pursuit of someone else's love or approval ever again.

Shortly after that night, I met someone who had values much more closely aligned with mine, and that was my first experience with practicing authenticity in dating. It was such a liberating moment. It felt like, *Wow, I don't actually have to drink on dates or pretend I like partying, and that can be okay, and I can be with someone who has values in common with me.* It gave me permission to expect more from relationships—and more from myself.

Connecting the Dots

If you have to change who you are to get someone to like you, then do they really like you? While compromise and openness to trying new things are important elements of a healthy relationship, shape-shifting is not. If you cannot show up as your fully expressed and unfiltered self, then either you have some inner healing to do or it's not the right connection for you.

What I know now is that betraying your values is not impressive. Abandoning yourself for the sake of fitting in is not impressive. Becoming aware I was doing those things, however, did give me valuable information about the unhealed wounds I still had. It's hard, but necessary, to examine the ways your childhood shaped you, no matter how much you logically know that your parents loved you and that they were doing their personal best. Connecting the dots isn't about blaming anyone—it's about learning where your core wounds come from so that you can take responsibility for healing them.

As an adult, I was used to abandoning myself and choosing people who weren't fully choosing me because it was all I had known most of my life. I didn't have a parent physically abandon me when I was little, but you could easily argue that growing up in a family with divorce, alcoholism, and emotionally unavailability feels a lot like abandonment to a child. What was more important for me to understand and acknowledge was how I learned to abandon myself for others at a tender and formative age. My young brain decided that the best way to handle the instability around me was to play the role of peacekeeper and do whatever I could to make other people happy, no matter the cost to me. I always knew as I got older that I had a tendency to people-please and "play the diplomat," as people around me pointed out. But what took me a lot longer to grasp is that people-pleasing is really just control disguised as self-abandonment. The by-product of making sure that the people around you are happy and stable is that *you* feel more secure. For a little kid in chaos, it can be a brilliant coping mechanism to try to get their needs met. But for an adult trying to experience healthy relationships, it can be hell. It communicates to yourself and others that you are inferior and your needs don't matter.

Coming to this realization was one of those decisive moments in life. Either I was going to keep participating in this pattern and end up selling my soul to get the wrong people to choose me, or I was going to draw a line in the sand. I had already been on my healing journey and practicing variations of self-love for five years at that point. I had no idea what it was going to take to finally stop self-abandoning, but I was willing to find out.

What I discovered to be a crucial step in the process was to identify my core values and decide what principles I wanted to live my life by (something I'll walk you through doing as well). I had a vague idea of the morals and general standards that mattered to me. But I had never gotten unambiguously decisive and put them to paper as a declaration of sorts. Guess what? It turned out to be really empowering to do so.

Try This

IDENTIFY YOUR CORE VALUES

What is a core value? It's a personal ideal or guiding principle that helps define your identity. When you home in on the most important values for you, it helps to inform your behavior and the choices you make. Basically, operating from your core values helps you become more of your true self. Now it's your turn. Spend some time journaling to identify five to ten of your core values so that you can let them be the driving force behind all of your life decisions. These prompts can get you started:

- Describe the top five people you admire and why you admire them.
- What do you regularly spend your time doing and why?
- If you could change one thing about yourself, what would it be and why?
- If you suddenly lost everyone and everything in your life, what are the top three people/experiences/things you'd want back?
- What do you consider most important in life? How do your actions currently align with those values? How could they be better aligned?

Here are some core values. Ponder the words and see which ones resonate with you: adaptability, advocacy, altruism, art, authenticity, balance, beauty, career, community, compassion, courage, creativity, curiosity, discipline, emotional intelligence, faith, family, freedom, gratitude, health, home, honesty, integrity, joy, justice, kindness, knowledge, leadership, leisure, love, loyalty, mental health, openness, optimism, order, patience, peace, personal development, play, purpose, relationships, resilience, respect, responsibility, self-expression, service, strength, travel, truth, wealth.

Once you've identified five or so core values that feel really potent and significant to you, write them in big letters in your journal and expand on what each one means to you and how you would like to see it actualized in your life. You might also reflect on where the gaps are: identify the areas of your life where you're not currently embodying these values and consider ways to actively lean into them. Next, write each one on a Post-it note and put them where you'll see them often as a reminder to use these values as your new inner compass. Anytime you're stuck on what to do or where to go or whom to be with, you can check in with your values as a guide.

Chapter 11

Drop the Judgment

Changing Your Relationship to Being Single

Uncovering all of those patterns to myself was a difficult and lengthy process. With each new realization, I thought I'd finally revealed *the* answer that would change my love life for good. Every discovery felt so significant—and they absolutely were—but I was approaching this process with the wrong intention. I thought that by identifying and fixing my issues, I'd finally be able to experience healthy love.

What I was missing was that I needed to become the source of love for *myself* first and foremost. I needed to stop outsourcing my self-worth to my relationship status and get comfortable with the idea of being single.

For most of my adult life, I approached dating the way most women do. It's the same way we learned to approach body image and weight loss. Diet culture has a lot of us feeling like we always have to be striving for some goal. There's this sense that it's not okay to just accept your body as it is. Think about how often we make excuses and issue disclaimers about the way our bodies look: "I've gained weight because I've been injured/sick/traveling/working/[fill in the blank]," or "When I get back in shape/lose this weight/add more muscle/[et cetera], then I'll finally..."

What we are really saying is that we don't feel good enough as we are, and we need other people to know that we intend to do something about how "not enough" we are. We assume others are judging us for our body size or shape, and we try to fend off the judgment by signaling that we are aware and actively doing something to change it. Because God forbid we could just accept ourselves at any size. God forbid people might think we don't care about losing those twenty pounds or growing our butt or revealing our abs.

I think the same is true for a lot of people, especially women, about being single. It can often feel like being in a relationship is the default that we should always be striving for. The thought of actively *not* dating had never once in my life occurred to me. Because if I took myself off the market, then what would that say about me? What would people think? And what if I missed out on meeting my person?

No, surely it's a safer option to be perpetually on dating apps and scanning every environment I enter into for potential matches. Never mind how utterly exhausting that all is—I must keep striving. Striving for love, striving for that perfect relationship, striving to finally feel good enough.

I remember having so much judgment in my twenties about women in their thirties or—*gasp!*—forties who were single. Where had they gone wrong, and what could I learn from them as a cautionary tale? Even when I saw women who seemed to be empowered in their singlehood, I felt like it was nice for them, but certainly my life would pan out differently. I was destined for love, and soon. Right? Please, God, let it be soon.

The judgments I was having weren't actually about these women. I'm sure they were all wonderful people with beautifully fulfilling lives. The judgments stemmed a lot more from my own insecurities, my fear that I had some blind spot that might keep me from love and I'd end up an outcast in the eyes of society. And it certainly didn't help that nearly every other conversation I was a part of centered around dating. Inevitably friends and family would always ask if I was dating anyone new, who I was interested in, what was going on in my love life. The insinuation was that my love life was the most interesting thing I could possibly have going for me as a young woman. Which of course just perpetuated my insecurities further.

And then one day it hit me: *If you can't be comfortable being single, then you're always going to be choosing a relationship for the wrong reasons. And if you're choosing a relationship for the wrong reasons, then you're more likely to choose the wrong person for you.* I generally don't like using comparative words, such as "good versus bad" or "right versus wrong," because I believe that being a human is an inherently messy endeavor with endless possibilities, not one ruled by a binary system. No one's going to come along to check that you are doing love "right."

That being said, I've also come to believe that a lot of people have misaligned intentions when it comes to love and relationships. We look to love to save us or a relationship to validate us. We settle for an almost love because we're convinced it's better than being alone. We enter into relationships as if they're business arrangements, hoping that they'll make the everyday logistics and financial aspects of life in a capitalistic society easier to handle. We make another person our idol in the unconscious expectation that focusing all of our love on them will make us feel loved in return and finally heal those childhood wounds.

We use love as a bargaining chip to avoid the discomfort of facing our own self-healing. These misalignments taint our love and make it feel compulsory. If we tether the experience of love to someone or something outside of ourselves, then we'll always feel separate from it. When you get out of your own way enough to realize that you yourself are the origin of love, then you can enter into relationships freely and authentically, in the right timing for you.

Are You Ready?

This is your moment to commit to fully choosing yourself, if you haven't already. Maybe you've gotten here out of necessity, or out of desire, or maybe out of sheer exhaustion. What matters is that you are here. I had done a *lot* of inner healing work before I was finally ready to lean into being single and explore the lessons that empowered solitude was eager to teach me. And, to be completely honest, I chose it from a place of necessity and exhaustion at first.

In early 2020, I had entered into a perfect storm of work burnout, undiagnosed chronic illness, and a couple of recent lackluster dates that were defeating enough to put me over the edge. I knew I couldn't attend to the physical healing that my body so desperately needed while also trying to entertain the game of dating in New York City, which was exciting but energetically demanding, to say the least. I was also finally in a place where I was more willing to trust the timing of my life, which gave me the faith to know that if I took time off from dating, I wasn't going to fall behind in life.

So that's exactly what I did. I made the decision to spend at least one full year intentionally single and focused on my healing. I deleted the dating apps, tied up loose ends with guys I'd been casually seeing, and shut down shop, so to speak. And . . . it felt really freaking good. A little scary, sure. But mostly it was liberating to know that I didn't have to strive anymore.

When you consciously take yourself out of the dating game for the first time, you begin to see all the little bizarre behaviors and beliefs that you adopted in an attempt to be liked by others. You might notice that you were dressing a certain way, or keeping a particular hairstyle, or speaking in a tone of voice that isn't authentic to you. When you drop the pretense of needing to impress or attract anyone, you might be surprised to see just how far you've deviated from your center. Do you have any idea how much energy, creativity, wisdom, and clarity you can free up when you're no longer obsessing over a crush?

One of the patterns I've observed in many women who date men is the way we adapt our choices in anticipation of some guy who's not even there yet. Women will often shrink or alter their desires in order to remain likable to a fictitious man who might come into their life and disapprove. The realm of home decor is a great example. I've known so many single women who live alone and feel insecure about the furniture they want to buy or the way they want to decorate *their own home*. As if a guy will come back with them after a date and immediately leave because it's too pink, or it's too feminine, or—God forbid—there's a cat.

It sounds silly, but many of us are conditioned to this kind of thinking. I remember furnishing my first place by myself and worrying that my love of velvet furniture was going to be off-putting. To whom? Here's what I have to say to those fears and insecurities: if someone you're dating is judging you for personal choices that bring *you* joy, then that is not the person for you. Full stop.

The right person for you will support what you love. And even if they hate your pink rug or your velvet couch, they won't make you feel bad about it, and they certainly won't run the other direction. Starting to make choices for you will only weed out the people who aren't truly meant for you. Being your authentic self is actually a great filtering technique and will save you a lot of time when you do decide to start dating again.

The more you systematically acknowledge and release your judgments around being single, the more you'll start to feel like yourself. It's really a beautiful thing to realize that you can take up space and be utterly honest about who you are and know that the right person for you will lovingly embrace every bit. Embodying that awareness is a milestone in your journey that will make being single feel infinitely more comfortable. It's like you're relaxing into your self-worth.

It's worth noting that the longer you spend in that space of self-worth, the more you'll grow to enjoy it. As you progress through this journey, you just might find that you prefer being single to dating or being in partnership. And that's perfectly okay. The tools in this book are meant to help you build a rich and fulfilling life, regardless of your relationship status or goals. The point is, you get to choose.

Reflect

FIND YOUR SELF-JUDGMENTS

All judgment is ultimately self-judgment. If we're critiquing someone for their life choices, then we hold a conscious or unconscious belief that we're not allowed to make those choices either or there's something wrong with us if we do. Taking time to identify your own hang-ups about being single will help build compassion for the part of you that has held rigid standards about the way your life must go in order for you to be "enough." The following questions will help you reflect on any judgments or blind spots you might have in the arena of dating:

- How do you feel when you meet people your age who are single? What do you think about them?
- How do you feel when you meet people much older than you who are single? What do you think about them?
- Do you feel like the most authentic version of yourself when you go on dates or meet new people?
- If you're really honest with yourself, how do you feel about being single and actively not dating?

If you need a few examples to get you started, consider these:

- Believing that there's something wrong with you, or others, for being single past a certain age (perhaps thirty, forty, et cetera)
- Feeling like it's not okay to go to social functions like weddings, parties, and holiday gatherings without a partner
- Judging the way you meet people (on apps versus in real life)
- Feeling like it's not okay for you to take dating off the table and focus on yourself; worrying that people might judge you
- Believing that you need to hide parts of your personality, your past relationships, your upbringing, or your lifestyle in order to be liked or to find a partner

Chapter 12

What Else?

All the Ways We Get in Our Own Way

I'll admit it up front: this part of the work that we're about to explore is not the most fun. We're going to get into the fun part soon, but calling ourselves out on self-destructive patterns is a necessary part of healing and being in integrity. It's not that you're inherently broken and don't deserve to experience joy until you've healed. I promise, that's not it at all. Coming from someone who used to believe that I had to have all my shit figured out before anything good could happen to me, I hope you know that you are enough exactly as you are. And, honestly, there is nothing to fix, because you're not broken.

It's just that taking a deep look at how we get in our own way can make life easier and more enjoyable in the long run. When you're not being driven by old conditioning, you're free to experience the type of life and love that feel best for you. Being in integrity with your truth just feels better than the alternative. Healing is for all the younger versions of you who didn't feel good enough. Because there will be hard and lonely moments with no one else around, and you deserve a loving presence at all times. And that's it. That's why we do this work.

The patterns and blind spots we've explored so far are not only the ones that I had to move through, but they are the ones that I see most frequently in my clients' lives. They're what I call the big blocks to love, and when we clear them, we learn to love in ways that feel better. Clearing these wounds happens through consistent practice of the tools you've been learning in this book, as well as through the support of a trusted professional. Modalities like EMDR (eye movement desensitization and reprocessing therapy), hypnotherapy, IFS parts work, and somatic trauma therapy can all have a powerful impact on your ability to show up for yourself and your relationships in new, more aligned ways. I'll share some of my favorite modalities in the "Recommended Resources" section in the back of this book.

But besides the big blocks to love common to many of us, we each have our own unique package of conditioning, childhood wounds, past relationships, parental experiences, and belief systems that can show up in different ways. I'll touch on a few more patterns that you might brush up against in your self-reflection process as you continue to move through this book: not giving the wound time to heal, not feeling attracted to healthy relationships, codependence, hyperindependence, unrequited love, and dating someone's potential. I'll then leave you with some prompts to help you contemplate how you might be getting in your own way, so that you can approach your exploration in a productive way and not an existential-dread sort of way.

Not Giving the Wound Time to Heal

I love ear piercings, but I hate having to deal with the aftermath of getting a new piercing. I'd probably have a couple more if the process didn't suck so damn much. As it stands, I have six piercings: two on one ear and four on the other. Anyone who has had multiple ear piercings before knows that the cartilage ones are *much* worse than the earlobe ones. They take about eighty-seven times as long to heal, and they hurt so much more. When you have a new piercing, it's excruciating to sleep on that side or hold the phone up to your ear; or God forbid someone brushes up against it or something catches on it. (I learned during the pandemic that catching a face mask loop on a fresh piercing is a whole new level of pain.) So you're supposed to take extra care not to irritate it and to clean it every day. But here's the thing: I'm oddly stubborn about things like that. For someone who is an ardent rule follower, I hate being told what I can and can't do with my body. If I want to sleep on my left side, then I'm going to do that, piercing be damned!!

That's the joy of being an adult. You get to make whatever choices you want to make, but you also have to be willing to accept the consequences. Time and time again, I'd get tired of sleeping on one side after a new piercing and rebelliously switch to the forbidden one. I'd pop an Advil and recklessly smoosh my ear into the pillow, and inevitably I'd wake up in the morning to a swollen and sometimes bloody ear. I was really bad at giving wounds the time they needed to heal, because I'm impatient and, like most humans, I have areas of life where I prioritize short-term gratification over long-term well-being.

And that's what I see so many people doing in their love lives. You know, the ones who jump from one relationship to the next without taking half a moment to come up for air. We're either impatient or lonely or just don't want to deal with our pain. There are many reasons we do it, but the reality is that the time after a relationship ends is a lot like the period after getting a new piercing. The wound is going to be tender and painful, and we need to allow time for it to heal on its own, rather than pretending that it doesn't exist.

Not Feeling Attracted to Healthy Relationships

You know the old sayings about how girls like bad boys and the nice guy never gets the girl? They're not entirely wrong. But here would be a more accurate way to phrase it: people with unhealed childhood wounds attract people who will trigger said wounds, and the emotionally available person will rarely get the one who's still stuck in old conditioning. Maybe that doesn't roll off the tongue as easily, but it paints a more accurate picture of what's really going on.

I've had so many women come to me with a pattern of toxic relationships and claim that they wish they didn't find healthy relationships to be so boring. What these women don't realize is that these relationships actually aren't boring—they just don't trigger the familiar feelings of chaos and instability that were modeled in their house growing up. When you learn at an early age that love means pain or yelling or fear, then someone who is safe and stable is understandably going to feel unfamiliar. When someone usually treats you poorly, it feels exhilarating to get any shred of affection from them. Those inconsistent rewards keep you caught in a dopamine-seeking cycle that feels both thrilling and exhausting.

That's why toxic relationships are often full of high highs and low lows. You're always waiting for the breadcrumbs of proof that you matter to them, that you're special. When you begin to do the work of healing your own relationship to love and regulating your nervous system, you no longer need to seek that roller coaster of familiar emotions. The more you heal, the more attracted you'll feel to the stable and available person.

Codependence

You might see the word *codependence* tossed around a lot in conjunction with the topic of toxic relationships. Codependency exists when one person in a relationship relies exclusively on the other person to validate them, meet their emotional needs, and make them feel safe. One partner is entirely dependent on the other person socially, emotionally, and even financially, in a dynamic that can sometimes enter the territory of relationship addiction. The codependent one is often sacrificing their own needs and desires just to make the other happy and keep the peace.

A codependent person is likely to enable bad behavior in their partner, because they rely on the validation they get from the relationship. The codependent person deeply fears abandonment, rejection, and loneliness. They get their sense of security from maintaining the connection, even if it means they abandon themselves in the process of turning a blind eye to their partner's dysfunction. This maladaptive pattern can be a hard one to break, and it is also one of the strongest cases for choosing to spend time intentionally single. Learning to meet your own emotional needs and depend on yourself for your feelings of worth should be at the top of your list of intentions for healing. We started to explore this work in part 1, and we will dive deeper into it in part 5.

Hyperindependence

On the flip side of the codependence coin, we have the folks who are so determined to maintain their sense of identity that in relationships they never really let their partner in. Having walls around your heart might keep someone from hurting you, but it will also keep them from truly loving you.

When you are hyperindependent, you refuse to lean on your partner for anything. That could include refusing emotional support, being unable to ask for or accept help, being overly controlling, or making decisions without considering your partner. This can understandably leave your partner feeling unwanted and unvalued.

This pattern is usually a response to abandonment, neglect, or having had your trust broken in significant ways. You can learn to let people in again while single by practicing vulnerability with a trusted therapist, trauma-informed coach, or close friends. This kind of practice starts with the communication work we explored in chapter 9, as well as the social regulation techniques in chapter 8.

Unrequited Love

My heart aches a little bit just talking about the subject of unrequited love, because I know how much it hurts to love someone deeply who doesn't love you back. Whether it's the best friend, the boss, or that guy at your gym, the subject of unrequited love always seems to be someone you have to interact with regularly, so you're just quietly pining for them while they go about their life completely unbothered. If that sounds at all familiar, I urge you to revisit the section on emotional availability in chapter 7.

Choosing to invest your attention and love in people who don't feel the same way about you is often a strong indication that you are emotionally unavailable yourself. When some part of us is scared of real, vulnerable love, it feels safer to choose someone who we know will never choose us back. We feel protected because we'll never have to truly open up and risk getting hurt.

It's also easier to fantasize about someone who isn't choosing you. That state of mind when you're flooded with obsessive thoughts about an unavailable or uncertain connection is sometimes called limerence. Limerence is often present when you lacked emotional nurturing as a child and then unconsciously project those unmet needs onto potential partners as an adult. Limerence creates an intense emotional roller coaster of cravings, ambiguity, and temporary euphoria. If you've experienced it, you know how consuming and confusing it can feel to be lost in a fantasy land that you crave to make real. The solution for limerence and for the pattern of pursuing unrequited love lies in healing the childhood attachment wounds that caused the pattern in the first place. (Don't worry, we're getting there.)

Dating Someone's Potential

Raise your hand if you love a good fixer-upper or DIY project. If your hand is raised, please save that interest for Pinterest projects and not for people. There's something potent about the desire to be the one who can fix, change, or save someone. I've seen it countless times among clients in my practice and a few times in my personal life as well.

You see the potential of who someone could be in a relationship and latch onto that idea while hoping that you will be the one who is special enough to change them. And it makes sense. I mean, the thought that someone could love you so much they'd do anything for you sounds romantic as hell. Until you remind yourself of something very important that we touched on earlier: if we have to change for someone to like us, then they don't really like us. This rule goes both ways. If you're falling for someone's potential and not the reality they're showing you, then back away from the crush. Not only is it not your job to be someone's savior, you can't be. We all have free will, and if someone doesn't really want to change, they won't. It's time for you to take your free will and do your own inner work rather than trying to do theirs for them.

Radical Responsibility

I believe that when we can take radical responsibility for the patterns in our love lives, every area of our life is impacted for the better. And it bears reminding you once more that this is not a blame game. I'm not sharing this in an attempt to point fingers at or shame you, or your parents, or even your past partners, culpable as they may have been. Radical responsibility is about knowing that you are the sole person who holds the power in your life. You get to decide how you show up, whom you choose to be with, and how you treat yourself on a regular basis. That's what choosing yourself means. Let's dive into this in the following practice.

Reflect

HOW YOU GET IN YOUR OWN WAY

Let me ease your mind by assuring you that you are not alone in these patterns. At some point everyone gets their wires crossed when it comes to love. What's special about you is that you're willing to do this investigative work in order to get out of your own way. And I think that's really brave. Spend some time reflecting on the journal prompts below. Be gentle and compassionate with yourself and take as much time as you need.

- What are the patterns I can see clearly? As a reminder, those we've discussed in this chapter include not giving the wound time to heal, not feeling attracted to healthy relationships, codependence, hyperindependence, unrequited love, dating someone's potential, and radical responsibility.

- What are some areas where I feel stuck but I can't quite see a consistent theme or pattern yet? Write them all down, even if you can't discern a throughline just yet.

- Have my adult relationships mirrored the relationships I witnessed or experienced in my childhood?

- Do I always gravitate toward the same type of person romantically? How has that been working for me?

- What role do I try to play in my relationships? Caretaker, savior, martyr, controller, peacemaker, overgiver, accommodator, protector, fixer? At what cost do those roles come?

In the next chapter, I'll first share a powerful release ritual, and then we're going to start the process of building a new foundation of self-love in your life. That's where choosing yourself starts to get really fun. Most importantly, remember throughout it all that I'm proud of you for being willing to learn to choose yourself. I hope you're feeling proud of you too.

Chapter 13

Dear John (or Kyle, Claire, Quinn, or Whoever)

Letter Writing Practices to Let Go of Your Past

That was a lot of heavy stuff to sift through. Are you ready to set some of it down, maybe even let it go for good? Some patterns will take time to unravel and lots of practice to reweave. But I'm a big believer that acknowledgment and some sort of ritual for energetic release can go a long way in helping to clear a pattern, or a person, from your life. My experience with Reiki and energy healing has shown me just how much power these kinds of energetic practices hold. So that's what we're going to do.

If spiritual or metaphysical practice isn't of interest to you, you can think of this activity as an exercise in mindfulness and intention. It's mostly just about doing something to consciously honor the role something or someone served in your past, and to declare that you're ready to move on and create space for a new experience. It's the start of a fresh chapter in your life.

Try This

LETTER WRITING FOR HEALING

Below you'll find some prompts for letters that I'm inviting you to write. These are *not* letters that you're actually going to send or show to anyone. They're just meant to help you in your healing. If you're wary of this process, I encourage you to give it a try anyway. I think you'll be surprised at just how cathartic letter writing can be.

Letter Writing Guidelines

I recommend writing no more than one or two letters in a sitting. If you're really on a roll and it feels good to write more, go for it, but don't force it. The idea here is that you only want to let go of what is ready to be released. It's a practice you can come back to whenever it feels relevant.

Here's a simple step-by-step approach to writing your letters and how to release what you've written afterward:

1. Begin by doing something that feels significant to you to make this process special. You can light a candle, or put on some music, or turn it into a whole ritual if you wish. This will signify to your subconscious that something important is about to happen.

2. Write your first letter on a loose sheet of paper or a page in your journal that you don't mind tearing out.

3. Don't filter your writing. No one is ever going to see this letter, so write anything and everything that wants to pour out from your pen. Set a timer for at least ten minutes or just write until you feel there's nothing left to say.

4. Once you're finished writing, pause for a moment, shake out your hands and arms (this helps to release energy and emotion from the body), and take a few deep breaths. Then, you may choose to read your letter either silently or out loud, go through the process again and write a second letter, or move on to the next step.

5. Now is when you get to symbolically release what you wrote. Your first option is to tear the letter up into as many little pieces as you want and throw it away. Your second option, if you have a safe space to do so, is to burn your letter. You can do this in an indoor fireplace or a firesafe container outside. Just make sure you have water on hand and don't go too crazy with the flames. You can then throw the ashes of the letter away or rinse them down the drain.

6. Finally, take a moment after the release to close your eyes and breathe into the space you just created for yourself.

Letter Writing Prompts

All of the letter writing prompts below are just suggestions. You can do one of them, none of them, or all of them. Choose the ones that resonate with you and feel free to bookmark this page to come back to again and again.

Letter 1: Dear Former Lover

This is a letter that you write to a specific partner from your past. In this letter you might address any of the things you left unsaid when the relationship ended, the things you hated about them, the things you loved about them, the reasons you're grateful for them, what you learned from them, and who you've become since they left. For particularly tumultuous relationships, I sometimes recommend writing two versions of this letter. The first is sort of a "fuck you" letter, with all of the angry things you might never have recognized or would never say out loud. The second is more of a "thank you" letter, acknowledging all the ways you've grown and expanded as a result of knowing them.

You can go through this process for any and all romantic relationships from your past.

Letter 2: Dear Past Loves (Collective)

This is a letter to the collective of all the people you've loved who have helped shape who you are now, for better or worse. You might write to them about why you chose to repeat certain patterns and how you're choosing differently now. Or you might explain who you were when you were with them versus who you are stepping into now.

Letter 3: Dear Love

This is a letter addressed directly to love itself. You might write about how you learned what love looked like when you were growing up and the misunderstandings you had around it. You might contemplate the ways you misinterpreted and misused love in the past and how you're learning to relate to it now. It could be an apology letter to love, or a grievance letter to love, or a love letter to love.

A fun follow-up to this practice is to then write a letter back to yourself from the perspective of love personified. What does love want you to know now?

Letter 4: Dear Former Me

The "Dear Former Me" is probably my favorite of all the letters because it tends to be the most tender and emotional. This letter is an opportunity for you to write to younger versions of yourself. I'll often have my clients write these when they're having a lot of self-judgment about having ended up with a toxic partner or repeated a lot of unhealthy patterns. When you write to the version of you who was with that person or chose that pattern, you can invite in compassion and understanding. What do you want those younger versions of you to know? Get it all out.

Letter 5: Dear Future Me

This is a special letter that helps you tap into the energy of the life you are now creating for yourself. When you write to your future self, pick a date in the future that feels far enough out that something will have shifted—maybe one year, five years, or even ten or twenty years from now. Share with your future self about where you are currently and what you are working to step into. Ask them for guidance and advice, whatever feels relevant. And please note: this is the one type of letter that you don't burn or release after writing. Instead, keep it in your journal or another safe space where you can revisit it someday in the future and smile as you see how far you've come.

The beauty of letter writing is that it's a tangible and holistic practice in letting go of the past and stepping into your power. It engages your conscious mind, your subconscious, and your body all at once. You get to create space for your feelings and let them have their voice while simultaneously releasing anything that no longer serves you. I find that this practice always leaves me feeling lighter, clearer, and more empowered.

I recommend that you try each of the suggested prompts at least once. If it feels good to write, keep writing until you feel complete. You can always return to this practice anytime you feel you need it, or you can plan to do a quarterly or annual check-in with yourself to see if it's time to let something go.

As you are releasing past relationships and old patterns and outdated experiences of love, I want you to remember something important. You're only letting go of all that is not really you and what you were never meant to hold onto. I've met many women who've been afraid to fully close the door on an ex because they wanted to maintain access to all the good things that ex brought out in them.

The people we love have a unique ability to ignite sparks within us—sparks of desire, not for them, but for who we are when we're with them. Maybe they help us discover a new hobby, or fall in love with new music, or find a part of ourselves that we never knew existed. It can feel like this person held the keys to our joy all along, and it's exhilarating when they unlock it. They have the power to guide us, inspire us, and remind us of who we are and what we love.

This is a beautiful thing, but it also has a downside. When a relationship ends, we often feel that we no longer have access to who we were when we were with them—that all those wonderful things they awakened are stripped from us in their absence.

What's vital to remember is this: the people who come into your life and gift you with these experiences and revelations and self-discoveries are important but not omnipotent. The fire they stoked was within you to begin with, and it doesn't go anywhere when they leave. They were simply the igniter of the spark, not the keeper of your flame.

PART 4

Making Magic on Your Own

> "The body is where life happens—both the beautiful and the painful, our individuality and our relationships, the now and the past—but many of us have forgotten ourselves as bodies."
>
> —Hillary L. McBride

When you allow yourself to be messy, authentic, and fully in your body, that is when your true power begins to emerge. After you have called yourself out and begun to excavate your old, outdated patterns in love, you're poised to make actual magic happen. The alchemy of healing your past pain and transforming it into self-love is one of the most remarkably beautiful parts of the human experience.

This chapter of your story is all about rebuilding a relationship with your body, mind, and spirit that feels like home to you. It's about coming into connection with the forgotten wild parts of you and learning that you are far more resilient than you've been giving yourself credit for.

In part 4 we'll look at some of my favorite practices in the realm of personal healing and your relationship with yourself. We'll explore inner child healing, the stories your body has been holding onto, and what it looks like to reclaim your relationship with pleasure. You'll also learn some powerful somatic practices to continue to strengthen the connection between your mind, your body, and your emotions. My hope is that you come out of this section with a sense of curiosity, wonder, and belief in new possibilities for your life. This is where things get fun as we explore the territory of play!

Chapter 14

Your Inner Child

The Part of You Who Needs Some TLC

Do you remember a time in your life when you felt completely uninhibited, curious, and full of joy? Maybe you were soaring on a swing set, or building a sandcastle, or hosting an imaginary tea party.

For many of us, our memories that involve feeling free and joyful come exclusively from childhood. It's when we have the least amount of responsibility, the fewest judgments and preconceived ideas about the world, and the highest amount of faith in the unknown. It's also when we encounter many of the life experiences that contribute to all of the patterns we explored in part 3. It's when you learned that maybe going into the world so openheartedly isn't safe and you'd better find ways to protect yourself.

When that shift happens, when we go from innocent and trusting to wounded and wary, we begin to lose touch with all of the gifts of childhood. If I asked the average adult when was the last time they played with their inner child, they'd probably look at me like I'm from another planet.

When I was first introduced to the idea of inner child work, I thought it sounded silly. *What does my childhood have to do with the problems I'm trying to fix now?* I thought. *And even if I can see the correlation, what's the point in pretending to talk to a younger version of me that no longer exists? What's done is done, and I can't change anything that happened anyway.* I thought it was a modality for people who were stuck complaining about their childhood all the time, and the truth was I couldn't have cared less about mine. I had moved on, a full-fledged twenty-two-year-old adult. Crying about my childhood seemed weak and sad.

I'm giggling as I write that, because I have so much compassion for twenty-two-year-old me who was trying so damn hard to keep it all together all the time. You don't know what you don't know, and I certainly didn't know just how much of my behavior was being driven by my wounded inner child. It wasn't until my mental health really started breaking down that I was willing to admit (okay, maybe forced to admit) that I still had a lot to learn.

But admitting that you don't know something can be scary. It feels like giving up, which would be a direct threat to your survival if you've learned you're the only one who's got your back. And returning to a childhood that held some painful memories doesn't sound too appealing either. But I'm so glad I decided to trust my mentors and explore the realm of inner child healing, because it has offered me many gifts along the way.

A lot of what we explored in part 3 are the downstream effects of issues from your childhood. The self-reflection you've done to become aware of your patterns and start to work through them is a powerful first step. And now we get to go back to the source and heal those past wounds and misunderstandings with the magic of inner child work. Giving your younger self a stable and nurturing experience of love can have life-changing effects, especially if you had a lot of unmet needs in childhood. It can boost your self-worth and confidence while also changing the way you show up in relationships for the better.

The main goal with this work is to build a safe space for the tender and vulnerable parts of you to come forward with all of their feelings and creativity and curiosity. Little kids just want to explore and learn about the world, as well as to feel safe and loved while doing it. It's when we don't get that healthy experience that things can become askew in our lives. But the good news is, it's never too late to create that space for yourself. You don't need a parent to do it or anyone else's permission to feel supported and cherished. All you need is a willingness to build a relationship with those innocent little versions of you. I say "versions" because your inner child is often made up of many different parts of you from various ages, not just one static version.

Try This

MEET YOUR INNER CHILD

Meeting your inner child is very much an internal process, as it involves you imagining that your younger self lives within your mind, body, and psyche. When doing the practice I'm about to describe, it can sometimes be helpful to look at a few pictures or videos of yourself from early childhood, especially if you're having a hard time connecting to the energy of younger you. But then, you'll want to go fully inward.

Start by settling into a comfortable space, closing your eyes, and taking a few deep breaths. Then, begin to picture your younger self in your mind as if they were sitting right in front of you. Notice what they're wearing, how their hair is done, and what their mood is like.

Next, it's time to introduce yourself. Imagine yourself saying, "Hi, little [*insert your name or childhood nickname here*]. I want you to know that you're safe, and I'm here to take care of you. What do you need right now?"

Give little you the opportunity to answer. You might feel silly at first, but just go for it. You might also notice lots of emotion well up. This is also completely normal. The more you talk to and work with your inner child, the more you'll have the opportunity to process emotions that were ignored when you were young. This is a good thing, because creating space to feel them now means that they can stop taking up space in your body and driving your unconscious behavior. When it feels like they've said everything they need to say for now, take a moment to thank this version of you for showing up. Let them know you'll be visiting them again soon. And when you're ready, you can open your eyes and maybe spend some time reflecting on how that felt for you.

Once you've made this initial introduction, I want you to think of interacting with your inner child as being like reconnecting with a lifelong friend. They're a part of your inner world that's always there, and you're just now beginning to open an ongoing conversation with them. When you're feeling triggered about something, get curious about their feelings and perspective on the matter. What might this situation remind them of, and what do they need to feel safe and seen? When you're out and about in the world doing something fun, tap into what it feels like to let this little kid part of you be silly and carefree and happy. And, most importantly, make a regular practice out of asking little you how they feel and what they need. You might be the very first adult to do that for them.

Try This

ADDITIONAL PRACTICES FOR INNER CHILD CONNECTION

Here are a several more ways that you can connect with your inner child. For those that involve letter writing, you may also try using your nondominant hand when you're writing as your inner child. This will help you access the right side of your brain, which is intrinsically connected to emotion and self-expression—plus writing with your nondominant hand (which can be difficult!) taps into the part of you that is still learning how to do something:

- **Write a letter to a younger version of yourself.** If you have a hard time with visualization or meditation, writing can be a powerful way to invoke the presence and emotions of your inner child. You can choose to work with your inner child at an age when you needed a little extra care and support. Maybe it was when your parents got divorced, or when you were being bullied in school, or when a best friend moved out of state, or when a grandparent passed away. Write a letter to yourself at that age and then give younger you a chance to write back.

- **Get creative.** Drawing, coloring, crafting, or painting are great tools to use to connect to your inner child. When we use our creativity, we're actually accessing that innocent inner part of ourselves. You might even draw a picture that represents your inner child, whatever that means to you.

- **Use guided prompts as your inner child.** You can either speak these sentences out loud or write them down.

Then just allow the blanks to be filled in by whatever pops into your mind, speaking or writing as the voice of your younger self. Try not to judge what comes up, even if it doesn't make any sense. Trust that your subconscious is processing exactly what it needs to.

"I'm ___ years old, and I'm feeling..."

"I'm just a little kid, and it's not fair that..."

"I wish that the adults around me knew that..."

- **Use guided prompts as an adult in dialogue with your inner child.** Similar to the exercise above, write or speak these prompts and follow your stream of consciousness to fill in the blanks with whatever needs to be said.

"I am here for you, and I want you to know that..."

"I am really proud of you for..."

"All of your feelings are valid, and I'm always here to listen. What do you want to tell me?"

Reparenting Yourself

Much of inner child work centers around the concept of *reparenting*. This therapeutic tool teaches that in becoming a loving and stable parent to your own younger self, you can heal a lot of the wounds, misunderstandings, and attachment issues that have been impacting your adult life. In doing so, you teach yourself what healthy love looks and feels like, so that you have an example of it for future relationships.

It feels important to note, especially for the recovering perfectionists and masters of self-sabotage out there, that your reparenting process should also include a check-in on your beliefs about the relationship between love and discipline. For the perfectionists among us, there can be a tendency to throw ourselves into doing *all* of the work and getting it all "right," as if we're going to get graded on our healing. Perfectionists tend to have a hard time with inner child work because they're too rigidly attached to structure and self-discipline, leaving no room for creativity and messiness and play. And on the other end of the spectrum are the people who lack the skill of discipline and end up self-sabotaging in an effort to avoid doing uncomfortable things.

Both of these traits are often learned in childhood. As children, we need structure and guidance. As much as kids might want to eat cake and watch TV all the time and never go to bed, adults know that wouldn't ultimately be good for them. Children need loving but firm discipline in order to understand limits and boundaries. We're not born with impulse control—we have to actually learn it from the adults around us. So if you lived in a household that didn't have that healthy balance, you might have a skewed relationship with discipline: either you impose much too stringent rules on yourself, or you live in chaos, with no structure at all.

Self-discipline is ultimately about learning to keep the promises that you make to yourself. There are many reasons why this is important, but in the context of our conversation about love and self-love, two stand out in my experience. The first is that when you know you can trust yourself to keep your own promises, you no longer have to worry about being with the wrong people. You can lean into your ability to set boundaries, to say no when something is not a good fit for you, and to stop participating in unhealthy relationship dynamics. Second, when you practice reparenting and keeping your promises, you realize that you no longer need to outsource your well-being to other people. You believe in your ability to create the life that you want for yourself, with or without a partner, because you know that you've got your own back.

Reflect

YOUR BELIEFS ABOUT DISCIPLINE

Discipline isn't necessarily about willpower or how strict you can be with yourself. It's more a matter of how comfortable you feel regularly giving yourself the care and boundaries you need to feel good and reach your goals. You might find that you prefer the connotation of a word like *devotion* or *commitment* more than the word *discipline*. The goal is to find the inner resource of a consistent and loving parent figure, so choose whichever language resonates most with you. Take some time to write down your answers to the following questions:

- When you think back to the ways that you were parented, what did you learn about discipline? What did you learn about love? And what did you learn about how to take care of yourself?

- If you're someone who is always striving and pushing yourself too hard, what would it be like for you to ease up and give yourself permission to rest?

- If you lack self-discipline, what would it be like for you to incorporate some structure into your life and to practice showing up for yourself with consistency?

Self-Care for Your Inner Child

Have you ever had one of those nights when you're tossing and turning with a cold or flu, unable to sleep, and suddenly you feel like you just want your mom or dad? Even if you don't have a good relationship with your parents or they're no longer around, that thought can pop in, and in that moment you're convinced that everything would be better if someone were there to take care of you. These kinds of thoughts can be especially surprising if you tend to be someone who's hyperindependent. But whether you judge that thought or lean into it, the desire to be nurtured and taken care of is primal and universal. We've all had moments when we wished someone was there to make all of our problems go away.

I always thought I had a good handle on taking care of myself, because I felt I'd been doing it from such a young age after my parents' divorce. What I later learned is that I really only knew how to take care of myself when things were going well and when there were tasks for me to achieve. I knew how to cook for myself, and wash my clothes, and work out regularly, and get enough sleep, and accomplish my goals. But I was completely clueless as to how to care for myself properly when I was really struggling. When I went through my first heartbreak in college, I handled it by throwing myself into whatever distraction I could find. I filled my schedule with classes, studying, work, volunteering, working out incessantly, spending late nights with friends, and taking on new leadership roles—all while falling back into a pattern of undereating and neglecting to nourish myself enough to keep up with my busy life.

That was a pattern I knew very well: do as much as humanly possible, starve yourself, and uphold impossibly high standards that will inevitably make you crash and burn. That strategy sort of worked for me, until suddenly it didn't. When I was faced with deep depression, chronic anxiety, and panic attacks at age twenty-two, I was woefully unprepared to care for a version of myself who was really unwell. My depression often had me chained to my bed, truly unable to move, so my usual coping strategy of "do all the things" was simply not possible. That only added to the crushing disappointment and shame I felt toward myself. Caring for yourself when you're depressed already feels like an insurmountable task, but it's even more hopeless when you don't have a framework for self-love to fall back on when all is not well.

After some time spent wallowing around in the depths of despair, I finally started to realize what self-care was all about. It's not necessarily what we've been told it's about, checking things off a list to become the supposedly best version of your adult self: the skin care, the workouts, the fad diets, the beauty routines. It's really about becoming a nurturing and loving presence for the many and varied parts of you who have felt unworthy in the past, including your inner child.

Reflect

WHAT DOES INNER CHILD SELF-CARE MEAN TO YOU?

Self-care is about teaching yourself that you are someone worth caring for, in whatever form that takes. Self-care is the very practice of reading this book and applying its contents simply because you know you deserve to be prioritized. It's the process of learning to stand strong in your self-worth and to let go of anything and anyone who doesn't affirm your truth.

Besides the definitions I've just offered, what else might self-care look like for you? If you're drawing a blank, read through the following list and circle ideas that feel most appealing to you.

All of these tools and practices fall under what I believe to be the definition of self-care. What else might you add to your own list?

- Breath work
- Creating art
- Cooking nourishing food and eating mindfully
- Engaging in prayer and faith practices
- Dancing
- Having a gratitude practice
- Honoring your needs and emotions
- Journaling
- Meditation
- Meeting your adult responsibilities with compassion
- Prioritizing sleep and rest
- Practicing positive self-talk
- Nurturing your connections and community
- Regularly connecting with your inner child
- Singing or playing music
- Spending time in nature
- Setting boundaries to protect your peace
- Taking care of your body with good hygiene

Starting Your Inner Child Self-Care Practice

The easiest way to go about self-care is to ask yourself this: *What can I do today to love myself better?*

When you're feeling overwhelmed, triggered, or emotional, you can also reflect on how you'd treat a small child if they were feeling that way. When you treat yourself in a kind and gentle way that embeds the experience of healthy love deep into your body, you're setting the stage for healthier relationships as well.

If you're not sure what first steps to take as you embark on self-care for your inner child, I recommend starting with cooking, especially if it's foreign to you or something you've not put much energy or love into before. Learning to cook nourishing and delicious meals for yourself as a single person is a beautiful expression of self-love. This act communicates that you're worth the time it takes to make something special and fill your cup, even if no one else is around to experience it. Plus learning to cook will go a long way toward making solo date nights at home that much more of an occasion. You don't have to become a master chef. Just build some basic skills and experiment until you have a handful of recipes that you love and feel confident preparing.

One of the most important components to any self-care practice is intention. I once had a therapist who was helping me work through some of the lingering patterns and emotions left over from my journey with chronic illness. Specifically, we found a ten-year-old version of me who was still stuck in the past carrying the old burden of feeling responsible for everyone and everything. She never got to internalize the experience of care, so it was foreign to her. My therapist's suggestion was that every time I performed an act of self-care, I should bring her with me. So I'd take myself on a walk and imagine her by my side. I'd set aside time to get still in meditation, and I'd tell her that this was for her too. Little by little, this younger version of me learned what it felt like to be cared for. She'd help me identify which practices were most supportive. This is how we heal. As our previously burdened parts begin to feel safe and nurtured, we begin to come home to ourselves.

I want to acknowledge that it's normal to experience feelings of sadness or grief as you work with your inner child. You might begin to see all of the ways that your needs weren't met or how you missed out on the playful innocence during some (or much) of your childhood. It's okay, and even quite valuable, to grieve those losses for your younger self. Acknowledging the injustice or heartache will ultimately create more space for a sense of lightness and play to return to your life.

When you've gotten clear on the habits and practices that make you feel most at home within yourself, it will be a lot easier to maintain that beautiful individuality when you are building a healthy partnership with someone you love. The more full you are able to fill your own cup, the more you will have to give from an authentic place in relationships with others. It's easier to show up as a more loving and compassionate version of yourself when your needs are being met, and self-care is how we learn to identify and meet our needs. I believe that when you spend your single time consciously building a foundation of self-care practices into your life, you'll go into future relationships with a stronger sense of self and a better ability to advocate for your needs.

Playtime

Have you ever been ice-skating before? It sounds like a fun winter activity (especially if you enjoy the cold, like I do), but it can be frustrating and even downright scary if you're new to it.

Picture this: I took my nephew ice-skating for the first time, full of excitement to see him experience some joy. At twelve years of age, he was already taller than me and had size thirteen feet thanks to his six-foot-eight-inch-tall dad (my brother). The biggest rental skates they had came with worn-out laces rather than the secure plastic bindings all of the other skates had. I could see that they were a little loose around the ankle, but we tied them as best we could and hit the ice.

If you've ever seen a newborn deer figuring out how to walk for the first time, you can picture my nephew's first time on ice skates. His ankles kept knocking in, and he was reaching to hold onto anything for dear life as he wobbled around the perimeter of the rink. It was difficult to watch, not because it was embarrassing, but because I know how hard he is on himself when he's not immediately good at new things. I wanted to see him having fun, and instead I saw him frustrated and discouraged as all he could do was attempt to remain vertical.

I figured it couldn't get worse, so I suggested that we trade in his skates for a smaller pair with the more secure plastic buckles to see if that made any difference. He went along with it, probably just to humor me, and we stuffed his feet into some size twelves and made sure his ankle support was good as could be. When I tell you it was a night and day difference, I'm not exaggerating. Suddenly he was speeding around the ice like a pro, lapping past me and his sisters with the biggest smile on his face. He circled the rink over and over again; as his confidence grew, so did his joy, and he even began to try tricks and spins. All he had needed was one little adjustment to his foundation, and he suddenly felt safe enough to have fun.

Here's the thing: most of us go around in our lives on rickety old skates with worn-out laces. When your only focus is doing your best to remain upright, there's not much room for joy or play. The big shame in that is that play often *is* the medicine we most need.

In my experience, the crux of inner child work is reconnecting to the part of you who knows how to play. Sometimes you may first need to make some adjustments that allow you to feel safe enough to play, like practicing nervous system regulation and self-soothing. Once you've done that, though, your goal is to invite in as much play as possible. And not adult versions of play that are really just a facade for dissociative behaviors, but real, childlike wonder.

Invite in curiosity and awe and silliness and uninhibited joy. Start by returning to the things you loved to do when you were a kid. Maybe that means setting aside time each weekend for arts and crafts. Maybe it means participating in physical activities that feel like play, such as dancing, swimming, sports, or jumping on a trampoline. Maybe it just means giving yourself permission to skip while you walk or sing while you drive.

The point is, when you bring those younger versions of you into your present-day life, you not only have more fun, but you also experience more healing. We were never meant to lose touch with our inner child. Yes, it's important to learn how to be self-sufficient and responsible, and aging is inevitable. But it's equally important not to take yourself too seriously along the way.

Try This

TAKE YOUR INNER CHILD ON PLAYDATES

Your homework is to set regular playdates with your inner child. Do things that sound like fun, even if they don't make logical sense. Allow yourself to be as carefree and openhearted as possible, without judging the things that bring you joy. The sillier it feels, the more on point you likely are. Here are some examples to consider:

- Take an afternoon off of work and go to an amusement park.

- Schedule an evening of watching your favorite childhood movies.

- Spend the weekend out in nature, frolicking with your imagination.

- Try something brand new, like rock climbing or ice-skating, to tap into that feeling of beginner's mind.

Play is an important part of our overall well-being. Consistently making time to get into that creative flow state will help you deepen your relationship with your inner child . . . and your adult self. I suggest checking in at least once per month, if not weekly, to see where you can fit more play into your life.

I want you to remember something very important: little you is rooting for you to succeed. Picture you at a younger age, filled with all of your hopes and dreams for what your life would one day become. You were full of belief and optimism and magic, and you didn't have any doubt that future you would make it all happen. Well, if your inner child still exists—and they do—then that means you have a built-in cheerleader with you at all times. A joy-filled little bundle of light who is encouraging you to keep going when things get tough. And you're right there alongside them, giving them the love and nurturing they need to feel safe. This is the start of a beautiful new relationship.

Chapter 15

The Body Talks

Learn to Befriend Your Greatest Ally

Bodies are interesting things, aren't they? These living, breathing, fleshy machines contain entire universes and brilliant ecosystems all of their own. And yet, without our consciousness inhabiting them, they're just animals. That's what is so fascinating about being human: your experience here doesn't exist without the body, but the body is pretty irrelevant without your psyche to animate it. One is no more important than the other, but most of us tend to choose just one to reside in.

Many people I meet, women in particular, have a challenged relationship with their body in one way or another. We can be

---

* This chapter includes discussions of eating disorders and body image issues. If you're in a place where those topics may be triggering, you are more than welcome to skip this chapter and come back to it another time, when you feel well-resourced, or not at all. Remember to go at the pace that feels nourishing to your nervous system.

extremely body focused, obsessed with appearance or just with the day-to-day physical realities of surviving this world. Or else we're extremely heady, stuck in patterns of intellectualizing and overanalyzing everything. Or—option three—we're entirely dissociated from both mind and body and spend all of our time in the clouds, so to speak, as is the case for a lot of what I would call spiritual bypassers.

I feel like I've had about a thousand different relationships with my body in my three-plus decades living in it so far. I've overidentified with it and underidentified with it. I've punished it and starved it and pushed it past its limits. I've both coddled it and neglected its needs. I've hated it and judged it and shamed it and objectified it. I've also loved it and appreciated it and been in sheer awe of it. At times I thought my body was my greatest adversary, but in reality it has always been my greatest teacher and my fiercest ally. Throughout all of that drama, what I've become certain of is this: if you can make your body a home in which you feel safe and grounded yet expansive and free, there is nothing you can't figure out or accomplish. Your body holds the answers to just about every problem you come across, and building a strong relationship with it is what helps you access that wisdom.

So that's a key reason why we're talking about your body in a book about choosing yourself. Trying to love yourself while hating your body is the ultimate example of cognitive dissonance. Your body is your home, and you can't separate yourself from it, at least not in this physical lifetime. Whether you like it or not, it's yours.

A few other reasons why we need to befriend our bodies have been shouted at me over the years:

- A complete experience of self-love requires unconditional respect and acceptance of your body.

- Your body is the recordkeeper of your past, and it can tell you about the wounds and pain you might still be holding onto from past relationships or childhood.

- Sex and intimacy are a really important part of relationships, but if you don't have a solid connection with your body, then your connection with pleasure is probably a bit distorted as well.

- Pleasure of all kinds is one of the most wonderful aspects of being human, but many of us are out of practice and out of tune with the sensations available to us through the body.

We place so much emphasis on what our bodies look like that we forget that their magic is in their ability to feel. It's kind of the whole point of being in a body with five senses in a world full of sensational things to experience. As illustrator and body confidence advocate Stephanie Chinn wrote on one of her artworks: "This body is just the keeper of my magic. Who cares where it folds or dimples."[1]

My own relationship with my body has been tumultuous. For a long time I made my body the sole focus of my worth, because it felt like something that was in my control. I couldn't control the heartbreak I felt, or whether a loved one got sick, or the chaos and injustice in the world, but I could control my body.

I became rigidly obsessed with what I ate or didn't eat, how many calories I burned in my workouts, and what size my clothes were. After six years of this, I knew it wasn't healthy for me, and I went through a round of outpatient treatment for an eating disorder. It helped for a bit, but it didn't really stick, because the next big life challenge I faced brought me right back to my old behaviors. I had a major car accident at twenty-two, and as soon as I finished my physical therapy, I went into training for bodybuilding competitions, the most extreme form of body mastery I could find. I'd train way too hard without any rest, scrutinizing every centimeter of skin and fat that I believed wasn't in the right place. But the truth was, the more I tried to control it, the more disconnected from my body I became.

My first real encounter with self-love, including love of my body, came at twenty-five, not long after that fateful birthday when I decided to choose myself. I had spent the entire previous year trying to win the losing game of vying for the affection of someone who wasn't the right fit for me. I had also decided to end my three-year pursuit of bodybuilding, as I could see the negative toll it was taking on my mental health. But that meant taking away my one true vice at a time when I had a lot of painful emotions to face.

One afternoon, feeling confused and unsettled, I decided to make my way to the beach for solace. There were plenty of downsides to living in Los Angeles during the hardest years of my life, but the Pacific Ocean was not one of them. It was my safe space, my source for answers. So I drove along the Pacific Coast Highway on a cloudy afternoon and found myself on a secluded beach standing in front of waves that looked slightly more ominous than usual. I've always had a healthy level of respect for the ocean and its vast power. But that day I didn't care.

I walked into the water and let the waves crash over me as I released the valve on the tears that had been begging to pour out of me. Standing there, sobbing in the ocean, I was suddenly overwhelmed with grief for my body. Grief for all of the years that I had spent hating it and punishing it and trying to control it. Grief not just for all of the trauma it had survived but for all that *I* had put it through on top of that trauma. If anyone had seen me on that beach, they probably would have thought I looked like a lunatic as I cried out, "I'm so sorry!" to my body, but it was one of the most transformative experiences I've ever had.

I won't say that from that day forward I loved my body and we rode off into the sunset together and everything was peachy. It's been a journey of high highs and low lows. But I can say that that was the day I made the conscious decision to see my body as an ally rather than an enemy or a thing to be controlled. That was the day I decided to play on the same team as my body and to learn from all of its wisdom. What I didn't know at the time was how much that decision would impact all of my relationships moving forward, starting with my relationship with myself.

To think that your body is something to be controlled is not only disempowering, it's off base. And also comically arrogant. How would you feel if I told you that you were suddenly responsible for consciously digesting your food, eliminating toxins, fighting off viruses, making your heart beat, creating new skin cells, growing your hair, and maintaining your internal temperature? You'd probably feel pretty freaking inadequate, because those are not things you know how to do. Those are, however, things that your body does every single day without your conscious help, and it's very good at them, which is lucky for you. So, no, your body is not something to be controlled. Your mind could use a little work though. The mind that tells you your body isn't good enough because of the cellulite on your thighs. The mind that tells you you should feel like a terrible person because you ate a cookie for breakfast. The mind that tells you no one is going to love you once they see you naked. That is the only part of you that needs changing.

And yet so many women are living with this fractured connection between mind and body. So many of us were taught to hate our shape, size, and the skin we were born in. So many women commiserate and even bond over the weight they want to lose, the calories they've eaten, and the shame they feel about their dimples and rolls. Or we're taught that our bodies are simply objects of desire for men. Either way, the spotlight is directed at what we look like rather than who we are. And when you've been fed that lie long enough, it's hard not to believe it.

In order to correct that misunderstanding within myself, I swung pretty far in the opposite direction for a period of time. I decided to go with the approach of "I am not a body, I am a soul" and focus on spiritual growth and improving my mental health. I think it was necessary for me to do that, because I needed to release all of the ways in which I was trying to control my body, and I could only do so if I pretended not to care about it anymore.

At first, separating my identity from my body felt liberating, like I was finally free of heavy chains I'd been wearing all my life. I was having super deep meditations and powerful spiritual experiences, enjoying the feeling of being up in the clouds most of the time. It also felt like I was giving a big middle finger to societal conditioning and beauty standards for brainwashing me with pictures of emaciated celebrities on magazine covers throughout my teen years and the prolific ads for diet products all over social media in my adulthood.

But after a while, I realized something important: detaching from my body is not the same thing as loving my body. I needed to detach from it in order to get to a space of neutrality, where I wasn't so damn triggered by it all of the time. But then I knew I needed to rebuild the bond from a new place, a place of acceptance and compassion. I finally started to see how being in your body holds so much value.

We're only able to experience the sensations of love and joy and connection because of the body. Our five senses aren't just evolutionary tools for survival, they're what animate our entire life experience. Because of your body, you get to watch beautiful sunsets, taste delicious food, smell the scent of fresh flowers, listen to music that makes you want to dance, and feel the warm embrace of a hug from your favorite person. And when you're fully present in your body, the dial on all of those sensations gets turned way up. I believe that true presence happens only when we've become willing to embrace and accept our body as it is and to care for it with sincere respect.

To me, that's what loving your body unconditionally is about. It's about caring for it as though it matters, just as you're learning to care for your inner child. The good news is, that doesn't mean you have to like what it looks like all of the time. You can love your body and still have days when you're not feeling great in it. You can respect your body and still have days when it's in pain or discomfort. Just as any loving relationship has ups and downs, so will the one with your body. The key is to learn to *stay* in your body, even when you're feeling something that you don't like.

On the surface, improving your body image will increase your confidence, which can change the way you show up in the world and in relationships. And on a deeper level, improving your body image can change your relationship with life entirely. When you learn to fill yourself with gratitude, appreciation, awe, and wonder for the legit miracle that is your body, you begin to enliven all of your experiences in the same way. Life just becomes a little more shiny.

Plus it makes dating a whole lot more fun when you're not constantly shaming yourself and criticizing the way you look. I truly cannot count the number of women who have come to me with mountains of disdain about their body to unpack. Usually by the time they've found me they've hit a breaking point. They carry massive shame about their relationship with their body and want it to be different, but don't know where to start—or if it's even possible to change it. And as they're explaining the pain they've been living in, they'll inevitably say something about how it's impacting their relationships. Either they can't bring themselves to date because their confidence is on the floor, or they're in a relationship with no physical intimacy because they can't stand the thought of being naked. Or—the worst one of all—they're dating, but they keep attracting people who are inconsistent and superficial, making them feel even more dismal about their bodies. I found myself in that category on quite a few occasions. Even if you're with a decent person who compliments your appearance, it can be hard to hear that if you don't believe it for yourself.

Healing Your Relationship with the Body

It's pretty astonishing, though, how quickly things can change for you once you address these patterns. This is a good time for me to tell you one of my favorite client stories. She's given me permission to share her story on multiple occasions, because it's such a beautiful example of what is possible when we invest in our healing. For privacy's sake, we'll call her Claire.

Claire was initially referred to me by a colleague who thought I might be able to support her with her body image struggles. We began as most of my client relationships do, by doing a deep dive into the current state of affairs in her life. We talked body image, food, her history of eating disorders, her career success, and, finally, relationships. At the time she was involved in a pretty complicated relationship dynamic. Simply stated, she was putting up with an unhealthy situation with a guy who didn't respect her. Her self-worth was at an all-time low. Claire was choosing to invest her time and emotional energy in a man who was never going to fully choose her, and in the process she was abandoning herself.

Our work together was not her first venture into self-healing. She had already done years of therapy and read many self-development books; she was an incredibly curious and conscious person. But we all have blind spots or areas that we need a little help in exploring. So, as much as she was comfortable with, we spoke lightly about her love life. But for the most part, I was giving her practical exercises and reflections to help her come into a healthier relationship with her body.

In the first three months of our time together, she encountered many of the usual challenges and triggers that I see women face when healing their body connection. At times it can feel futile, like you're pushing a boulder up a hill only for it to roll back down. But Claire was committed. She kept showing up for our sessions and doing her practices in between and trying on what it felt like to treat her body with more compassion.

And little by little, she started to experience some real wins. She was building the confidence to do things like work out in just a sports bra and to be more present on outings with friends rather than consumed with worry about how she looked.

That confidence gave her the boost she needed to make decisions she had never made before. She was truly showing up in her life as a new version of herself. So when the opportunity presented itself to go on a tropical retreat where she'd be spending most of her time in a bathing suit around other people, she went for it. It was something she had always wanted to do but had held herself back from because of her body image issues.

It was on that retreat that Claire met her now husband. When I tell you that she was glowing the next time I saw her, I'm not lying. She was *radiant* from the inside out, and I could tell that it was less about meeting a guy and more about who she was finally allowing herself to be. In healing her relationship with her body, she was giving herself permission at last to be fully in her worth and enjoy life, rather than holding back and waiting until she "lost the weight."

The most important weight she lost was the weight of her prior unhealthy relationship and the shame that went along with it. She had stepped into her most authentic self and in doing so was able to say yes to the retreat and yes to the wonderful guy she met there. She was able to recognize him as a healthy partner and feel confident enough to date him because she'd done her inner work first.

Watching their relationship unfold ever since has been such a joy for me. Claire is not the only one of my clients who has gotten engaged or married shortly after our work together, but her story is a reminder of something very important. How we treat one aspect of ourselves or our lives will have a ripple effect into all other areas. You might think that learning to love your body just isn't a priority, but I'd say it's *the* priority. Start with self, always, and the rest will follow without much effort at all.

The Recordkeeper

Your body is your one true home while you're here. And if you don't feel safe within yourself, then it's going to be very difficult to ever feel safe with other people. This goes back to the conversation we had about nervous system responses. When you're stuck in a pattern of fight, flight, fawn, or freeze, it's because your body is remembering a past threat and trying to keep you safe from a future one.

Your body is the keeper of your stories. Your tissues hold records of the trauma you've endured, whether physical, emotional, or psychological. Your cells have a memory of what's happened to you, even if your brain has blocked it out.[2] Your body is wise and will tell you what it needs in order to heal and what it's ready to let go of. The problem is, we let our ego get in the way and think we know better. We disregard the many signs our body sends us until they turn into symptoms that are screaming so loudly we can't ignore them anymore.

The pit in your stomach, the lump in your throat, the tightness in your chest . . . they're not just random and frustrating bodily functions. They are messages that your body is sending to get your attention. To tell you when something feels off, or when a person isn't safe, or when it's a yes or a no. Most of us aren't in tune with these messages because we weren't taught that our body is someone to listen to, only something to look at. And on top of that we're often numb or dissociated from our feelings thanks to being overmedicated, overstimulated, and undernourished in our modern lives.

When you do eventually start to tune back into your body, it might feel pretty uncomfortable and even overwhelming. To suddenly feel all the things that have been bottled up for so long and not know how to process them is a heavy experience. One of the most common remarks that I hear from new clients is, "I hate crying. It's so embarrassing. I don't want to start, because I feel like I'll never stop."

Crying and expressing emotion can be especially difficult for those of us who weren't taught growing up that it's okay to feel our feelings, even when they feel big and scary. But I like to think of it like this: you've experienced a finite amount of trauma and pain in your past that your body has been keeping track of for you. By allowing yourself to cry (or yell or shake or hit some pillows), you're allowing that old energy to literally discharge from your body. Eventually, there will be no more old energy, and no more tears to cry, about that particular issue. By allowing yourself to feel it, you drain the emotional charge from it.

Our emotional reactions also give us very compelling information about the elements of our story that need some attention and healing. I'm talking about those moments when you're not even sure where the emotion is coming from, and you couldn't hold it back if you tried. I'll give you an example from my own life.

I noticed in my late teens and early twenties that I struggled to have conversations with authority figures. Oftentimes I'd even find myself welling up with tears during a basic, nonthreatening conversation. It would happen when I had to talk to a professor about a grade, or ask my boss for a raise, and definitely any time I had to admit a mistake. I always felt so embarrassed by my reaction and wondered why I couldn't control my emotions. It even started to show up in my dating life, because I often perceived the men I dated as more powerful than me and put them on a pedestal.

Eventually I realized that the question I was asking myself, "Why can't I control my emotions?" was the wrong question. The question should have been, "What are my emotions trying to tell me?" When my heart raced and my body felt flushed and the tightness in my throat indicated that tears were on their way, my body had a message for me. That message was that I'd been programmed to avoid getting in trouble or being judged at all costs. My body still believed that someone being upset with me would lead to a loss of love. My body remembered moments from my past when I had felt this shame and pain, and it wanted me to avoid that again, no matter what it took. Our bodies are always trying to protect us. So my work was to create space to allow those stuffed-down emotions to flow and to rewrite that narrative so that my body didn't need to get my attention at inconvenient times anymore.

Sometimes we don't even need to consciously address what's ready to be let go of—we just need to breathe and move our body and cry or make sounds to let it go. When I first began the work of healing from my past, I was trying to deal with the real-time traumas of the car accident and emotional abuse simultaneously. I often had that fear of not being able to stop crying once I started, but the problem was that I didn't seem to have any control over when I started anymore. I fought it at first, but sooner or later I just gave in and let it happen. In my car, in the gym, at the grocery store, at the beach.

My life felt like such a confusing mess at that point that crying in public places didn't make it that much worse. My first indication that my body was holding onto more trauma than I realized was that I couldn't do any physical or somatic practices without crying. For (many) months I cried in every single yoga class I took and every single breath work practice I participated in. Sometimes it would just be a few subtle tears letting themselves out, and other times I felt like I was literally crying all of the moisture out of my body. I mastered the art of silently sobbing so as not to freak people out. I also had a knack for choosing teachers who used playlists containing songs that devastated me every time I heard them. The combination of their music, the deep breath work and healing movement I was doing, and my weary surrender to this pain was apparently the key to unlocking years of repressed emotion.

Having emotional releases like that often feels a bit draining afterward, like you've just run a marathon and feel slightly shaky and nauseous. After it happened enough times, though, I started to notice that I actually felt lighter when it was over. It was like my armor was being chipped away. Which was partly scary, because it left me vulnerable, but also relieving, because it meant I wasn't carrying as much weight around. I kept chipping away at it until eventually I wasn't crying in yoga classes anymore, and things that used to feel triggering and heavy started to feel much easier.

Giving myself space and permission to feel my feelings, including the old ones, has completely altered the way I show up in my life and my relationships. There's so much more space to be myself when I'm not carrying around stifled stories from my past.

Stuck Emotions in the Body

Here are some signs that you might have old emotions stuck in your body:

- You always feel tired and drained.
- You have a hard time regulating your emotions.
- You carry chronic pain or tension in your jaw, neck, shoulders, and/or hips.
- You feel like you overreact frequently.
- You have digestive issues or other chronic symptoms that are unresolved by medical treatment or diet.
- You feel like you really need to cry, but can't.

While these signs can be related to other issues as well, starting with the body is always a good idea. One useful practice is to close your eyes and mentally scan every part of your body, asking it what it needs and seeing what arises. These are a few other practices you can try in order to access, process, and release any trapped emotions:

- Breath work
- Gentle or restorative yoga
- Nonchoreographed or freeform dancing
- Shaking or bouncing

Try This

SHAKE, SCAN, AND BREATHE

This is one of the simplest and most effective practices for moving an emotion through your body, even if you're not sure which emotion you're moving. You can choose to do this practice in silence and just listen to your breath, or you can put on some background music if that helps you get out of your head and into your body.

Start by standing with your feet about hip distance apart. Then raise your arms out to your sides in a T shape and shake them out as if you're trying to fling something off of each hand. As you continue to shake your arms, introduce a gentle bounce into your knees. Slowly speed up the bounce as you tap your heels into the ground and maybe even take some small jumps if that feels good. Continue to bounce and shake your whole body for at least one minute, or more if you'd like.

After a minute, or after you feel complete, bring yourself to stillness and begin to internally scan your body from the crown of your head down to your feet. Observe what each body part feels like and notice any sensations that have shown up or shifted. Notice if the emotion you were feeling before this practice still feels present. Is it stronger, diminished, or about the same in intensity?

Now, for another minute or so, intentionally slow your breathing. Inhale through your nose to the count of five and exhale through your mouth with pursed lips (like you're blowing through a straw) to the count of seven. Repeat this for about five or six rounds. Then do another body scan and notice what you feel.

The goal isn't to "make an emotion go away." It's simply to let the energy of that emotion move through your body and allow a release if that's what's needed. The breathing at the end of the practice should ground you and help you feel more connected to your center.

You can repeat this practice as often as you like. I do this practice at the end of most workdays or even in the middle of the day if I'm feeling overwhelmed and need to move some energy.

Whenever I forget that my body has always been my wisest and most patient teacher, my yoga practice reminds me. Slowing down to be present in every inch of this body of mine is my favorite medicine. Your medicine might look different, and that's okay.

Those moments when you get out of your head and drop down into your body, feel an emotion wash through you, and savor the lightness and relief once it has said its piece—those moments are proof that this thing we've been trying to control all these years has always been on our side, waiting patiently to be our friend.

Chapter 16

It's Okay to Feel Good

Reclaim Your Relationship with Pleasure

Once upon a time, I lived with the belief that pleasure was something to feel bad about. The term *guilty pleasure* was frequently tossed around and led me to believe that feeling good was something you did in secret—or not at all. You ate delicious foods late in the midnight light of the refrigerator so that no one would see you indulging. You kept your voice down and laughter quiet in public so as not to offend people around you. And you certainly felt shame about that fun tingly feeling in your body every time you saw your crush. Carrying that heavy guilt alongside every

---

* *This chapter includes discussions of sex and sexual trauma. If you're in a place where those topics may be triggering, you are more than welcome to skip this chapter and come back to it another time when you feel well resourced, or not at all. Remember to go at the pace that feels nourishing to your nervous system. The topic of sex may or may not be of interest to you to explore, and either's okay.*

experience of pleasure made it quite difficult for me to develop a healthy relationship with sex, intimacy, or my body for that matter. Because, if you haven't noticed by now, your body has a whole bunch of nerve endings that deliver an endless number of sensations to you on a daily basis. You smell the sweet scent of roses, taste the juice of a fresh strawberry, and feel shivers running up your spine when something tickles your skin. Your body is a sensation-making machine, and a lot of those sensations are meant to feel good. What's more, it's actually okay for you to *enjoy* those good feelings.

Let's Talk about Sex

If your body remembers everything that has happened to you, that means it also has a record of all of your sexual encounters, for better or worse. From your first kiss on, your body has an imprint of all the intimate experiences you've shared, how they felt, and what they meant. It also has a memory of all your strong feelings associated with conversations about sex.

Let's start by acknowledging that for some of us, talking about sex can be exceedingly uncomfortable. You may have been taught that sex is something bad or shameful, or it's a secret act not meant to be discussed. You might still be carrying those feelings of shame with you on a conscious or unconscious level, and that's exactly why we're going to spend some time talking about it. Sex, intimacy, and pleasure are wonderful and important parts of adulthood. It's just that most of us have a disempowered relationship with our sexuality. And I believe that originates from the disconnect with our bodies.

You can see this play out in many different ways. It shows up in women who feel an intense amount of shame or disgust about their body and have difficulty experiencing pleasure or orgasm. It shows up in women who are dissociated from their body and aren't attuned to what they like and don't like. It shows up in many women who've experienced sexual trauma and have become hyper- or hyposexual as a result. People with anxious attachment patterns often use sex as a means to get their need for physical and emotional closeness met, whereas avoidant people may abstain from sex to avoid intimacy or participate only in casual sex with emotionally unavailable people.

I haven't met a person yet who hasn't at some point in their life had a complicated relationship with sex—particularly those who identify as women. When you think about it, the physical act of sex is inherently more vulnerable when you're a woman, because you are literally being penetrated. Someone is inserting themselves into a part of your body that you may already have mixed emotions about. And maybe it feels great, but if you were taught that it's bad and wrong, that's confusing—what does that say about you? Or maybe it actually hurts, but all the media and messaging you've seen is that sex is supposed to be amazing, so again you're left feeling confused and full of shame. And, as many women experience, when your body carries the memory of shame long enough, it can lead to patterns of sexual dysfunction, numbness, and pain.

There are some great books out there about reclaiming your relationship with sex and sexuality, so we won't go too deeply into this topic. But I cannot understate the importance of taking a thorough inventory of what your sexual journey has looked like and assessing how you feel about it now. As the shy and timid youngest daughter of a noncommunicative household, it was painfully hard for me to talk about sex with anyone—or to even know that it might be helpful to talk about. I only became willing to explore this side of inner work out of necessity. I had traveled far and wide across the spectrum in my relationship with sex without ever having actually talked about it with anyone. I loved it, I feared it, I craved it, I felt ashamed of it, it was mind-blowing, it was painful, it made me feel loved, it made me feel devastatingly sad, and then at times it was completely uninteresting. Complicated to say the least.

There were very few things that I knew for sure when it came to sex. One of them was that I wasn't capable of having casual sex and feeling safe and secure within myself. But that's a tough pill to swallow for an insecurely attached twentysomething who keeps choosing emotionally unavailable men and just wants to feel loved. I convinced myself that I was okay with just "having fun" and experimenting. But in doing so, I got myself into a lot of situations where I said yes when I really wanted to say no.

I eventually learned that my body really didn't like that. I started to struggle with pain during sex, lack of sensation, and inability to orgasm. I ignored all of these issues for as long as I possibly could and just wrote the problems off as "bad sex." It didn't help that I had never heard these issues talked about before and had no idea where to turn for help. *Cosmo* articles on how to have better orgasms were the closest thing I had to advice, and they didn't seem relevant or helpful at all. Intuitively I knew something was going on with my body and that it was trying to tell me something; I just didn't know what.

So I did what I knew how to do: I sought out every professional I could find who specialized in this area—sex therapists, energy healers, tantric masters, and eventually a pelvic floor physical therapist. What I discovered was that my body was holding onto an incredible amount of tension in an effort to protect me. It was holding onto the memory of past sexual trauma, emotional pain, and all of those times I didn't really want to say yes. Even though I had already processed a lot of this in talk therapy years prior, I hadn't yet given my body the chance to process it and let it go.

It was an incredibly powerful and cathartic unfolding for me to truly connect with this part of me for the first time. Most women I meet aren't taught about the profound wisdom and power that their bodies hold. Returning home to this truth is an act of liberation.

Reflect

CONTEMPLATE YOUR SEXUAL JOURNEY

Exploring your own relationship with sex may take some time and bring up complex emotions. Don't feel pressure to do every bit of this reflection all at once. Your subconscious will reveal to you what you're ready to process at any given moment of your healing practice.

Set time aside to reflect on your sexual journey in your journal. Here are a few questions to get you thinking about your own relationship with sex, intimacy, and dating:

- How was sex talked about or addressed in your household?
- What were your first sexual experiences like?
- What's your relationship with your own sexuality like? How attuned do you feel to your sensual side?
- How comfortable are you with physical intimacy in relationships?
- Do you use sex as a means to get closer to the people you date?
- Do you feel confident in your ability to say no when you're not interested in sex?

- Have there been times in your past when you said yes just because it felt easier, but it wasn't really what you wanted?

- If you have a history of sexual trauma or abuse, is that something you have gotten professional support in working through?

- If you have a history of pelvic pain or conditions that make sex painful or intolerable, how has that impacted you?

- If you have a history of STIs, chronic illness, or medical trauma, how have these experiences impacted your relationship with sex and your body?

- How have your sexual orientation, gender identity, and sexual preferences shaped the way you relate to dating and intimacy?

Conscious Celibacy

The big question that comes up for a lot of people when considering spending time intentionally single is: "What about sex?" That's a great question, because sex can be an important part of overall well-being. Sex and physical touch cause your brain to release a bonding hormone called oxytocin. It also stimulates the release of other feel-good hormones, like serotonin and dopamine, while reducing stress hormones, like cortisol. Humans have evolved as social creatures, and touch improves our mental, physical, and emotional wellness.

For a lot of people, the only form of regular touch they receive happens in romantic relationships. But it's worth noting that these same health benefits occur with forms of nonsexual touch, like hugging, self-massage, and even petting an animal. If you're single and choosing to abstain from sex or if you identify as asexual, it's important to know that your need for touch doesn't magically go away. You will want to actively seek out other ways to get that healthy connection.

Physical touch will feel more significant to some than to others, so your level of openness to my suggestion here will be highly individual. But if you've never thought about it before, it might be worth considering having a period of conscious celibacy. That means you consciously choose to abstain from sex altogether rather than not having sex simply because you don't currently have a sexual partner. There are many reasons you might make this choice. If you have a history of losing yourself in the pursuit of love and connection, conscious celibacy can help you to draw your energy back into yourself. If you've used sex as a tool to distract yourself and numb your emotions in the past, celibacy can also be a great way to reset that pattern.

Simply put, sex has the tendency to complicate things, especially when you have a history of misaligned dating patterns. Consciously choosing to withdraw your energy from those patterns allows you to come back into integrity and clarity within yourself. The parameters and boundaries are up to you. You may choose to abstain for a month, six months, a year, or longer. You may swear off all physical intimacy, or you may decide that kissing is okay for you. The most important thing is that you are honest with yourself about your emotional pain points and your purpose for taking this time to yourself. The more clear you are in your intention, the easier it will be to honor your boundaries if they're challenged. And the fun news is, just because you're celibate doesn't mean that pleasure is off the table . . .

Feel Something

Remember when I talked about how being present in your body turns the dial up on all the sensations you feel? I have come to believe that that's kinda the point of all this. We all have different beliefs, but I have a spiritual belief that who we really are is infinite. We're so much more than just a body, but we chose to come here to experience life in these physical bodies. That's it, that's the whole point: our higher self wanted to experience *feeling*, which is only possible through our physical senses. And if that's true, then our whole goal should be to feel all the things as much as possible.

So many of us spend our lives avoiding real pleasure and favoring the mundane comfort of our routines and responsibilities, with quick hits of shallow gratification to fill in the gaps in our days. We go to work, stare at screens, maybe get in a quick workout, then have some drinks and eat some food while we lie on the couch staring at more screens until we go to bed. And don't get me wrong, I love a Netflix binge just as much as the next person. But I also know that when I disconnect from my body for too long, I'm not a happy camper.

Pleasure is something we have to be intentional about attuning to. We have to get out of our comfort zones and be willing to feel things that maybe even scare us a little. Think of the best sex you've ever had in your life. If you're honest with yourself, there might have been a little fear or exhilaration mixed in with all those gooey, wonderful sensations. That's because losing control and fully surrendering can feel a little scary. And because there's this part of us that fears those big feelings, we learn to stay contained and play small. We start to delay our pleasure, because what if it hurts, or what if it runs out, or what if we can't handle it? So we hold back, we save our favorite perfume for special occasions, we save our favorite candle for the right moment, we save our sexiest dress for when we've lost enough weight to feel confident in it.

My invitation to you is to let today be the day you stop delaying your pleasure and your joy. It's time for you to get back in tune with the natural inclination of your body to experience pleasure. Not just on special occasions, but every single day.

First, let's redefine our understanding of the word *pleasure*. We often think that pleasure is reserved exclusively for sex, whether solo or partnered. But pleasure is so much more than that. Pleasure comes in that drenched-in-sweat glow you get after an amazing yoga class. Pleasure comes in feeling the soft fabric of your favorite blanket as you cozy up by the warm fire. Pleasure exists as you soak up the sun on your face while walking to your car. Pleasure is slipping into freshly washed sheets with freshly shaved legs. Pleasure even exists in the simple sensation of your full-bodied stretch when you first wake up on an average Tuesday morning.

Pleasure is what you make of it. It's ultimately about being present enough in your body to enjoy the sensations of even the most simple moments throughout your day. And that's why pleasure is a choice. The really cool thing about making that choice is that your whole life feels more vibrant and full when you give yourself permission to attune to your pleasure. You also realize that your pleasure was never dependent on another person, and it was never just about sex. You don't need a partner in order to access those juicy feelings. In fact, when you make a practice of this, a happy side effect is that when you *are* ready to choose sex and intimacy in a relationship, it will be infinitely more enjoyable.

Try This

BODY CONNECTION THROUGH PLEASURE PRACTICE

Pleasure is your birthright. Isn't it time for you to celebrate your innate human capacity for joy in your body? If this is brand new territory for you, the secret sauce will be patience. You may meet some resistance, discomfort, and self-judgment as you explore a relationship with pleasure. It might feel like a huge sigh of relief, or it might feel a bit forced at first. Either way is okay. These are some of my favorite pleasure practices, but I encourage you to add your own to this list as well. My recommendation is to experiment with different practices on different days and times as you learn what feels good for your body. Try them out to help you get back into your body and turn up the sensations.

- **Hip circles.** Start by coming onto your hands and knees on a yoga mat or soft carpet and gently sway your hips in a circular motion. Put on some good music to get you out of your head even more. Don't judge what the movement looks like—just let your hips move in all different directions, following what feels good. You can also do this practice while standing. Feel the blood start to flow more freely in your pelvis as you unwind all the tension you've likely been holding there.

- **The exaggerated sigh.** Take a deep breath in through your nose, then sigh it out with an audible *haaaa* or *hmmm* sound. Imagine you've just arrived at a beach vacation and are lying down in a hammock for the first time with nothing to worry about. That's the kind of sigh we're going for. Notice how it feels in your body.

- **Mindful eating.** Take a small piece of fruit, like a strawberry, or a square of chocolate and eat it as slowly as you possibly can. Notice how it feels in your mouth, how it tastes, the temperature, the texture, and all of the sensations you get while eating it.

- **Moving through honey.** The next time you take a yoga class or go for a walk in nature, move as if your body is moving through honey. Slow way down and imagine what it would feel like to embody that gooey, luxurious sensation.

- **Self-touch.** One of the best ways to figure out how you like to be touched is by exploring yourself. Set aside some special time for a self-massage. Maybe even light a candle and put on some sensual music. Start by closing your eyes, taking a deep breath, and checking in with your body. In order to teach yourself what healthy consent feels like, see if it's a yes or a no to keep going. Then slowly trace your fingers along your face, neck, and shoulders. Moving mindfully along your whole body, explore how different amounts of pressure feel and stay in areas that are asking for more attention. There is no goal other than discovering what feels good for you.

The point of developing a pleasure practice is to remind you that your life is actually meant to be enjoyed. Sure, it's not going to be joyful all of the time. There will be challenging chapters. Some of this deeper inner work and moving through heartbreak can often feel really heavy. Hell, life itself can often feel really heavy. But no matter your background, your limitations, or your level of privilege, we all have access to experiencing pleasure: no one can take that from you. Embracing your body, your desire, and your pleasure gives you direct access to finding more fulfillment in being single and ultimately, if you choose it, more embodied and healthy love in your future.

Chapter 17

Your Wild Moment

Do the Things You Think You Need a Partner For

The plot of most of our favorite self-discovery books is that the author's life completely falls apart, and in the midst of their pain, the only option is to do something drastically new in order to find themselves. That's how we got Cheryl Strayed's stunning account of grappling with her mother's death by hiking 1,100 miles of the Pacific Crest Trail in her memoir *Wild*, and it's also how we got the epic three-country healing journey of Elizabeth Gilbert in *Eat, Pray, Love*. Oftentimes the heroine's journey isn't a grand adventure around the world, but the fulfillment of a courageous commitment to finding a path to healing that works for them. In her memoir *What My Bones Know*, Stephanie Foo poignantly shares her process of healing generational trauma and complex PTSD and shows us the beautifully brave work of finding herself in the process. What all of these women have in common is that they are launched into growth by reaching their breaking point—that potent moment in time where someone decides to draw a line in the sand and find their true self on the other side of it, no matter what it takes.

If you're a *Gilmore Girls* fan, then you know that the plot from *Wild* even made its way into the *GG* reboot. *Gilmore Girls* was one of those shows that I always heard everyone talk about but I never got into when it was on air. In my mid-twenties, a Gilmore-obsessed friend pleaded with me almost weekly to watch it so that we could talk about it. I was in a tough place emotionally and wanted a new comfort show, so finally I binged all seven seasons, along with the six-hour reboot, in a very short span of time. (I don't generally recommend this for good mental hygiene, but like I said, I was struggling.) I could see why she loved it so much. It's witty, nostalgic, and comforting, and it gives you the sense that everything is going to be okay.

Near the end of the reboot, Lorelai (mother of Rory and one of the Gilmore girls in question) is feeling unsettled in her relationship and decides she needs a fresh perspective. She tells her partner that she's flying to California to "do *Wild*" (that is, hike the Pacific Crest Trail), which is a hilarious plot point because Lorelai is notoriously unathletic and antioutdoors. She arrives at the trailhead and is met by a dozen other women who are there for the same reason. The women share stories about their recent divorces and major life crises that led them to this adventure. They all set off the next day, but Lorelai misplaced her hiking permit, so she ends up killing time waiting for a coffee shop to open. While overlooking a beautiful view, she has *the* epiphany she was hoping for. The irony is, she never needed the hike in the first place. She just needed the fresh perspective that accompanies being the kind of person who makes bold choices.

What If You Could Stop Waiting?

My question for you, sweet reader, is this: What if you didn't have to wait for your life to implode in order to do something bold, uncomfortable, and epic? What if losing yourself isn't actually a prerequisite for finding yourself? To be clear, I do believe that taking brave, new action is a phenomenal way to find meaning in extraordinarily painful circumstances. When life throws a heavy curveball your way, it's nice to know that if you really wanted to you could sell all of your things and move to Bali on a whim. But I also believe that if we just gave ourselves permission to self-explore well before the shit hits the proverbial fan, then we'd actually be on much more solid ground when it does.

This goes back to that idea of the Plan that I shared at the beginning of this book. When we're so busy focusing on our path to the perfect job, the perfect marriage, the perfect family, and the perfect life, we actually lose the plot. The real plot of our lives was never supposed to be about those external accomplishments. It's about our return home to ourselves. We think that we lose ourselves in the wake of catastrophes and gigantic events like divorce, death, and addiction. But the truth is we lost ourselves much earlier.

We were born wild and uninhibited and sure of ourselves. But little by little we learned to dim our light to make others more comfortable, to be quiet and ignore our needs, to feel ashamed of our desires, and to care what other people think. In childhood we learned that if a boy is mean to us, it's a sign that he likes us, while we also absorbed the Disney-fueled message that girls need a prince or knight in shining armor to make their story interesting. It's one of the many reasons why women stay in unhealthy relationships to begin with. We're taught both to expect subpar treatment from men at best and to believe that we need them in order to save us or make our lives worthwhile.

My entire life changed when I realized that I could give myself all of the things I was waiting for a partner to give me. I started small, buying myself flowers while secretly wondering, *Is this completely pathetic that I am paying for my own red roses?* (Answer: no. Pathetic is my ex who refused to buy me flowers because he thought they were cliché, even though he knew I loved them.) After roses, I graduated to solo coffee dates. Not a coffee run, where you quickly grab your order and go home, but a proper date. I'd put on a cute outfit, grab my journal and my book of the week, head to a café, and slowly sip my drink while learning to enjoy my own company. Often I'd sit there fidgeting, going between my phone and my book and my journal just to keep my hands busy and avoid having to make eye contact with anyone.

It took me a long time to graduate from solo coffee dates to solo meals, probably because it's socially acceptable to be alone at a coffee shop but not at a nice restaurant. I spent plenty of time in my head wondering if people were judging me. The truth is, no one cares. And the only people who are looking at you who really matter are the other women around you whom you're inspiring to invest time in their own company as well.

When I finally made that leap, suddenly the world opened up to me in a new way. I used to spend an inordinate amount of time thinking about this insane dessert at one of the fancy restaurants that Love No. 3 used to take me to. I'd crave it and then feel sad because I had no one to take me to that restaurant. Until I realized: *Holy shit, if I'm craving that cake, I can just go get it myself.* Sometimes I ordered it to go, but one time I got dressed up just to go inside and eat cake at the bar with absolutely no shame, because I had learned that our little pleasures aren't guilty.

Instead of waiting for a partner to go with me to do the things I loved, I just started doing them, by myself or with friends, completely unapologetically. It was a revelation. The first time I went to the movies by myself, I realized how nice it is to not worry about what someone else is thinking the whole time. Because I've always been hypersensitive to the moods and emotions of those around me, I used to spend most of my time in a movie theater assessing whether the person I was with was having a good time or not. God forbid I suggest a movie that they then disliked. Instead, by myself, I was able to simply watch the movie and form my own opinions and enjoy my popcorn in peace. What a concept.

The first time I went to a concert by myself was admittedly a little awkward. Before the band came on, I was roaming the venue with a club soda in hand (again, gotta keep the hands busy), feeling overly self-conscious. But as soon as the lights went down and the music started playing, I was in heaven. I love live music, and I was so proud of myself for doing something I was excited about even though no one was free to go with me. That's how you build your self-identity and make empowering memories that will last a lifetime.

The last concert I went to solo was in February 2020. I was living in New York City at the time, and on this particularly cold winter night a singer I liked was playing just eight blocks from my apartment. It was pretty last-minute, so none of my friends could go. I'm a homebody by nature, so I sat in my cozy apartment for quite some time seriously contemplating skipping it. But finally I tapped into my empowered choosing-myself energy, put on a cute outfit, and made the five-minute trek to get there. (File this away under "Reasons I Miss Living in New York.")

Given the timing, I'm unbelievably grateful that I got out of my comfort zone and went. I had no idea that would be the last live concert, or any large event for that matter, that I'd be able to go to for more than two and a half years. Entering the COVID-19 pandemic single and living alone was the most profound test imaginable of all these skills I'd been building in this journey of self-love, but that's a story for another time. What's important to focus on now is all the ways we delay our joy because we haven't met the One yet.

Take the Trip

One gift I inherited from my mom that I will be forever grateful for is my love of travel. Because she was both a flight attendant and a European citizen, when I was growing up we had some incredible opportunities to travel that wouldn't otherwise have been possible for our family. We didn't travel an insane amount, but I spent enough time in Ireland as a kid that it felt very familiar to me. So familiar, in fact, that my mom would let me ride around Dublin on buses and explore the city all by myself by the age of twelve. I reflect on that a lot, because I know it's a big part of what instilled my confidence in my ability to navigate the world alone. That independent and adventurous spirit stayed with me until the age of twenty-one. After graduating college, I decided to take a two-month solo trip to Europe. I had never done anything like that before, and the job I had lined up to start after graduation had just fallen through, so I figured this was my moment.

I began the trip on familiar turf with a visit to my family in Ireland, then went on to explore England, France, Switzerland, and Italy. I revisited old favorite places and ventured out of my comfort zone by going to new places on my bucket list. I made a point of making friends wherever I could and immersing myself in the local cultures. I people watched at Parisian cafés and walked along the waterfront of Lake Geneva. I took myself out for dates where I'd indulge in smutty romance novels and copious amounts of fondue. I wandered quaint little farmers' markets and delighted in the flavors of local produce. I also sweated profusely hauling my overpacked luggage on and off trains under the hot European summer sun, so it wasn't all glitz and glamour.

But I learned one very important thing about myself on that trip: not only was I capable of traveling alone, I actually loved it. Like, *really* loved it. I enjoyed the freedom of being able to walk for miles to my heart's content as I wandered a city, stopping only when I felt like it. I liked moving at my own pace at museums and shops and cafés. It was truly an eye-opening experience for me to interact with the world without taking anyone else into consideration. But somewhere underneath all of the excitement and croissants and macarons was a sinking concern that I needed a partner to make those memories count.

I returned home feeling accomplished, as if I had checked off an important box on my trusty Plan. Now that I had traveled solo, I could return to my regularly scheduled programming of launching a successful career, meeting my soulmate, and getting married. And over the next few years, I noticed an interesting pattern emerge. Anytime an opportunity to travel presented itself, I hesitated to commit. If a group of my friends were planning to go somewhere, I'd hold out because I wanted to keep my calendar clear in case my (not-yet-existent) partner wanted to do something else with me during that time. Or I'd procrastinate on RSVPing to destination weddings, thinking *surely* I'd be with the love of my life six months from then and I wouldn't want to go without him.

I was constantly leaving space for someone special to come in and create memories with me that would be more significant than if I created them myself. Because every time a milestone passed and I didn't have someone to go with, I'd feel that much more behind on the time line of my Plan. I spent so much time fantasizing about what it would be like to travel and have adventures and do life with a partner that I wasn't allowing myself to have those experiences on my own.

It finally hit me when I was twenty-seven, nearly six years after my European solo tour, that I had put my life on hold in my effort to be ready when my person showed up. I was the one making myself feel lonely by telling myself that there were certain things I couldn't do or didn't have access to without a partner.

We miss out on delicious meals, epic concerts, romantic movies, and life-changing adventures just because we're waiting for someone else to share them with us. And don't get me wrong, it's a wonderful thing to create memories with someone you love. But in the absence of a relationship, you *still* have access to creating amazing memories with someone you love: you. As long as *you* are fully present to experience a moment, it will become a meaningful memory. Your presence is enough, and there is nothing a partner can give you that you can't first give to yourself. Instead of focusing on who's not there, give all of your love and attention to the amazing person who is there. Make moments special for yourself. You deserve that.

Once I had this realization, I dusted off my passport and committed to having more adventures. No more waiting for people or permission or perfect timing. I decided to start saying yes to life again. I said yes to travels with friends, planned more solo trips, and tapped back into a side of myself that had long been dormant.

During this period I visited a friend who had moved to New York. It was my first proper visit to the big city, plus it was Christmastime and I was buzzing with excitement to take in all of the holiday cheer. I returned to my practice of wandering miles and miles as I explored the city, stopping at cafés to people watch and sipping hot cider at the Christmas markets. I spent only three days there, but I felt an instant kinship with the streets of Manhattan and knew I'd be back (which probably had something to do with the fact that I had the lucky experience of witnessing fresh snow fall in Central Park while carolers sang in the background, aka the most idyllic version of New York).

I visited a few more times over the next two years as I slowly grew restless with my life in California. I wasn't considering moving and really had no reason to even think about it. But I'm not kidding when I say that one morning I woke up and I just knew I needed to move to New York. I couldn't explain it, and it really didn't make any sense. I thought I'd be staying in Los Angeles for the long haul, so this gut feeling seemed ridiculous. There were still a few things keeping me tethered to LA, and I really wasn't in a financial position to make a cross-country move. But this was one of those moments when logic just couldn't defeat emotion and intuition.

I'd always been so pragmatic that taking a big risk, like doing the whole year-in-Bali thing, seemed like a nice idea for other people, but not me. But somehow I knew that my soul was guiding me toward a new chapter in my life, if I would only be willing to take the leap. I started by testing the waters first. Within weeks of that impulse to move, I sublet my apartment in LA and went to New York for two months in the middle of winter to see how I liked it. The verdict? I loved it. I felt at home there in a way that I never expected to.

I returned to Los Angeles to tie up my loose ends and noticed, ironically enough, that my life there was crumbling before my eyes anyway. I went through a lot of loss in those few months; it felt like the universe was unceremoniously kicking me out of that old life and into a new one. Rather than fighting it (which I very much would have in the past), I leaned into it. I put my things in storage and decided to spend a few months traveling to visit friends and family while saving up money before apartment hunting in my new city.

It was the first time in my life that I didn't have a home address, and it was equal parts unsettling and liberating. Surrendering to the flow of life and building a deep level of faith in the universe was a new practice for me, one that forever changed me. I ended up making that cross-country move and another one three years later, with plenty more adventures in between.

There's something about throwing yourself into the fire of your fears that serves as a catalyst for fast-paced growth. When you get comfortable with discomfort and are at peace with uncertainty, it feels like you've reached a secret level of this game of life where anything is possible. It's in that space that you finally realize all the things you were looking for outside of yourself really do exist within you already. The love you wanted from a partner, the validation you wanted from a job, the security you wanted from money . . . all of those experiences originate from within you. And when you tap into the part of you that can experience all of that right here and now, you stop putting your life on hold until everything falls into place so you can be happy.

While accessing all of that is certainly possible in the middle of the day on an average Monday at work, most people need to get pretty uncomfortable first. But you don't have to move across the country or take a sabbatical from your job or have a glamorous international adventure. All that's required is that you do something bold and outside of the confines of your usual routines. Something that makes a statement that you are no longer holding back on life until your person shows up—that you are instead *becoming* your person, now. Something that marks a before and an after in the story of your life. Your *Wild* moment. Your *Eat, Pray, Love* moment.

I have a friend who recently went through a particularly emotional divorce. From the outside looking in, it seemed like she had it all together: as they were separating, she was stepping more and more into her power, building the most beautiful and expansive life for herself. She is a profoundly spiritual and self-aware person, and she did a lot of the inner work to let go of their relationship and heal from this loss. It was a gorgeous transformation to witness.

And then one day we were catching up on the phone, and she shared how challenging it was for her to be single for a long stretch of time. She was explaining how her loneliness felt and then suddenly cried out in frustration, "I just want someone to make me eggs! I'm not good at making them, and when I'm tired and hungry I just want someone there to care for me in that way." We laughed a little at the silliness of the moment, and I spent some time validating her very real feelings and telling her how completely normal it is to want to feel cared for. But then I asked her to consider another option: "What if you could make your own eggs, and make them well?"

We walked through a scenario of how empowering it might feel to know that she could make her own eggs in exactly the way that she likes and have access to fulfilling that culinary desire anytime she wanted. I could hear the relief in her voice once she appreciated that this was a real possibility. To be clear, there's nothing wrong with enjoying the feeling of someone you love making your favorite food for you. But it's even better when you get to a place where your happiness isn't contingent on the presence of someone else.

Reflect

WHAT'S YOUR WILD MOMENT?

When you can make your own eggs, you're free to enjoy remaining single until the right person comes along. And maybe you'll discover when you meet them that they can't make eggs, but that will be okay because you've already learned how. Sometimes that's your bold and uncomfortable thing. Your *Wild* moment could be an eggs moment. There's no right or wrong way to show up for yourself.

I've applied this same principle anytime I've found myself feeling like something is out of my reach (which is really just a way of saying I'm disconnected from my personal power). I challenge myself to give myself the things I think I need a partner for. Whether it's taking myself on a trip to the flower market or stretching my limits by treating myself to a first-class plane ticket, I've made a regular practice of showing up for myself in new ways. It's without a doubt one of the biggest factors that has changed my relationship to being single.

Now it's your turn to get a little wild. Get out your journal:

- Make a list of all the things you think you need to have a partner in order to experience.

- In what ways are you holding yourself back from fully living your life until you meet someone?

- In what ways do you withhold love from yourself?

- What is something you have always wanted to do, but it feels a little scary and uncomfortable?

- If you're really honest with yourself, why haven't you done that thing?

- Is there anything you feel like you're waiting for permission to do?

- What is one small thing you can do today to give yourself the experience of love? Once you've identified something that feels empowering but doable, go do it!

- What's one small step you can take this week to work toward one of the bigger goals you identified above? Maybe it's researching flights, hotels, or camping sites; maybe it's finding a new course to sign up for. Schedule time into your calendar this week to take that small step. Then once you've completed it, identify the next small step toward that goal and schedule it into your calendar. Keep going until you do the wild thing!

PART 5

Something New

"Though fairy tales end after ten pages, our lives do not. We are multi-volume sets. In our lives, even though one episode amounts to a crash and burn, there is always another episode awaiting us and then another. There are always more opportunities to get it right, to fashion our lives in the ways we deserve to have them."

—Clarissa Pinkola Estés

When you end your quest for love as something separate from you and outside of yourself, you tap into the awareness that love is a boundless experience that can only start from within. The way you're going to relate to and interact with love from here on out will be distinctly different from anything you experienced in the past. With this new understanding, you'll approach all of your relationships in a fresh way. Love will no longer just be something that you look for—it will become *who you are*.

In the final part of this book, it's time to tie together everything you've learned and transformed so far and apply it all to building the kind of life you want to live. We'll navigate community building, demystify loneliness, get clear on what you want, and set high standards for ourselves. You'll continue to find exercises and reflection questions woven throughout these chapters to support you in putting these concepts into action. Because the goal isn't just to read about self-love, it's to choose it and fully practice it.

Chapter 18

Building Community

Romantic Love Is Not the Only Kind

In recent years I've had a lot of women come to me saying that they feel insecure because they've never dated anyone or have never been in a "real" relationship. They often feel like there's something wrong with them or that no one will ever want to be with them because they haven't learned how to be in a relationship. And while this logic makes sense—that it's hard to feel confident at something you've never done—I also think it's based on a flawed premise. Romantic love, contrary to the image that pop culture paints, is not the only kind of love that exists.

Western society in particular glorifies and idealizes romantic love, to the disservice of all the other types of love that are equally important. Platonic, familial, community, and self-love are all just as valuable to our overall well-being as romantic love, if not more so in many cases. Whenever I make this argument, I'm inevitably met with cries of "But it's just not the same!" And no, it's not. But that doesn't make these other forms of love any less significant.

I'm not arguing that we forgo romantic love altogether and replace it with our other relationships. But I am certain that in the absence of a romantic relationship, you will still find endless opportunities to practice your relationship skills and experience connection, love, and intimacy. In fact, we deeply *need* those connections. As empowering as it is to learn to meet your own needs and become your own best friend, we were never meant to do life entirely alone. Because of that, a conversation focused on self-care would be incomplete and irresponsible without also addressing community care.

The key is, we have to be intentional about nurturing our friendships and communities. We have to begin to prioritize the platonic love in our life as much as we've prioritized romantic love. And I promise this isn't just a general platitude meant to make you feel better about being single—this is rooted in actual science. Dr. Robert Waldinger is a professor of psychiatry at Harvard Medical School, as well as the fourth director of the Harvard Study of Adult Development. For over eighty-five years, the Harvard study has been tracking individuals and their families to discover what factors contribute to robust physical, mental, and emotional health and longevity. Dr. Waldinger even cowrote a book on this study called *The Good Life*. Do you want to know what the researchers identified as the number one contributor to living a fulfilling and meaningful life? Relationships. As Waldinger states, "Good relationships make us happier and healthier. Period."[1]

The wonderful thing about this study is that it didn't conclude that *romantic* relationships make us happier and healthier. The study is very clear that relationships of all kinds contribute to our overall well-being. That means your friends, family members, coworkers, workout buddies, book club buddies, baristas, and peers are all equally important. The strength of your connections is what matters. And if you're worried that you don't have any strong connections, the study also shows us that there is no wrong time to strengthen current relationships or even seek out new ones.

I think that the main reason connection and community are so important to our well-being is because they give us a sense of belonging. I define *belonging* as feeling safe, accepted, and understood by those around you. It's the sense of being an important part of a body bigger than yourself, one that will always have your back. This type of support and acceptance can help us to feel more resilient, more capable, and certainly less alone.

I clearly place significance on building a healthy sense of independence and individuality, as evidenced by my urging you to have solo adventures. I really do believe there's much value and empowerment in learning to love your own solitude and knowing that you are fully capable of meeting your needs. But that doesn't mean I think you should be a hermit and forever isolate yourself from other people. We need other people. We need that sense of belonging, and we need our connections and communities. We need them not just to support us during times of trouble but to cheer us on when life is good, to laugh endlessly with us at the silliest things, and to provide a safe space in which we can practice opening our hearts and loving.

We also need to experience the empowerment that comes from contributing in impactful ways to our communities and relationships. I recently spoke to a psychologist on my podcast *Well, Then* about the process of healing from particularly difficult breakups. An expert in this arena, Dr. Cortney Warren had much valuable wisdom to share about the topics of love addiction and letting go of an ex. She told me her research has shown that our connections are a vital factor in healing from a breakup and that, most importantly, we have to take an active role in our relationships and communities in order to get the greatest benefit from them.² That means being proactive about deepening your friendships, nurturing your relationships with acquaintances, and showing up for others as much as you want them to show up for you.

Life gets busy, and some of us tend to isolate when shit hits the fan, but that's when we need to lean into our communities the most. That might mean scheduling a weekly coffee date or nature walk with your bestie or FaceTime dates with your friends who live out of town. It might also mean committing to being part of a healing community, group therapy, or book club. The idea is to make a point of showing up consistently for the relationships in your life in order to experience and nurture accountability, connection, vulnerability, and reciprocity.

The Importance of Friendship

Another reason our friendships are so valuable in the context of ending unhealthy relationship patterns is because they allow us to become aware of our behaviors and triggers with a lot less emotional charge attached. All of our relationships are mirrors for the beliefs, patterns, and conditioning that we carry, but we tend to pay attention to these themes only in romantic relationships. Again, this is because most people are socialized to prioritize and invest in romantic relationships more than any other kind. But when you learn to approach your platonic relationships with just as much attention, care, and curiosity as you do your romances, your emotional intelligence and relational well-being will skyrocket.

To give you some concrete examples, you may have read through "Called Out," chapter 4 of this book, and wondered how you're supposed to work on healing your relationship patterns while you're single. Like, how are you supposed to become a better communicator if you're not dating anyone to practice communicating with? How are you supposed to work through your codependent tendencies without a partner to show you where you still get triggered?

How? Friendships. Seriously, our friendships provide the most wonderful space in which to heal and practice new skills. If you can't speak your truth or set a boundary with a best friend, how can you expect that you'll magically be able to once you have a romantic partner? We often project idealized versions of ourselves into our future relationship, fantasizing that when we meet our soulmate, all will be well. We assume that things will just be easy and our problems will go away once we meet the right person. But the truth is, if we want to change a pattern, we have to take an active role in our healing.

Reflect

FRIENDSHIPS INVENTORY

Every time we're willing to get curious and ask ourselves a nuanced question, we access parts of ourselves that were previously hidden. Observation leading to awareness is the first step to being able to choose a new way of being. How you experience friendship can tell you a lot about your attachment patterns, conflict styles, and inner child wounds. Here are some valuable questions to ask yourself as you reflect on what there is to learn from your friendships:

- Do you trust your friends?

- Do you choose friendships that really challenge and support you, or do you go for more surface-level connections that serve as distractions?

- What do you think gets in the way of you having even deeper connections with your friends?

- Do you allow yourself to be vulnerable and lean on your friends in time of need, or do you refuse to ask for help? Are you the one whom everyone else goes to for help, but you never ask for it when you need it?

- Do you push friends away or stop reaching out when you feel anxious and overwhelmed? Have your relationships suffered because of tendencies to isolate and be overly self-sufficient?

- When you don't feel included by your friends, what do you do? Do you withdraw and isolate yourself? Or perhaps get angry and blame others?

- Do you spend time with other people 24/7 as a means to avoid your own emotions?

- Do you often feel unheard, unimportant, or misunderstood?

Try This

STRENGTHEN YOUR FRIENDSHIPS

If observation leading to awareness is the first step, taking action is the second. So if you discover, by taking the inventory above, that you haven't been investing much energy into nurturing your platonic relationships or that you don't feel as close to your friends as you'd like, you're now aware of those patterns and can make different choices. That doesn't mean you have to go out and become a social butterfly if that's not in your nature. It's just an invitation to be more intentional about how you cultivate your connections. And now that you know how vital relationships are to your overall well-being, doing so is a no-brainer.

While exchanging memes and funny videos is a fun way to keep in touch, it's not enough to nurture a deep connection. Here are some creative ideas to help you strengthen your existing friendships:

- Exchange written notes or postcards. (This is an especially fun way to connect with long-distance friends!) I also make a point of sending postcards every time I travel, and my friends love it.

- Start asking your friends questions to promote vulnerability and connection. Using a card deck like *We're Not Really Strangers* can be a great place to start.

- Plan theme nights with friends. My friends and I used to rotate houses to watch our favorite show each week, and we would set a new theme for each get-together. We'd also have what we called "family dinners," themed potlucks that got everyone involved.

- Start a book club. Even if it's just with one friend, getting together to talk about shared interests like books is a terrific way to nurture your connection. It could also be a podcast club!

- Have one activity that you and a friend do every week together like a workout or a coffee date. Honor it as you would any other important commitment.

- Send check-in texts. Little messages can go a long way. It can be a simple "Hey girl, I was thinking of you and hope your presentation goes well!" or "How can I help you feel supported today?" One of my friends will periodically check in with the question "How is your heart today?" and he always has a knack for sending those texts right when I need them. Never underestimate the power of kindness to nourish a friendship.

Having healthy long-term friendships provides you with the experience of being in secure relationships, even if you've never been in a secure romantic one. Our friendships are a safe space to learn what it feels like to be emotionally invested in someone and have them be equally invested in us. They teach us what it looks like to oscillate between being the supportive one and being the one supported, just like in any other relationship.

Our long-term friendships even show us what it looks like to disagree with someone, to have a fight, or to grow and evolve and still be in the relationship. When you're intentional about nurturing mutual trust and security, your friendships can actually be one of the biggest contributors to your emotional well-being.

The Celebration Hack

Another impactful way to nurture your friendships is by celebrating one another's wins. This topic deserves its own section, because there's a bit of nuance to it. The types of celebrations we're used to having with our female friends are pretty firmly tethered to romantic relationships: engagement parties, bachelorette parties, weddings, and baby showers. If you're a woman between the ages of twenty-five and forty, chances are you've gone to your fair share of these celebrations of love and love-adjacent life milestones.

In fact, one of the biggest frustrations I hear from the women I speak to often sounds something like this: "I'm so tired of going to all of my friends' weddings and celebrations and feeling like it will never be my turn." Not to mention all the money that gets spent on these parties—gifts, outfits, and travel add up fast. Our cultural overemphasis on celebrating partnership and underemphasis on celebrating anything else of value leaves a lot of women feeling less than. It can be exhausting and demoralizing.

Love is a wonderful thing to celebrate, but we have to be intentional to make sure it's not the only thing we're celebrating. We should also celebrate our friend who just got her master's degree, and the one who opened her own business, and the one who bought her first home all on her own. We should celebrate our friend who quit drinking and the one who just started therapy for the first time. We should celebrate our friends who are doing the hard work of showing up for themselves and healing from their pasts. We should celebrate ourselves for rejecting societal norms and choosing to be single in order to end unhealthy relationship patterns and build a better relationship with ourselves.

All those things deeply matter, and they are worth celebrating. That doesn't mean we need to break out the confetti cannons or throw a huge party every time we set a boundary or crush a presentation at work. But normalizing the practice of acknowledging these wins in our friend group is one of the most powerful joy hacks that I've discovered in life. I'll do things like plan an impromptu dinner to celebrate a great week at work or take my friend out for dessert because she finally ended her situationship. Building this habit within your friend group will require communication, because it may not come naturally at first. You will want to let your loved ones know what types of things you'd like to be celebrated for and ask them the same in return. We have to learn to cheer each other on, not just in good times, but in times of overcoming challenges too. Even just a simple "I'm so proud of you" can go a long way.

Chapter 19

The L Word

Redefining Your Relationship with Loneliness

It's hard to have a conversation about loving yourself without also having a conversation about loneliness. It's the inevitable fear that surfaces for most people when they think of being single.

There's a distinct difference between being alone and being lonely—they are not the same thing. You can spend a night alone at home and feel endless amounts of joy and fulfillment, just as you can be surrounded by people and feel lonelier than ever. Being alone is a binary condition: either you are by yourself, or you are with other people. Loneliness is an emotional state of distress or discomfort when there's a perceived gap between your desire for connection and your actual experience. That's how you can end up feeling lonely even in a romantic relationship. If you have a desire for a particular experience of connection that your partner is not able or willing to offer you, then there's a disconnect.

I used to think that my deeply rooted feelings of loneliness and not-enough-ness would completely disappear once I met my soulmate, as if there were one single person out there who had the power to magically flip a switch and make me feel connected and loved all of the time. I experienced feelings of loneliness in groups of friends who didn't really get me; I felt lonely at events that were supposed to be fun and happy; I felt lonely even when I was pretending to love my independence.

I assumed that romantic love must be the solution to my loneliness problem, because it was the only thing that I believed was missing from my life. When some part of us deeply craves meeting our counterpart and can vividly envision what life might look like with them, then it makes sense that life would feel empty without them. I'll even hear successful and empowered people say things like, "I'm so grateful for everything I have and the amazing life I've created, but it just feels like I'm *missing something*, and it's all meaningless until I have someone to share it with."

The hopeless romantic in me used to love hearing things like that, because it validated my inherited view of the world: romantic relationships and nuclear family are the ultimate sign of success, and if you don't have that, then your life is pointless. As silly as it may sound, I unconsciously loved believing this, because it affirmed both my low self-esteem and the notion that some guy would swoop in to save me someday. Now, I don't disagree that sharing life with someone you love is a really special experience. But having done the work of building self-love and nurturing my community as my strong base, I no longer believe that it's the only way to find meaning and fulfillment.

The Real Disconnect

I've discovered that at its core, loneliness is not a disconnection from other people—it's a disconnection from self. We're inherently social creatures, and we need intimate connections in order to thrive, that much is true. But it's unreasonable to think that our life doesn't begin until we meet our soulmate. Or if, God forbid, we lose them and that relationship ends, does that mean our life is over? Many people would say it certainly feels that way. I believe the reason so many people would say that is because they haven't built an enduring relationship with themselves that serves as the foundation for a deeply fulfilling life.

Occasionally, feelings of loneliness will be caused by not having enriching friendships and social connections. But even then it ties back to a root cause of disconnection from yourself. The more aligned and connected to your authentic self you are, the more you will attract people who are on your wavelength, and the more willing you are to put yourself in positions where you'll meet those people. On the other hand, the more you're hiding or showing up inauthentically, the more empty and fragmented your connections will feel.

Assuming that loneliness is, as I previously defined it, an emotional state of distress when there's a perceived gap between your desire for connection and your actual experiences, this is a powerful opportunity for a perception shift. If you feel fulfilled in all other areas of your life and your experience of loneliness truly is coming from your lack of having a partner, then I'm going to invite you to consider a new perspective.

Right now, you desperately want this one thing (a romantic relationship), and you're convinced you can't feel content until you have it. But what if you could hold enough space for two possibilities to be true? Multiple truths can coexist. It's what we call "both, and" in the therapy world. You can both deeply desire a relationship *and* be absolutely thrilled and delighted with your current life experience. You can be both excited to meet your partner when the time is right *and* happy that you get to spend this special chapter getting to know yourself better.

You close that perceived gap by accepting that your partner isn't here yet and knowing you don't have to suffer as a result of that simple fact. Your loneliness only comes as a byproduct of you convincing yourself that there's a person out there who holds the sole set of keys to your happiness and fulfillment. But *you* are the one who holds those keys, and you have the ability to free yourself right here and now.

Plus when you get better at being alone, your future relationships will be better as well. Significantly. Or at least to the degree that you commit to improving your relationship to being single. Whereas if you are sulking in the murky waters of loneliness for too long, you might find yourself in a dynamic you don't want to be in. The opposite of loneliness in this scenario tends to be an unfulfilling partnership. Meaning, we settle for people we wouldn't normally want to be with, just because we're resistant to being alone. The irony is, we often end up feeling more lonely in a bad relationship than we were by ourselves. The goal should be to get to the place where your solitude is so sweet, you're not willing to spoil it with inauthentic connections. If a potential suitor doesn't add value to the standard you set for yourself in your singlehood, they're not worth investing your time and energy in.

By the way, there's nothing inherently wrong with feeling lonely. Loneliness is just an emotion like any other, and all of our emotions are welcome messengers that give us valuable information about the state of our inner world. We don't have to push loneliness away or distract ourselves when we feel it; rather, we can get curious about why it's there and what it wants us to know. Loneliness might tell you to call a friend and get a dose of connection. But if you listen hard enough, I think you might also hear loneliness telling you to forge a deeper connection within. To get to know yourself on a more profound level and to find fascination in your own company.

The Loneliest Hour

Let's look at a practical example using one of the biggest sources of loneliness for most people: nighttime. I cannot count the number of times someone has told me that they feel okay during the day, but once the night rolls in, they are consumed with loneliness, sadness, and self-pity.

Nighttime is often when our vices and unhealthy coping mechanisms sneak their way in as a Band-Aid for all those heavy feelings. We attempt to mask our discomfort by drinking, smoking weed, endlessly scrolling through social media, binging TV, overeating, online shopping, or texting that ex we promised our bestie we wouldn't. Anything to avoid feeling the searing pain of being alone. Self-love just feels so much harder once the sun has gone down. It's easy enough to stay distracted during the day, but at night it can feel like the darkness somehow illuminates all of our feelings of not-enough-ness and convinces us that we will surely be alone forever.

The solution lies in correcting the perceived gap between your desires and your current experience. Your suffering comes from your belief that you should be experiencing something other than what you're currently experiencing. That you should have a partner, that you'd be so much happier if only there were a warm body next to you to keep you company. But again I'll challenge you to reflect: What if you could hold space for that desire and simultaneously not find any fault with being alone? What if you could actually find joy in being alone and making your solo evenings feel more special?

That's what I did, and what I have coached hundreds of other women to do, and I can tell you that it truly works. This shift doesn't have to be over-the-top either. It's just about showing up for yourself with intention, as you would if a date were sharing the night with you. I started making myself fancy mocktails after work to mark the transition into relaxation mode. I'd put on my favorite music and dance around the kitchen while cooking dinner, infusing love into every meal. I started using evenings to do things that had been on my bucket list: learn to play piano, practice Ayurvedic self-massage, experiment with new recipes. Suddenly nighttime became something that I looked forward to rather than the lonely part of the day that I dreaded most.

I promised you at the beginning of this book that you'd never be bored when you learned to become your own best friend. This is where I make good on that promise. When you become willing to admit to yourself that maybe it's possible to tap into happiness and fulfillment while single, a whole new world of magical experiences opens up to you. I honestly never would have believed someone if they'd told me that I'd be deeply content and joyful on my own—that in fact I'd often prefer it to the company of others. I genuinely thought that people who said they were happy single were lying.

When I finally made the decision to spend a year intentionally single, I thought it would involve a whole lot of painful loneliness. As it turned out, that chapter was the first time in my life when my loneliness fully disappeared. The more I committed to showing up and loving myself, the more fulfilled I felt in my own company. And when I realized just how much I loved it, that one year turned into three.

Getting to the place where you can go anywhere and do anything alone and find enjoyment in your own company is an experience of liberation that I wish upon every person reading this book. Because your single life shouldn't be a series of moments spent waiting for someone else to arrive and complete your story. It should be a collection of the most exciting, joyful, love-filled moments and epic stories that you're proud of. You can fill it with love, joy, adventure, play, connection, passion, and all the other things that you thought you had to wait for the perfect person to experience. You are that perfect person, and that time is now.

Your life isn't on hold—it's happening right now. And when you become an active participant in it (or, even better, the main character), you'll be surprised at how quickly your loneliness dissipates.

So to recap:

- Romantic love is not the only type of love that exists. Invest in your connections and community. Celebrate and nurture them just as you would soulmates (because, hint: they are).

- Multiple truths can coexist. It's okay to want to meet your person and simultaneously give yourself permission to live your life at full volume before you meet them.

- Loneliness is only showing you where there's a disconnect. Become your own best friend, and everything will feel clearer and easier.

Try This

SOMATIC HEALING FOR LONELINESS

When we're craving connection and it doesn't feel available in the moment, one of the most powerful things we can do is enlist the help of our own body to make us feel connected. This practice may feel silly at first, but give it a try. You might be surprised at how nourishing it feels.

The first step is to find or create the coziest possible area in your home. That could be your bed, the couch, or a comfy setup on the floor with yoga props and pillows. Personally, I like grabbing my softest blanket and plushest pillows and setting them up in a space that feels safe. You might try dimming the lights and lighting a candle to make the environment feel even more intimate and peaceful.

Then wrap yourself in that blanket and either lie on your side in the fetal position, resting your head on your arm, or stay seated and wrap your arms around your body. Whichever position you choose, begin to take some slow and deep breaths as you feel your rib cage expand and press up against your arms or the floor you're lying on. Take a moment to appreciate the gentle pressure of that sensation combined with the feeling of being held by the surface you're on, your blanket, and yourself.

Now close your eyes and imagine a time you felt really loved, special, or seen. If you can't recall a specific moment, just imagine what that feeling might be like. As you conjure it, imagine that with every inhale you take you are literally filling your body with that feeling. And with every exhale you take, practice allowing your body to soften and let the feeling penetrate deeper.

Continue like this for at least five to ten minutes, then check in with how you're feeling at the end. This practice might bring up some big emotions, and that's okay. Just see what it's like to become the source of your own connection, filling yourself up from the inside out. It's more than okay to get connection from the outside world, but it's also beautiful to learn to source it from within yourself.

Chapter 20

Mining for Gold

Getting Clear on What You Really Want in "the One"

If there were only one person who could give you all of the love you've ever wanted, do you know who it would be? It's you, babe. You are your One. Anyone else who comes along and has the privilege of loving you, whether for a long time or a short while, is only going to reflect what's already there.

That being said, I've found that being clear on what you want in the realm of love and relationship can actually make relaxing into your singledom much easier. It makes you settle-proof. This chapter is going to help you create that clarity so that if and when you decide to start actively dating again, or if someone interesting shows up in your life unexpectedly, there will be no more guesswork involved. It takes the drama out of the dating experience and helps you focus on what really matters. I call it "mining for gold," because you get to extract the good and leave the rest.

We're going to make some lists that will serve as somewhat of a compass for your life. But before we make the lists, I want you to start to call to mind every experience or observation of love you'd ever had. Relationships you've been in, your parents' relationship, your friends' relationships, what you've seen on social media and movies and TV, what you've read in novels—all of it. With all of these examples of what a relationship could look like, you're going to sift out what you want and what you don't want. It's also a great opportunity for you to review the assumptions you've made about love based on the stories you've witnessed.

As an example, maybe you believe that all men are bad communicators, because that's all you've seen. So if you want to be with someone who has healthy communication skills, you'll have to challenge that narrative and be willing to put something on your list that you've never seen before. Lists are helpful because they bring tangible clarity to what we're looking for in a relationship and can help us to avoid falling into old patterns. Lists become unhelpful when we get lost in little details that don't really matter and that distract us from our core values.

Try This

LEAD FROM YOUR VALUES

Speaking of core values, let's return to yours. If you remember from chapter 10, your core values are five to ten guiding principles that help you to remain in alignment and integrity in your life decisions. You may have one list of values that applies to all areas of your life or separate lists of values (though some may overlap) for each major area of your life. For the purposes of this exercise, you're going to come up with a list of core values that apply to your relationships.

It's pretty easy to identify your current core values by observing what you spend the most time doing and thinking about. If you always prioritize going to the gym before work and cooking healthy meals at home, then wellness is likely one of your core values. If you go out of your way to volunteer and take part in community programs, then service might be one of your values. What you're currently prioritizing is most often a direct reflection of what you currently value.

Another way to go about this process is by reflecting on an existing list of words (see below) and circling all the ones that resonate with you. Then, narrow your own list down to the top five values that are most important to you to bring into a relationship. Often people have a hard time refining which ones are most important. If you have a tough time narrowing it down, think about what would come first if you could only express a limited number of values in each day; that's how you identify your priorities.

The values on this list are not the only ones to choose from, so if something comes to mind that you don't see here, feel free to add it to your list.

Examples of Core Relationship Values

Achievement	Cleanliness
Adaptability	Commitment
Adventure	Communication
Balance	Community
Beauty	Connection
Clarity	Creativity

Curiosity	Love
Discipline	Loyalty
Empathy	Nature
Emotional intelligence	Open-mindedness
Environment	Partnership
Faith	Peace
Family	Personal growth
Fitness	Playfulness
Flexibility	Purpose
Freedom	Respect
Friendship	Romance
Fulfillment	Security
Fun	Self-care
Generosity	Self-expression
Gratitude	Sensuality
Health	Service
Humor	Spirituality
Independence	Success
Integrity	Trust
Intimacy	Wealth
Joy	Wisdom
Leadership	

Once you've identified your top core relationship values, spend some time reflecting and writing about what each one means to you. Why is it on your list? How does it show up in your life now? How do you envision this value showing up in future relationships?

Then, write down your values and put them someplace where you will see them often for the next few weeks. Anytime you need to make a decision or don't know which direction to take, allow yourself to be guided by your values.

Try This

IDENTIFY YOUR NONNEGOTIABLES

Now that you've got your core values as your compass, we can move on to building some of the more specific lists that will help you step into your worth and raise your dating standards. It's important to note that these are not wish lists of random qualities that make up the seemingly perfect person.

Having higher standards is not about being nitpicky or judgmental. It's about acknowledging that you hold certain values that guide the way you live your life, and any partner you choose to be with should be aligned with what matters most to you. It's not about saying, "He has to have brown hair and green eyes." Instead, it's an opportunity for you to be honest about your most authentic needs and desires and to finally give yourself permission to have them met.

A nonnegotiable is exactly as it sounds: something that, for you, is a must-have in a partner or a relationship dynamic. It's something so important to you that you know you couldn't truly have a happy, fulfilling relationship without it. The cool thing is, you get to decide what your nonnegotiables are. They'll be different for each person. Your list is uniquely you.

That said, there are some foundational relationship elements that many people's lists may have in common—things like healthy communication, trust, honesty, and love. You can get as specific or as broad as feels supportive to you. You might feel you have a complete list just by carrying over your core values. Or you may want to elaborate and add clearer examples of those values.

For instance, maybe you put family as a value and a nonnegotiable. Does that mean that you want to be with someone who has a good relationship with their family? Someone who prioritizes spending time with your family? Someone who wants to have children and build a family of their own with you? These are all different possibilities for the same word, which is why getting specific can be really useful.

Here are another few examples of how a core value can translate into a nonnegotiable relationship experience:

Value: Curiosity

Nonnegotiable: Continuous desire to try new things together.

Value: Adventure

Nonnegotiable: Willing and able to travel together or explore local hiking trails.

Value: Integrity

Nonnegotiable: Someone who does what they say they'll do and honors their word.

Value: Personal growth

Nonnegotiable: Both partners are committed to self-exploration, going to therapy, and other forms of growth.

You don't need to write every single thing that you want to experience in a partner on this list, only the most important ones. These are the things that you have to be prepared to draw a line in the sand for. That means that if you are dating someone really wonderful but they're missing one of your nonnegotiables, you have to be willing to honor yourself enough to walk away. That's why it's important that this list be comprised of the things that really matter to you. You probably wouldn't walk away from an amazing connection because of the color of their eyes, so we don't add those types of fun preferences to the list. (We'll explore the idea of fun preferences in a bit.)

Try This

IDENTIFY YOUR DEAL-BREAKERS

After you've identified your nonnegotiables, it's time for you to identify your deal-breakers. These factors might sound similar, but there's a distinct difference: nonnegotiables are the things you absolutely need to experience in order to have a secure and healthy relationship, whereas deal-breakers are the things that you're absolutely *not* interested in experiencing. Deal-breakers are the "don't wants" that help guide you to end a connection when it's not the right fit for you.

There are a couple of examples that I love to offer, because they tend to be pretty clear-cut and even divisive. The first one is smoking. If someone is a smoker, typically either you care or you don't. And if you do care, it's usually because you have a strong aversion to smoking, so you know that you cannot be with someone who smokes. That's a pretty undeniable deal-breaker.

We could also use drinking as an example. Many people drink socially, but maybe being with someone who is a heavy drinker is a no-go for you. Or perhaps you're sober and you've identified for yourself that you can't reasonably be with someone who drinks at all. Politics and religion are other great examples. For some people, being with someone who holds different beliefs is no big deal. For other people it's a deal-breaker. The point is, only you know what your limits are. It's important that you be honest about them.

Deal-breakers can also be your opportunity to get clear with yourself about what would and would not fly in your ideal relationship. If your partner cheats, is that the end of the relationship, or is it something you could forgive? You don't have to have all the answers to hypothetical scenarios, but it can be helpful to become clear about where you stand on certain issues in an effort to avoid old patterns and uphold a new standard. Because choosing yourself sometimes means being able to walk away from the wrong people, no matter how hard it feels.

Once you've identified the behaviors or patterns that you wouldn't be willing to tolerate in a relationship, then it's up to you to set and maintain those boundaries. It becomes a practice in learning to trust yourself enough to say no to what isn't right for you.

Just like with nonnegotiables, there are a few foundational deal-breakers that you might want to consider adding to your list:

Any sort of abuse

Disrespectful communication

Inconsistency

Irresponsibility

Not wanting the same things as you

One-sided interest (aka lack of reciprocity)

Keep in mind that your goal in dating shouldn't be to look for deal-breakers and try to find things wrong with potential partners. It's not about actively searching for red flags and reasons why someone isn't a match. Your goal should just be to keep an open mind and observe the person in front of you. Don't project stories from past heartbreaks onto each new person and expect the worst from them. And don't wear rose-colored glasses and refuse to acknowledge reality when those red flags do pop up. Hover somewhere in the middle and just enjoy the experience of getting to know someone new with your fresh clarity on what it is that you want (and what you don't).

Fun Preferences

If you're a digital nomad and you travel and work from different countries all the time, it's probably going to be essential for you to be with someone who also has the flexibility to work remotely. In that case, career flexibility and love for travel might be nonnegotiables for you. If, on the other hand, you're someone who has an in-person job and has never really traveled much but loves the idea of it, then you might add "desire to travel" to your preferences list. You can think of preferences as "the things that are nice to have" list. They're not things that are required for you to be happy and fulfilled, but they're fun bonuses that you might enjoy getting to experience.

You don't need to have a preferences list at all, but it can be a fun way to envision what life might be like with your future partner while making a clear distinction between what you need versus what you'd appreciate but could live without. This list tends to include what we think of as the more superficial qualities—things like height and hair color, but also taste in music and personal style.

You can think of preferences this way: while it would be really fun to share the same taste in music or home decor as your partner, it's probably not going to be a deal-breaker so long as they have all of your nonnegotiables and your core values align. Or say you meet your dream partner who embodies everything you've always wanted, but they're a couple inches shorter than you expected your soulmate to be. Is that a deal-breaker? Probably not.

Try This

THE MAIN CHARACTER LIST

Now that you've made all these lists about your ideal partner, it's time to make one more. I want you to set a timer for twenty minutes and write down everything that *you* bring to the table in a relationship. We often get so caught up in defining who this other person needs to be that we forget how much we have to offer. Write down anything and everything that comes to mind, from your adventurous side to your love of baking. Write about the ways that you give love to others, and how well you're learning to take care of yourself, and the fact that you're investing serious time in your healing and growth.

Get it all down on paper so that you can plainly see what a catch you are. This exercise may be uncomfortable at first, since we're not used to celebrating and bragging about ourselves. But it's important, because if you want a partner who embodies all of the wonderful qualities you desire, then you need to unapologetically own your wonderful qualities as well, as the main character of your life. And when you realize how great you really are, you're a lot less likely to settle for someone who doesn't see, love, and embrace all of you.

Making this list also gives you the chance to notice where there are any gaps between what you want and who you are. If you really want to be with someone who's a great communicator but that's not a strong suit of yours, then you know that's something you need to start practicing. If you want to be with someone who's well traveled but you've never left your home state, then it's time for you to book some plane tickets. It's not that you're doing these things to become more worthy of love. You're doing them because they bring you joy and because they make you more of an energetic match for the type of love you want to experience.

It might sound cheesy, but a lot of this work is about becoming your own soulmate. Something magical happens when you put the focus on yourself rather than on the relentless search for someone outside of you. You free up your time, mental space, and emotional energy for yourself when you're no longer caught in the obsession of finding the One. Instead you get to relax into the knowledge that you're cultivating a life you absolutely love. You'll recognize the right person for you when they show up, but nothing is missing in the meantime.

Letting Go of the Wrong People

Part of your growth process also entails setting boundaries and being honest with the people who are wrong for you. This is your opportunity to tend to any relationship housekeeping that you didn't do in chapter 4, "Called Out." That means choosing to no longer participate in connections or dating dynamics that are not aligned with this newfound clarity of yours.

I'll give you a personal example. Some time after I'd begun to explore this work in my own love life, I realized I was still participating in a dynamic that wasn't healthy for me. I'd maintained a friendship with one of my ex-situationships and convinced myself that it was no big deal, even though I knew I still harbored some feelings for him. I'd go for long stretches of time not thinking about him and assumed that meant I'd moved on. But as soon as he'd (inevitably) text me, the door to my repressed feelings would unlock. And then, when we'd (predictably) meet for coffee to "catch up," all of those feelings would come rushing to the surface.

I was living in a state of cognitive dissonance: I knew I didn't want to be with him and logically understood the reasons why we'd never work as a couple, yet my body told a completely different story every time I interacted with him. I'd feel anxious butterflies in my stomach, wondering if maybe he still had feelings for me. It was confusing, to say the least.

Because of those repressed feelings, I hadn't been willing to cut off connection with him and lose him completely. Even though it hurt me every time I saw him, I feared the finality of closing that door completely. The text exchanges kept me tethered to him. But eventually I got fed up with this pattern. I was tired of the self-imposed drama it caused. I didn't like the fact that he could derail my sense of stability with a single text—and that his texts were quite lazy in the first place. He was never really interested in how I was doing or what I was up to; he was interested in seeing if I was still hooked on him. So that was one of the major boundaries I knew I needed to set. No more pointless, lazy texts. No more pretending to be friends when clearly some part of me still craved more than that. I finally became ready to admit that participating in this dynamic was in no way supporting my love life, so it had to go.

Taking time to assess whether the connections in your life are aligned with your values helps you create more room for yourself. You can also practice leading from your values when you meet new people. For instance, let's say you're asked out by a nice person who just isn't a match for your values. A pattern of people-pleasing might cause you to go out with them out of politeness or fear of confrontation, whereas the authentic response would be to turn them down. This may not seem like a major issue, but it can be a potent opportunity to practice using your voice and owning your truth. Saying something like, "I appreciate it, but I'm not interested" may feel really uncomfortable at first, but it's honest. And honesty means alignment with our values, which ultimately means a stronger connection with ourselves. Practicing honesty in this way can also make it easier for you to cut ties with potential suitors when you discover they aren't the right match for you. Rather than stringing them along or ghosting them, try communicating truthfully by saying something like, "I've enjoyed getting to know you, but I don't think we're a good fit for what I'm looking for." Statements like that have a special way of placing you firmly in your power.

For something new to come in, we have to be willing to let go of the old in order to create space. Healing old wounds, shifting patterns, and creating new clarity all ultimately help you experience more spaciousness in your love life. As you practice setting authentic boundaries, give yourself a moment to enjoy what it feels like to have all of that newfound space, and trust that in doing so you've laid the foundation for the right person to come in. You can relax into being single and choosing yourself when you know that you've cleared the space for healthy love and that you're not interested in settling for anything less. At the end of the day, it's far better to be single than to be in the wrong relationship.

Chapter 21

Love Me Well

What It Looks Like to Choose Love from Your New Standard

The point of choosing and dating yourself is to learn what it feels like to be loved, to be treated well, and to become the source of your own joy. When you do that long enough, you'll naturally attract partners who are ready to love you well and higher caliber people into your life in general. Best-selling poet, meditator, and speaker Yung Pueblo expressed it beautifully when he tweeted, "People who have healed deeply and know their worth cannot help but emit 'love me well or leave me alone' energy. They only allow real connections with people who are emotionally ready because they know relationships take a certain degree of maturity to work."[1]

The final piece of the work we've been doing in this book is to put into practice the new standard you've declared for yourself.

It's about learning to trust your decisions when it comes to love and to trust that you are learning how to choose people who will love you well because you've shown yourself what that looks like.

When Is the Right Time?

The question I often get asked is, "How do I know when I'm ready to begin dating again?" And while I wish I could give a clear-cut formula that in X amount of days, weeks, months, years, you'll be ready to get back out there, it's not that simple. It really depends on your history, the patterns you're healing, and your intentions for dating. There's also a big difference between being aligned with your authentic self enough to start dating again and actually being ready. Relationships take time and investment, and being ready implies that you're prepared to carve out the space in your life for someone else—without losing yourself in the process. You might find that as time goes on you actually enjoy being single and value being able to invest so heavily in yourself and your goals. Maybe you want to savor this chapter a little longer before opening up to a relationship again. Maybe you decide that you prefer single life entirely. There's nothing wrong with choosing to be single simply because you're enjoying it. If and when you're ready to get back out there and actively date, it's important that you feel you have a strong sense of self-identity and a solid foundation on which to build a relationship. Once you have those things, the rest of the process becomes much easier. Sharing a life with someone is still going to come with its challenges, but your self-awareness and self-love will help you stay grounded as you face them.

Reflect

ARE YOU READY FOR A RELATIONSHIP?

Because being partnered is the conditioned default goal for many people, we often neglect to ask ourselves if we're actually ready for the demands that a relationship brings. Wanting someone to keep us company is not the same thing as being ready for a relationship. Here are a few questions for you to reflect on to help determine your readiness:

- Are you looking for a relationship to complete you or make you feel better about your life?
- Do you find yourself trying to be someone you're not in order to impress other people?
- Are you still hurting from a previous breakup and feeling consumed by thoughts of your ex?
- Do you still harbor feelings for someone you used to date or hopes that you might get back together with an ex?
- If you're honest with yourself, do you think you need more time to heal? Do you want to tend to yourself before adding another person into the mix?
- Do you want the freedom to devote all of your time to any projects or areas of your life right now?
- Are you interested in facing the challenges that come with nurturing a healthy relationship, like facing triggers, openly communicating, and investing time in getting to know and meet your partner's needs as well?

If you answered yes to any of the questions above, that may be a sign that you should lean into your single chapter for a while longer. Think about it from the other perspective: Would you want to invest time in dating someone who isn't over their ex or isn't fully available? Probably not. And the second question is important to reflect on because it shows you where you're still straying from your authentic self in order to pursue a connection. If you find yourself falling into patterns of trying to be the cool girl or the chill girl, there's likely some more identity work for you to do. Same thing goes for the pattern of trying to be the good girl who does and says everything right and feels the need to be perfect in order to be loved.

This is coming from someone who used to be entrenched in all of those patterns I've just described: your job is not to convince someone else to choose you. I believe that when you step fully into your worth, the natural by-product is that you no longer accept anything less than being well loved. It doesn't mean you won't ever attract people who reflect your old patterns, because the truth is they'll probably still show up. But you'll have a new ability to recognize the patterns and be willing to walk away in service of choosing yourself.

All Trust Is Self-Trust

I have one final reminder for when you do decide it's the right time to open yourself to partnership: trust yourself. When you're questioning if it's the right thing, it can be so easy to default to asking everyone else's opinion or consulting tarot cards or looking for signs. But by now you've done a lot of work to become your own best friend, and that means you can trust that you have your own best interests at heart. You know when someone is good for you and when they're not. And if you really aren't sure because you have a history of unhealthy relationships and no reference point for what healthy feels like, seek the opinion of one trusted person, like a therapist or a close friend. Allow them to reflect back what they're seeing in you and trust that you can never get it wrong—you can only learn.

Many people worry about whether or not they can trust someone else with their heart. You may be one of those people. And while it's important to be discerning about whom you choose to invest in, the real fear beneath that worry is that you can't trust yourself. That if someone hurts you or betrays you or leaves and breaks your heart, you won't be able to pick up the pieces and learn to love again. The real work isn't about trusting that you'll find the perfect partner. It's about trusting that you'll be okay, no matter what happens. Because even healthy relationships are imperfect. And you're likely to end up with someone who at times lets you down, makes a mistake, or unintentionally triggers your childhood wounds. So the real question is: Can you trust in your tools and your ability to lean into vulnerability for the sake of deeper connection?

Even if a relationship doesn't work out, you will always learn from it. And with your new tools, you'll know how to keep your heart open and rediscover more of yourself along the way. So trust your heart to love again and trust yourself to have your own back in the process. You've got this.

Conclusion

Happily Ever After

You Are Perfectly on Time

I feel like I should throw you a party. Seriously, the work that you've done to reflect on some really difficult things and to practice showing up for yourself in new and more loving ways—it's a big deal. You are a big deal. We'll do some more celebrating in a bit, but first I want to share a story that's going to help you bring all of the lessons of this book along with you into the next chapter of your life.

A few months ago I took myself on a little solo adventure. I'm well practiced at this point, so I had no fear or discomfort about taking this road trip. But for some reason, I'd been putting off this particular bucket-list item for a while. There's this adorable little Bavarian town about three hours outside of where I now live in Seattle. You feel like you're in a fairy tale when you go there, especially if you visit in the winter. The town gets blanketed in snow, and they string up holiday lights on every available surface, so it's pretty much the epitome of my favorite things (cozy weather and Christmastime).

I've been to this town quite a few times in the summer, as it has some epic hikes nearby. But I'd never been in the winter, and I wanted to give myself that experience. I knew how much I would love it. Yet I kept delaying it or making excuses for why I couldn't go. I realized that some part of me was trying to save that memory-making event for when I could do it with a partner. The moment I realized that, I did two things.

First, I acknowledged my feelings and validated the part of me that wants to build a life with someone. Second, I acknowledged the dual truth that it's possible both to create happy memories now all on my own and to share special experiences with a partner in the future. Those things are not mutually exclusive. *Duh.* I mean, it seems obvious, but sometimes I forget.

So off I went. I put on my coziest winter outfit, gassed up my car, and hit the road. I blasted my favorite music and sang all the way through the snow-covered mountain passes. I don't know what it is, but every time I see snow, I feel like a little kid who's been given keys to the candy store. So with a smile plastered on my face, I pulled into town after a few hours of scenic driving. I was ready to start exploring.

One of my favorite things to do when I'm going on a solo adventure is to pick a fun starting point and let the rest of the day unfold from there with no specific plan. I've found that when I try to structure new experiences too much, I'm more focused on controlling them than actually living them. So I parked near my favorite little coffee shop to start my day with some sustenance. I ordered an avocado toast and something called a "yuletide latte," which had a delightful blend of clove, cinnamon, and orange peel. I sipped my coffee with a firepit on one side of me and a snowbank on the other, feeling a massive swell of appreciation for this simple little moment.

The rest of my day was spent slowly wandering the streets of this storybook town, bobbing in and out of shops and stopping wherever I felt called to. That's the beauty of solo travel—you get to do exactly what you want, on your time line. I sniffed locally made candles, tasted locally sourced honey, and bought a locally knit beanie, feeling delighted to support all of these small businesses. I watched kids go sledding down a hill that had clearly been appointed the official town sled spot, and I smiled as a happy family rode by in a horse-drawn carriage, for real. I wasn't kidding when I said this place is something out of a fairy tale. And I was savoring every moment of my perfect day.

I was nearing the end of my wandering when I happened upon a bookstore, one type of establishment I can never pass up. When I explore a new bookstore, I don't head straight to any specific section; I allow myself to be intuitively guided. I've found that to be the best strategy for finding the books that are precisely what I'm meant to be reading at that moment in time (or, rather, letting them find me).

As I slowly walked around, I ran my fingers across a few intriguing titles before feeling led to park myself in front of one particular shelf. I reached for the first book in my line of sight and quite literally laughed out loud when I read the title: *The Princess Saves Herself in This One*. A book of poetry by Amanda Lovelace about a woman learning to become her own savior. It felt like a perfectly orchestrated moment, a divine wink from the universe telling me that I was exactly where I needed to be.

I left the bookstore feeling a kind of magical glow and decided to take myself for an early dinner before heading back home. I sat at the bar sipping some hot cider and gazing out of a picture window while waiting for my meal, thinking to myself how grateful I was that we can't see the endings of our stories before they happen.

If you'd told twenty-five-year-old me that I'd be thirty-three and still single, she would have been horrified. And if you had tried to convince her that I was actually incredibly happy and fulfilled without a partner, she would have thought you were insane. I had no foresight and no faith back in my youth. I thought there was only one way my life could pan out that could possibly make me happy, and anything else felt like failure.

So if there were one piece of wisdom I could instill in my younger self, and in you, it would be this: trust the timing of your life. As Steve Jobs once said in his famous 2005 Stanford commencement speech: "You can't connect the dots looking forward, you can only connect them looking backwards."[1]

You have to learn to trust that things are unfolding for you in a way that is for your highest good, even if you can't see it right now. The lessons you're learning and the person you're becoming are precisely what will lead you to the places you want to go and the person you want to be with. And when you don't get what you want, trust that it's because there's something better headed your way. The timing will rarely be what you want it to be, so let go of arbitrary time lines altogether. Allow life to surprise you a little bit.

And in the meantime, give yourself permission to love what is. Not just to tolerate it or to use it to kill time until something better comes along. But to truly love, embrace, and enjoy this particular season of your life. If you knew, beyond a shadow of a doubt, that you would meet your person exactly one month, one year, or even ten years from today, what would you do differently? If you knew that this was the last chapter of your life where you'd have all of this time and freedom to invest in yourself, would you embrace it a little bit more closely?

Well, it's time to start treating it that way. This moment of your life deserves your attention. *You* deserve your own love and attention. You don't get to know exactly when you'll meet your person or even how long you'll have with them or what your future will hold. But you're here right now, and there is so much joy to be had and life to be lived. You are your person. The moment you give yourself permission to simply love what is without resisting or trying to force it to be different is the moment your life begins.

Maybe this isn't the love story you imagined you'd have, but it's the one you needed. You've come home to yourself and learned to become your own best friend, and anyone else who gets to love you along the way is just a bonus. And if you ever waver in your self-worth along the journey, just remember this: Love is not something you earn or a reward you get for being good enough. Love is who you are.

With Love

Thank you to everyone who made this book possible.

To my clients: thank you for your courage to break cycles and learn new ways to love yourself and others. Thank you for your commitment to this work and to yourself, and for the many ways your stories will change the lives of women who read them.

To my sweet friends: thank you for teaching me so much about love. Thank you for answering my calls and being my sounding board and letting me practice my vulnerability with you again and again, no matter how awkward that felt. Thank you for continuing to choose me, no matter how many miles may separate us.

To my family: thank you for accepting me as I've grown into myself and for letting me do life on my own time line.

To my agent, Michele: thank you for immediately seeing the vision I had for this book and being a fierce advocate for bringing this message into the world. Thank you for believing in me.

To my editors Angela, Diana, and Jade, and the Sounds True team: I'm so grateful for your invaluable guidance throughout this process and your commitment to helping me empower women to live life on their terms.

To all of the women who are doing the work: you inspire me so much, and I'm so proud of you.

With love, Megan.

Recommended Resources

If you haven't gathered by now, building a relationship with yourself is an ongoing story. There will be chapters of meeting past versions of yourself and editing outdated beliefs. Those chapters may feel a bit heavy at times. There will also be chapters of levity and celebrating both small wins and massive growth. You'll continue to get to know yourself in the context of new and old relationships, and the more aligned you feel with your authentic self, the better you'll be able to connect and relate to others.

Throughout all of those chapters, it's invaluable to have a support system. I'm a big advocate of having people in your corner, both platonically and professionally, who can help you see your blind spots and hold you through tough times. I'm not a huge fan of talk therapy just for the sake of venting about the same thing for years and years. I am, however, a fan of identifying modalities that really work for you.

Healing Modalities

Here is a list of healing modalities that you might want to explore if this book has made you aware of some patterns or emotions for which you'd like support in working through. It's not an exhaustive list, nor is it one-size-fits-all. These are just some of the tools that I've found to be useful for me, both in my own healing journey and in my work with clients.

- Dialectical behavioral therapy (DBT)
- Emotional Freedom Technique (EFT) tapping
- Eye movement desensitization and reprocessing (EMDR) therapy
- Holistic Pelvic Care
- Hypnotherapy
- Integrative Somatic Trauma Therapy
- Internal Family Systems (IFS) or parts work
- Psychedelic-assisted psychotherapy (PAP)
- Rapid Transformational Therapy (RTT)
- Somatic Experiencing (SE)

Reading

For a deeper dive into some of the specific topics we explored in this book, here's some recommended reading. It's important to note that if you are someone who tends to spend a lot of time in your head, intellectualizing your feelings and patterns, there will come a time where you need to put the books down and put the work into practice directly in your body. I love self-help books as much as the next gal (hello, I wrote this), but at a certain point I also had to stop all of the obsessive externalized seeking and take the plunge to go within. Now I advocate for a balance of both. Just something for you to consider and tune in with yourself about.

Astrology and Healing

- Tahir, Lisa. *The Chiron Effect: Healing Our Core Wounds Through Astrology, Empathy and Self-Forgiveness.* Rochester, VT: Bear & Company, 2020.

Body, Femininity, and Sexual Healing

- Boehm, Michaela. *The Wild Woman's Way: Reconnect to Your Body's Wisdom.* New York: Enliven Books, 2018.

- Kent, Tami Lynn. *Wild Feminine: Finding Power, Spirit & Joy in the Female Body.* New York: Simon & Schuster, 2011.

Breakups

- Warren, Cortney Soderlind. *Letting Go of Your Ex: CBT Skills to Heal the Pain of a Breakup and Overcome Love Addiction.* Oakland, CA: New Harbinger, 2023.

Love

- hooks, bell. *All about Love: New Visions.* New York: HarperCollins, 2001.

- Williamson, Marianne. *A Return to Love: Reflections on the Principles of A Course In Miracles.* New York: HarperCollins, 1992.

The Mother Wound and Reparenting

- Gibson, Lindsay C. *Adult Children of Emotionally Immature Parents: How to Heal from Distant, Rejecting, or Self-Involved Parents.* Oakland, CA: New Harbinger, 2015.

- McDaniel, Kelly. *Mother Hunger: How Adult Daughters Can Understand and Heal from Lost Nurturance, Protection, and Guidance.* Carlsbad, CA: Hay House, Inc., 2021.

Patterns

- Beattie, Melody. *Codependent No More: How to Stop Controlling Others and Start Caring for Yourself.* Center City, MN: Hazelden, 1986.

- Levine, Amir, and Rachel Heller. *Attached: The New Science of Adult Attachment and How It Can Help You Find—and Keep—Love.* New York: TarcherPerigee, 2010.

- Mellody, Pia. *Facing Codependence: What It Is, Where It Comes from, How It Sabotages Our Lives.* New York: HarperCollins, 1989.

Shadow Work

- Elliott, Carolyn. *Existential Kink: Unmask Your Shadow and Embrace Your Power.* Newburyport, MA: Weiser Books, 2020.

- Ford, Debbie. *The Dark Side of the Light Chasers.* New York: Penguin Group, 1998.

Trauma Healing

- Maté, Gabor. *The Myth of Normal: Trauma, Illness, and Healing in a Toxic Culture.* New York: Avery, 2022.

Notes

Chapter 1: The Real You

1. Will Durant, *The Story of Philosophy: The Lives and Opinions of the World's Greatest Philosophers* (1926; repr., New York: Outlook Verlag, 2012), 87.

Chapter 8: Getting to Know Your Nervous System

1. Nikolai A. Shevchuk, "Adapted Cold Shower as a Potential Treatment for Depression," *Medical Hypotheses* 70, no. 5 (2008): 995–1001.
2. Deb Dana and Dr. Scott Lyons, Integrative Somatic Trauma Therapy Certificate program, Embody Lab, 2022, theembodylab.com/integrative-somatic-trauma-therapy-certificate.

Chapter 15: The Body Talks

1. Stephanie Chinn, "This body is just the keeper of my magic," stephaniechinn.com/product-page/original-this-body-is-just-the-keeper-of-my-magic.
2. Antje Gentsche and Esther Kuehn, "Clinical Manifestations of Body Memories: The Impact of Past Bodily Experiences

on Mental Health," Brain Sciences 12, no. 5 (2022): 594, doi.org/10.3390/brainsci12050594.

Chapter 18: Building Community

1. Robert Waldinger, "What Makes a Good Life? Lessons from the Longest Study on Happiness," TEDxBeaconStreet, November 2015, ted.com/talks/robert_waldinger_what_makes_a_good _life_lessons_from_the_longest_study_on_happiness.
2. Megan Sherer, "How to Let Go of Your Ex with Dr. Cortney Warren," *Well, Then* (podcast), March 22, 2023, podcasts.apple .com/us/podcast/how-to-let-go-of-your-ex-with-dr-cortney -warren/id1482678110?i=1000602549378.

Chapter 21: Love Me Well

1. Yung Pueblo (@yungpueblo), Twitter, April 11, 2022, 2:13 pm, x.com/YungPueblo/status/1513626263960891401.

Conclusion

1. *Steve Jobs' 2005 Stanford Commencement Address*, YouTube video, 15:04, posted March 7, 2008, youtube.com/watch?v= UF8uR6Z6KLc.

About the Author

Megan Sherer is a holistic therapist, coach, and wellness expert who specializes in love, self-worth, and relationships. She is also a writer, speaker, and the host of the *Well, Then* podcast. She serves as a mentor and guide to women who are ready to find alignment within themselves and in their love lives.

Megan's mission is to help women connect to the most authentic expression of love in their lives in order to have more self-confidence, healthier relationships, and a stronger sense of purpose. She pulls from a wide range of expertise and personal experience, along with her strong intuitive abilities, to take a truly holistic and personalized approach to helping you get to the root of what's going on for you and how to effectively change it.

In addition to her private practice, Megan is the founder and CEO of The Self Care Space, a self-guided therapy app and community for women. She also founded the nonprofit organization Be More, which teaches young people the importance of mental wellness and self-esteem in the digital age. Her passion ultimately lies in empowering people with the tools to advocate for their own health and strengthen the quality of their lives.

Megan happily resides in the Pacific Northwest and can often be found traveling to California, New York, and international locations where she leads retreats. To learn more, check out her website at megansherer.com or follow her on Instagram at @megansherer.

About Sounds True

Sounds True was founded in 1985 by Tami Simon with a clear mission: to disseminate spiritual wisdom. Since starting out as a project with one woman and her tape recorder, we have grown into a multimedia publishing company with a catalog of more than 3,000 titles by some of the leading teachers and visionaries of our time, and an ever-expanding family of beloved customers from across the world.

In more than three decades of evolution, Sounds True has maintained our focus on our overriding purpose and mission: to wake up the world. We offer books, audio programs, online learning experiences, and in-person events to support your personal growth and awakening, and to unlock our greatest human capacities to love and serve.

At SoundsTrue.com you'll find a wealth of resources to enrich your journey, including our weekly *Insights at the Edge* podcast, free downloads, and information about our nonprofit Sounds True Foundation, where we strive to remove financial barriers to the materials we publish through scholarships and donations worldwide.

To learn more, please visit SoundsTrue.com/freegifts or call us toll-free at 800.333.9185.

Together, we can wake up the world.